THE
TUSCAN YEAR

ELIZABETH ROMER

NORTH POINT PRESS

Farrar Straus Giroux

New York

North Point Press
A division of Farrar, Straus and Giroux
19 Union Square West, New York 10003

Library of Congress Cataloging-in-Publication Data
Romer, Elizabeth.
    The Tuscan year / Elizabeth Romer.
      p. cm.
    Subtitle on cover: Life and food in an Italian valley.
    Originally published: 1st American ed. New York: Atheneum, 1985, © 1984.
    Includes index.
    ISBN-13: 978-0-86547-387-4
    ISBN-10: 0-86547-387-0 (alk. paper)
    1. Cookery, Italian—Tuscan style. 2. Tuscany (Italy)—Social life
and customs. I. Title.

TX723.2 T86 R65   1989
641'.0945'5—dc19

                                      88-37226

www.fsgbooks.com

P1.

❧ CONTENTS

🌿 ACKNOWLEDGMENTS

Senza l'amicizia e la generosità
della mia amica e insegnante
Silvana Cerotti
questo libro non sarebbe mai stato scritto
e vorrei ricordarla qui
con molto affetto e gratitudine.

Writing this book has been an important and enjoyable part of my life. I have derived great pleasure and satisfaction in learning from my friend Silvana Cerotti. We have spent many happy hours together, cooking, walking through the fields and simply chatting. Without her friendship and willingness to teach me, this book could never have been written and I am very grateful to her.

I should also like to thank my editors Vicky Hayward and Anne Dobell for their invaluable help. Caradoc King and my husband John Romer have also greatly helped me with their constant interest and encouragement.

-Elizabeth Romer
Aiola 1984

❧ INTRODUCTION

This is a book about the food grown and prepared by a family who live in a green and secret valley joining Umbria and Tuscany, two of the most historic and beautiful areas of Italy. It is is also about this family's everyday life and the culture of their region, for Tuscan cuisine is inextricably bound to the culture and personality of Tuscany and its people. I do not mean by Tuscan cuisine the elaborate food that one might eat in one of the region's many grand and elegant restaurants; I mean the sort of food that the waiter will eat when he goes home, the recipes that the grandmother of the chef might cook every day.

I fell in love with Italy in the traditional English manner when as an art student I travelled from Rome through the Tuscan cities to the north. I was dazzled by the art, the architecture and the landscape but even more by the Italians and their food. I loved the noisy market women of Rome who pressed bunches of cherries into my hands to taste before buying; the impressive arrays of cheeses in the food shops, the vast loaves of rough bread and the wine with which we filled our bottles from the big barrels kept in the dark depths of the tiny shops. It was not until some years later that, engrossed in a life of archaeology in the Middle East, my husband and I decided that the most logical place to have our home was between Egypt and England. So, armed with the small amount of money that in those days one was allowed to remove from Britain, we set off to find a house in some Mediterranean country. After dallying with a Turkish house in Greece we sailed for Italy and went straight to Tuscany.

My first impression of the house that was to be ours was of a grey stone building with a lichen-encrusted red-tiled roof standing above green and scented fields that were studded with the brightest scarlet poppies and blue cornflowers. The surrounding hills were green and lush with chestnut trees, and the valley was bisected by a dusty white road and a stream which we crossed by footbridge to reach the house. It was June and the air was full of the steady drone of bees. The crickets, disturbed by our footsteps, leapt before us as we walked through the meadows. After exploring the house we went up to see its owner at the *fattoria*, the home farm, and we walked into their huge dark kitchen. There was Silvana Cerotti with an enormous bowl of pasta in her arms serving food to the work people, about twenty or so they must have been. Immediately chairs were shuffled around and she insisted that we join them for lunch. It was the first of many meals that I have enjoyed at the Cerottis' house.

Over the years we have become friends; I have spent many hours sitting in Silvana's kitchen watching her cook, walking with her through the fields where she has taught me which greenery can be picked to make an *insalata di campo*, a wild salad: and most enjoyable of our expeditions remain the *funghi* hunts in the woods where I have learnt which mushrooms are edible and which poisonous. When we first came to the valley Silvana did her ironing with an antiquated tall hollow iron that was filled with wood embers. One day when I wandered into the *fattoria*, she was using an electric one and chuckling with glee at the ease and convenience of the new iron. Then I realized that this old fashioned life could change: perhaps the next generation of country women would forget how to make cheese, maybe the *prosciutto* would be bought from the store and the old skills would be gradually forgotten. This is one reason why I started to write down all the things that I have learnt from Silvana; the other reason for writing this book is that her Tuscan way of life is so satisfying and her way of cooking so delicious that they deserve to be known by a greater number of people. When I told Silvana what I was doing she was delighted at the thought that other women in far off lands might read about her way of life.

Life in the valley is still firmly moulded by the past. The two regions that meet in the valley – famed for their art, architecture, traditions, cuisine and landscape – are the cradle of the classic image of Italian culture. Those who dwell here live in mediaeval houses, pray before altarpieces painted by Renaissance masters and prepare their food with the grace and balance instilled into them by hundreds of years of measured civilization. They use recipes handed down from mother to daughter, based on home-produced ingredients.

This ingrained tradition is typified in the life of the Cerotti household. Both Orlando and Silvana are strongly Tuscan in origin, coming from small enclosed communities in the remote mountain area between Cortona and Castiglion Fiorentino. They have one remaining young son, Sauro, the elder, Pietro, having been killed in a farming accident some years ago at the age of sixteen. A giant new tractor overturned on a slope and pinned him underneath. Silvana herself took him from the field and he is buried in the little churchyard on the hill above the house. Every Sunday she visits his grave with fresh flowers that she grows in a plot laid aside by the kitchen garden, and on the anniversary of his death priests come from Cortona to celebrate a memorial mass in the eighteenth-century chapel that stands next to the house. She makes them a splendid lunch and it is a comforting occasion.

The Cerottis come from old farming stock and they run their estate and live their lives in a traditional manner. This they do from choice not necessity. Their lives are bounded by the land, which they use to its fullest extent, and in this way they are virtually self-sufficient. Their property is extensive, stretching over 400 hectares, and includes acres of forest and arable land, streams, vineyards, many small houses and their own imposing *fattoria* with its surrounding walled kitchen garden, olive groves, chapel and outbuildings. They utilize each part of their domain and grow and gather in the fruits of the seasons helped by their *contadini*, or farm workers, who live with their families in the surrounding stone houses. Years ago it was common for the *contadini* to be turned out of their homes and off the land that they may have toiled over for years by the whim of an absentee landlord; today the workers are better protected. However, the children of the *contadini* drift away to the towns and the sons who stay on the farms have difficulty in finding girls who are willing to marry them and share the drudgery and discomfort of the draughty stone houses and the everlasting toil of the farmyard. Those who choose to remain on the land are those who have a taste and love for it.

The Tuscans are a sober and even severe group of people, or so it is said in other parts of Italy. Although the Cerottis have been highly successful in a modern world, their values are rooted firmly in the country traditions of a past age. It is possible even to perceive the sort of values inherent in ancient Roman family life in their family group. The old virtues of *Gravitas, Pietas* and *Simplicitas* still remain. *Gravitas,* or taking life seriously and treating each day's problems, however small, with care, is a strong trait. *Pietas,* the acceptance of authority, whether human or divine, and discipline before that authority, is still to be seen in the family structure: father's word is law and he himself is law abiding. *Simplicitas,* or the ability to see things clearly and as they really are, is perhaps an adjunct to country life where actions and their consequences are very clear. If you do not water your crops they will die. If you do not reply promptly to a business letter the outcome may be less obvious. Vesta, the hearth, is still of paramount importance. The Lares and Penates of ancient Rome have evolved into small plaster sanctuaries devoted to the Blessed Virgin or the Sacred Heart. The family is extended as in Roman times from father, mother and the children to dependent workers and other relatives. Father is still judge and supreme authority of what actions are to be taken and mother is still arbiter of morality and behaviour. The supper table is where matters are discussed and decisions taken.

All the year round, the produce of the farm is grown, gathered and stored following a pattern laid down centuries ago. The days begin early, end late and there are no holidays. As Silvana often observes, if you want to eat genuine food then you must work hard to make it. The tasks vary according to the changes of the seasons and the phases of the moon, the lunar rhythm dictating when to move the wine, sow the seeds and gather the herbs. The labour is divided. Orlando has the responsibility for the fields and their crops, the woods, the vineyards and the flocks. Silvana's domain is the house, the kitchen, the store-rooms and the kitchen garden, though this is dug and planted by one of the men. She also tends the domestic animals, which she feeds - walking miles to gather the best fresh herbiage - fattens, and finally kills. Hers, too, is the job of cheese-making and preserving the fruit and vegetables.

Silvana's style of cooking is not ornate, nor has she ever bought or read a cookery book, but from traditional knowledge handed down to her she produces wonderful Tuscan country food: her repertoire of recipes is large. Each month has special dishes appropriate to the season; produce is grown, gathered and stored to provide variety in the kitchen throughout the year. Silvana's cooking derives its immense character from the freshness and simplicity of the ingredients and the balance with which she combines them. The grace and economy of her food depend to a great extent on the ready availability of the traditional supplies in her *dispensa*, or larder. Her broad beans taste so good because it is easy for her to dash to the pantry and slice of a lump of *prosciutto* to flavour them; it is just as simple to add a glassful of wine to the cooking pot from the two-litre jugs of red and white wine on the kitchen table. Like most Italian cooks, she gives vague answers to most questions about quantities in any given dish: as much as is needed, a handful, a bunch, *un pò* – a little. Yet the proportions of her dishes are always nicely balanced by experience. She does not slavishly weigh out ingredients according to recipes, but has learnt by example from her elders, her mother and grandmother, then embroidered upon this education with her own experience and taste.

The character of Tuscan food is rather like the character of the Tuscans, sober and severe. This is not to say that their food is dull or that they have no sense of humour. Their food is simple, and consists of the freshest ingredients of superior quality unadorned with unnecessary items that would mask the intrinsic excellence of the basic food. Which is nothing more than our old virtue of *Simplicitas* – recognizing things for what they really are.

The appearance of a traditional Tuscan field demonstrates amply the basis of Tuscan cooking. The alternating rows of vines and olive trees around which corn is sown provide their essential staples: bread, olive oil and wine. Each part of Italy has its traditional staple: in the south it is pasta, in the north rice and *polenta*, but in Tuscany the basis of many country meals has always been bread. Similarly, there are areas in Italy that use butter as their chief cooking medium. Tuscany is not one of them. Here good olive oil has always been used for cooking even for the frying of sweet cakes. The wines of Tuscany are of the best in Italy; of course the Tuscans would say they are *the* best. And these excellent heavy red wines perfectly suit the good quality meat which also plays a great part in Tuscan cooking, again often prepared in the simplest way, that is, grilled over an open fire of sweet smelling wood. Tuscans are also partial to beans, which they eat seasoned with their best olive oil. The nickname for Tuscans in Italy is in fact *mangiafagioli* – the bean eaters. Although the basic characteristic of Tuscan food is simplicity, this does not signify that its preparation is easy and needs no care. From the market or garden to the table great attention and concentration are applied to the choice of the ingredients and the preparation of the dishes.

I have tried in this book simply to describe a great living tradition of good eating that has not yet succumbed to the pressures of modern life. It is not a conventional cookery book, but it is about real food. I hope that it is discursive enough to be read in bed and will fill the reader with pleasant dreams of the Italian countryside and new ideas for good food.

The activities I describe throughout the book generally happen during the month in which I have placed them. Of course much depends on the weather. In some years, for example, a cold wet spring might delay sowing and planting. Easter may fall early or late or early frosts ruin crops. The altitude, too, affects the growth and blossoming of plants and trees. Man's efforts to cultivate the land are in the end controlled by the elements.

✿ JANUARY

In January, when the mountains surrounding the *fattoria* of the Cerotti family are usually covered with thick snow and the thrice-daily bus is stopped until the snow ploughs can clear the road, the best way to approach their house is by the dirt road that leads from the Umbrian *pianura*. This narrow road, which in winter looks like a slick dun ribbon, passes through scattered grey stone villages, the prettiest of which is dominated by an elegant seventeenth-century church. Then bending sharply round this church past the post office with its art-nouveau letter box the road continues alongside flat fields edged with winter-naked vines planted in the ancient Roman manner.

The road passes the *castello* of a nobleman whose great-grandfather planted the magnificent line of umbrella pines that crown the ridge behind the castle. Roman columns powdered with snow lie like fallen trees in its grounds. Facing it across the bare cornfields on the other side of the valley another great house rears up from the wooded slopes, a classic shape in a rustic landscape, reputedly designed by Palladio, though thought by some to have been conjured up in the course of one night by the devil, a common legend about old houses in Italy. Continuing on its way the road passes the small walled cemetery where every evening someone comes from the village to light the red glass lamps beside each grave, so keeping the dead company through the night by illuminating the icy air. Outside the grey stone houses with their snow-speckled roman-tiled roofs, the geese and hens stray onto the road to peck and scratch at its stony surface, tame rabbits hop on the verges in search of the scanty grass and occasionally flocks of sheep block the road.

Past the last farmhouse adorned by a *madonnina* standing in a crumbling baroque niche the valley grows narrower. The hillsides, covered in woods of turkey oaks that still carry their rusty dead leaves, interspersed with juniper and ginestra, close in upon the fields and soon the road, wedged between lichen-coloured rocks, reaches the old customs-house on the borders of Umbria and Tuscany. Squat and square it stands on the verge, dating from the time before Garibaldi gathered Italy's separate kingdoms together. Here at the border the valley bells out once more and the road, curving beside a small stone monument, turns sharply back upon itself and winds upwards through the snow-blocked pass to Cortona, the market town whose massive Etruscan walls enclose silent alleys and steep sunless lanes, tall secretive houses and churches reputed to be haunted by lines of shuffling monks. A perfect mediaeval hill town.

It is at this bend in the road at the head of the valley, where the mountains rise steeply, that the Cerotti *fattoria* lies, placed on a small hill with the fields spread like skirts about it.

The house is very large and square with a classic aspect, built of finely cut stone, the façades decorated with pilasters. Five massive and majestic black cypresses surround it. The roof has a shallow pitch and under the deep eaves there are small round holes cut in the stone for swallows to nest in. The space around the house is paved with grey flags, now coated with treacherous black ice, and a *breccia* strewn drive leads up from the road to the front door with its sentinel pine trees, then circles around the house. At the back a courtyard contains the old chapel on one side and on the other a domed bread oven. Kindling for the fire is kept by the bread oven and stacks of logs by the garden wall. The large double back door of the *fattoria* leads straight into the heart of the house, the kitchen, a high square room with the customary red tiled floor and massively beamed ceiling. The most important feature of the kitchen, and possibly of the house, is the fireplace, around which, especially during these cold months, the life of the household is centred. Vast logs burn brightly all day and no one willingly leaves the warm kitchen for the icy chill of the upper rooms. Those neat piles of brushwood and logs that have been conscientiously gathered and stacked throughout the warmer months lie near the kitchen door so they are handy for quick forays to replenish the fire.

The Cerottis' fireplace is large and consists of a flagstone platform raised about two feet off the floor, with room on this platform on each side of the fire for two wooden chests, the best seats on these cold winter nights. The chimney breast soars to the ceiling. Fuel, logs from the forest, is supported by massive iron fire dogs trimmed with brass knobs. From a hinged triangular bracket placed high on the back wall of the chimney hangs a sooty iron chain with round links as big as teacups. From the chain hangs a copper cauldron which holds about ten litres of boiling water. When there are a great many people to feed Silvana cooks the pasta in this and fishes it out with a pear-shaped strainer. The quantities of pasta that the cauldron holds are too large to pour out into any normal colander. She makes *ricotta* cheese in it too. Around the fire there are all sorts and sizes of trivets to hold the pots and pans, for Silvana does much of her cooking over the open fire. There is a hollow under the stone platform, with a small entrance to it, in which dough wrapped in a cloth is left to rise. It also provides a refuge for tiny chicks and even at times for the cat. The huge carved mantleshelf that runs the length of the chimney breast is frequently garlanded with herbs, mushrooms, wet boots, and even pigs' intestines, put there to dry in the wet winter months.

Most of the rest of the space in Silvana's kitchen is occupied by the heavy wooden kitchen table, covered with a gaudy oil cloth. This table has deep drawers at either end in which Silvana keeps kitchen utensils of antique design, odd heads of garlic, a few mushrooms in season and, on occasion, game, a few birds or even a hare, as well as ammunition for the guns that are hung in the corner by the kitchen door. The old stone sink is by the wall near the door and over it is a favourite Italian device, an open-bottomed cupboard containing a wooden rack for draining the dishes, the drops falling into the sink below.

Opposite the fireplace, below the window with its view down the valley, there is a new gas stove with an electric oven, an expensive efficient model. But Silvana prefers to cook on the open fire or on the old wood stove beside it. She is convinced that food tastes better when cooked over a natural flame, so most things from meat to bread are cooked on the fire which burns perpetually with fuel obtained easily and at little cost from their own forests. The large stone oven outside is also heated with wood but is only used in the summer when there are twenty to thirty farm hands to feed.

Off the kitchen lies the *dispensa*, the pantry, where sacks of flour ground at a local mill are kept. Tuscan bread, large appetizing loaves made from unbleached, only partially refined flour, is now bought from the village store and Silvana keeps it in an old wooden bread chest, a long shallow lidded box on tall legs that is called a *madia*. The chief characteristic of Tuscan bread is that it is unsalted. Although this can be disconcerting at the first taste, when one remembers that it is often eaten with the very salty *prosciutto* or as the basis of well flavoured soup, salt in fact is not a necessary addition. Besides, this sort of country bread was designed to be baked only once a week. The addition of salt would attract water to the loaves and make them mouldy, whereas without salt they remain dry but can always be softened with a little soup. A glass-fronted cabinet contains row upon row of home-made tomato conserve made by Silvana at the end of the summer from the abundant crops in the kitchen garden, to last for sauces all the year through. From the beams in the ceiling hang bundles of dried herbs, both for cooking and for medicinal purposes, and also bunches of grapes which will remain fresh for months after the *vendemmia*, the picking, if hung in an airy place. The large wooden table is used for making pasta and pastries, and the *pecorino* cheese, Silvana's speciality, is left in its deep drawers to drain in earthenware moulds overnight. Large bowls of Cortona ware contain eggs fresh from the farmyard and there is a collection of bottles with china stoppers on wire catches. These are filled with wine for the labourers to carry in an old satchel with their breakfasts of rough bread and *salame* when they are working in far-off fields.

Through the pantry there is a long narrow passage lined with a tall dresser, its frame doors covered with fine meshed wire screens, a larger version of the old-fashioned English meat safe. In this are kept the *prosciutti*, whole hams, and the ripest cheeses. High on the ceiling dangle fat *salame*, sausages, and more *prosciutto* made in the house from home-killed meat by a butcher from Castiglion Fiorentino.

These bitter months, when no work can be done in the fields, are the ones when the Cerottis' lives most resemble those of their parents and their own as children. Their forbears would have filled the time with making baskets for collecting the olives and grapes and would have fashioned wooden sleds and carts to be drawn by the oxen and mules. Now the men occupy themselves with checking over and repairing the farm equipment and tools. The women would have spun and woven woollen cloth and embroidered their own trousseaus of fine cotton, voluminous chemises and nightgowns edged with crochet and decorated with complicated inset panels of lace. They also decorated their heavy linen sheets and made elaborate fringes for their hand towels. Now,

Silvana concentrates on knitting thick socks and shawls, spinning her own wool from their flock of sheep. She uses two intertwined wools, one light, the other dark, to enable her to see her stitches when working by firelight.

Silvana in her mid-forties is a sturdy handsome woman, still what the old fashioned Tuscan men would call *grassa*, which does not mean fat, but ripe and pleasing although her face has now lost the pretty smooth plumpness of her wedding photographs; the years have planed away the flesh to reveal the prominent high cheekbones and her splendid dark eyes are cradled deeper in her face. She wears her long black hair severely combed back and folded up over tortoiseshell combs; gold earrings dangle next to her creamy skin and glint in the firelight.

Both Silvana and Orlando remember that when they were very young, in their isolated mountain communities no one had cars or even motor cycles; all movement was accomplished on foot or with the aid of mules. This, says Orlando, is how each small group of mountain people came to have its individual dialect: no one travelled far to mix with other villagers, so they evolved their own private language to embellish their basic Tuscan. They still regard the speech used in the television news broadcasts as Italian, different from their own way of speaking.

To the right of the house above the kitchen garden a path leads to a house lived in by Andrea the shepherd, who tends the flock of about 120 sheep. One of the major tasks of this winter month is the feeding and tending of the animals, who rely on the stored grain for their fodder while the grass is well covered and flattened by snow. The folds under Andrea's house are full with ewes and so far sixty-three lambs have been born. Some nights he must sleep in the fold with the tiniest new born lambs held close to his body for warmth - the ancient way of ensuring that the small creatures will not perish in the bitter temperatures. In the morning he and Silvana will have the finger-numbing job of de-icing the water pipes from the spring to keep the drinking supply going to the folds. Another of Silvana's early jobs of the day is to soften up the grain for the animal fodder in hot water; she slings a huge can on to the hook and chain over the fire and the grain simmers away over the blaze. Later she carries it up the hill to the sheep and pours it into the low wooden troughs for the older lambs to gorge themselves. At this time of year the ewes' milk is reserved for the lambs; it is too cold for the cheese to form properly so there can be no cheese making until later in the year.

As January is the traditional month for pig-killing, much of Silvana's time now goes into curing *prosciutti*, the large succulent salt-preserved hams that form such an important part of Italian and Tuscan cooking. In previous years the Cerottis had over a hundred pigs of their own housed in sties some distance away from the house. It was Silvana's job to look after them and she would walk out in all weather to feed and tend the beasts. But after a while the work became too much for her, so the herd was sold and now they buy a fine pig each year for their supply of hams and *salame*. The big decisions to be taken are from whom to buy the pig and which animal looks the healthiest and most likely to produce the best *prosciutto*. This year they disagree over which pig they should buy: Silvana is in favour of a smaller animal, as she says it will have less fat on the carcass, but Orlando has set his mind on a creature of gigantic proportions. His is the casting vote and the fat pig is brought over the mountains in a truck. The animal is handled carefully to see that it sustains no injury or bruising, which would adversely affect the curing of the meat.

In years gone by the slaughtering of the pigs was a messy noisy business. Silvana remembers when she and her sister were girls and used to feed the pigs on their little farm high in the mountains. When the day for slaughtering came her sister would rise early and run far up into the woods so that she would not hear the pigs screaming and there in the shelter of the trees she would cry her heart out. Silvana, being made of sterner material, would often assist in the killing and hold the bowl for the blood. Orlando is also soft hearted and insists that a humane killer be used to prevent the creatures suffering; a small pistol fires a retractable bolt into the pig's brain and death is instantaneous. Then the heart is pierced to let the blood flow. Silvana stresses that the animal must be properly bled or the *prosciutto* will not cure properly. She also observes that the only animal whose death the old Tuscan people really mourned was the ox, the beautiful white beast that drew the plough; they were mourned almost as if they were human because they too need nine months in the womb before they are ready to be born.

After the pig is killed the butcher comes to divide the carcass into its different parts. The Cerottis have a butcher in Castiglion Fiorentino whose skill they trust and he comes every January to butcher their pig. He brings with him about ten kilos of the best *vitellone*, beef from young oxen, plus a large quantity of the ox intestine, *budello*, which he uses as skins for the sausages; the pig's intestines are used in a different manner. Every part of the pig has its uses and most will be preserved in some way to form part of the basic ingredients and necessities for the larder.

After the four quarters of the pig have been laid aside in a cold place the butcher makes the *salame*. Happily, there are wide differences of opinion in different parts of Italy as to what goes into the best *salame*, which means there are many different types to enjoy. In Milan the meat is ground very fine and the texture of the sausage is close-grained with the fat distributed evenly through the meat, giving a uniform pale rosy colour. Tuscans, however, prefer their *salame* to have a deep wine-red meat studded with large pieces of the white fat and a great many whole black peppercorns. This type is usually referred to as '*nostrano*', simply, our own make. Another very popular Tuscan variation is *finocchiona*, a fairly fatty loosely-packed pork *salame* flavoured with fennel seeds, which is truly delicious and makes a pleasant change when served together with more traditional sausage at the beginning of a meal. The Cerottis themselves like a mixture of pork and beef, as they find that pork alone is too rich and indigestible.

The butcher minces up the mixture of meats and fat in careful proportions, adding first a little nitrate to aid the conservation of the meat, then garlic juice, which is obtained by putting several large cloves of garlic into a muslin and sharply battering the garlic until it can be squeezed through the muslin to drip into the sausage mixture. The butcher also adds salt, whole black peppercorns and enough white wine to bind the mixture. He then stuffs the skins, forcing the mixture through until they are fat and rather knobbly, and finally he ties the ends firmly with twine.

Then the butcher takes the pig's head and parts of the belly and kidneys and he cuts them up and cooks them in the great cauldron over the fire. When the meat has been boiled to a state of tenderness he takes out the pieces and lays them all on the bare, well-scrubbed wooden table. Then with an iron curved-bladed chopper held in each hand he quickly chops the meat into small pieces (discarding the bones) making a great thundering noise on the table as he works. He seasons this mediaeval-looking mixture with chopped fresh orange peel, salt and a great deal of black pepper to make a deliciously perfumed brawn which is a real delicacy, the pungent orange making a surprising note in the flavour. The brawn is stuffed into soft fibry paper cases and tied at the ends with string, then the sausage is put into a net so it can be hung from the pantry ceiling. These brawn sausages, called *carne di testa di Maiale*, *coppa* or *capocollo*, are perhaps six inches in diameter and a foot or so long.

Sausage making would seem to be a masculine preserve. Silvana merely fetches and carries and watches the proceedings. She also washes the pig's intestines very thoroughly in many changes of water. Later she will lay them for days in a mixture of coarse salt and fennel seed, after which they will be hung around the fireplace to dry, looking like ribbons of yellowish fat. This '*budino*', as Silvana calls it, although *budino* can also refer to a blood pudding, will be cut into short lengths which are toasted on a trivet over the fire until they are crisp and crackling. They taste rather like the fatty crackling from a joint of roast pork though the flavour is slightly more gamey. Sauro enjoys them for breakfast with fresh bread on cold mornings. Just the thing to sustain you on a cold six o'clock morning bus ride through the mountains.

The remaining meat is minced and stuffed into small soft sausages which are either put into glass preserving jars and covered with olive oil or eaten fresh. The mixture for these sausages is pork, *vitello*, crushed garlic, salt and lots of ground black pepper; sometimes a little dried oregano is included as Silvana likes the flavour. In Arezzo there is one butcher's shop that sells wonderful sausages made of very lean meat and flavoured with ginger, *zenzero*; these are exceptionally fine. The spice does not give an actual ginger flavour but is lightly *piccante*. The pig's forelegs, or the skin of them to be more exact, are stuffed too, and sewn up to form *zampone*, a boiling sausage eaten with lentils or creamed potatoes.

To make the fresh sausages, *salcicce*, the butcher attaches a tubular nozzle to the old fashioned mincer which is clamped to the end of the kitchen table. He then opens the end of the longest ox intestine he can find, slides it over the nozzle and feeds the pre-minced meat again through the mincer and into the skin; he tries to make the longest, most even sausage he can manage. Guido, Orlando's foreman, who along with two other neighbours is helping the butcher, stands to receive the emerging sausage and winds it around like a Catherine wheel or Cumberland sausage on a large square board. He has a ball of thin twine and starting with a knot at one end he makes individual sausages by extending the twine the required length of the sausage, about two and a half inches, then, looping the twine around the sausage and pulling it tight, he is ready to proceed to the next *salciccia* link in the chain. The sausage-making is accompanied by a great deal of bucolic ribaldry of an obvious nature, in heavy dialect. Orlando, who does not actually join in the work, stands on the hearth and shouts instructions to everyone else and succeeds in keeping them all in continuous fits of laughter. He helps himself now and again to the wine which is always to be found at one end of the kitchen table. At very nearly fifty he is a good-looking man with a burly thickset figure and a pair of flashing, surprisingly blue eyes in a broad brown face. His taste in clothes is also surprising. He is sometimes to be seen in spring, wearing a very old suit of superlative brown velvet, which must have belonged to his father; which he adorns with a large purple bog iris in the lapel, the whole crowned with a brown velvet cap. On market days of course he wears a sober suit and a brimmed hat when he goes to stand and chat with his peers in the marketplace at Cortona. It is he, in fact, who does the marketing for such items that they do not produce themselves and he has excellent taste and discrimination when it comes to picking out a fresh fish, the most delicate fillet of veal or a tender artichoke.

When the butcher has finished his work and the sausages have been put away in the pantry, and the table cleared, Orlando brings out a bottle of his own *grappa*, lovingly distilled from their own wine. He pours out a glass for everyone and they relax after their hard work. Silvana chats to the butcher and asks for news of various relatives who live in his town. She enjoys hearing all the latest gossip about old friends whom she does not often have a chance to see. This is partly why they always ask him to butcher their pig, the other reason being that he is Tuscan, and can be trusted to do a proper job in the way of which they approve. Although Italy has been unified for more than a hundred years the inhabitants of small towns, not to mention whole provinces, are deeply steeped in their own very independent history and cultural traditions. There is enormous competition between the various regions in Italy and this is shown in the proud preservation of their regional differences. One of the strongest expressions of these differences is in the food of each region. The Cerottis would not trust someone from a different area with such an important task as the curing of their hams. This year, as Silvana predicted, the pig was too fat and she murmurs to the butcher about the amount of waste there was on the creature. The butcher tries to remain non-committal and to change the subject Orlando chases Silvana around the kitchen with a broom.

Later in the day the pig's blood is made into *sanguinaccio*, a blood pudding flavoured with pine kernels, currants, candied fruit, cinnamon and nutmeg and thickened with breadcrumbs, and this is Orlando's favourite dish from the pig. The *sanguinaccio* has several different names. *Biroldo* is a common name for a version of the pudding which is boiled in a skin like a sausage. *Burischio, migliaccio,* or *mueccia,* the latter a dialect name used in Silvana's native hamlet, are the names for the pudding that is cooked solely in a flat pan or *tegame*. Orlando prefers the *mueccia* which is a mixture of the pig's blood, grated *pecorino*, lemon peel a small amount of bread crumbs, nutmeg, a little sugar, salt and wine. Silvana puts this mixture into a *tegame* and cooks it over the open fire. She covers the pan with an old tin lid and on top of the lid heaps hot embers; this has the effect of cooking the top of the pudding until it is quite crisp.

 To make the **Sanguinaccio** you would need 1 kg or 2¼ lb of blood, 200 g or 7 oz of bread crumbs, three glasses of stock (in Umbria they use the stock from a boiled tongue), 100 g or 3½ oz of pine kernels, 50 g or 2 oz of sultanas, 100 g or 3½ oz of candied fruit, a pinch each of cinnamon, coriander, nutmeg, white pepper and salt. You also need a sausage skin. The method is as follows. First you must sieve the blood. Then simmer the breadcrumbs in the stock for ten minutes, drain them and squeeze them dry. In a bowl mix the blood and breadcrumbs together. Add the fruit and the pine kernels, a pinch of salt and a good sprinkling of all the spices. When the pudding is thoroughly mixed stuff it into a well-cleaned skin. Tie each end but leave a little empty space so that the contents will have room to swell in the cooking and in that way you will prevent the skin from bursting. Place the sausage in a pan full of cold water; bring to the boil and boil gently for thirty minutes. Remove the pudding from the pan and allow it to cool. When you are ready to serve the dish slice the cold pudding into thick slices, remove the outer skin and fry the slices in a pan with a little butter. This is an interesting and very old recipe which combines sweet and savoury elements.

The old country people made another interesting dish with the *sanguinaccio*, a **Frittata di Sanguinaccio**. This consists of fried slices of the pudding with beaten egg poured around them in a hot pan to make the *frittata*, or Italian omelette. The main ingredient of *sanguinaccio*, the fresh pig's blood, is probably not easily obtained in England. However a friendly butcher might be persuaded to make up the pudding if provided with the spices and the dried fruit.

Meanwhile, the hams are taken up to the attic storeroom. Here they are placed in wooden boxes and covered with a mixture of coarse salt and chopped garlic prepared by Silvana. The hams must lie in the salt for about a month, a little longer if they are very large. Silvana does not use nitrate, which is commonly used as a preservative and keeps the meat a rosy colour. She has to turn the hams frequently to make sure that each part is well and equally treated. In the Parma area, perhaps the most famous for *prosciutto*, some housewives pride themselves on not using large quantities of salt but rely on the pure air to cure the meat successfully. After they have been a month or so in the brine Silvana will move the hams to the kitchen to start the next step in the process of curing. It is easy to identify in old country houses the rooms in which the *prosciutti* were hung. The *mattoni*, the brick floor tiles, are often corroded and worn away in patches under the beams where the hams were strung and their salt dripped to the floor. Careful housewives would put down a layer of ashes to protect their tiles.

These good hams and sausages play an important role in Silvana's repertoire of recipes and her mode of serving food. Jars full of sausages line the pantry cupboards next to the tall jars of tomato conserve. The *prosciutto*, as well as being eaten in slices with fresh bread, is also used as a flavouring for all sorts of meat and vegetable dishes.

Food in the household in January is obviously as warming and nourishing as can be devised. Fresh vegetables from the *orto*, the kitchen garden, are at their very minimum, so Silvana relies heavily on her stocks of preserved vegetables; tomato *conserva*, stored apples and pears, walnuts, strings of onions and garlic, dried herbs, dried white beans and finally *funghi secchi*, the *porcini* she has lovingly sliced up and dried in the sun when there was a glut of the tasty wild mushrooms during the summer.

Every day Orlando and Sauro expect *pasta* or some such filling course with which to start their lunch. Since at this time of year there are at most five or six people at the midday meal Silvana often prefers to make *gnocchi*. In the summer, when there are more likely to be twenty-five to lunch, she invariably serves a *pasta*, as this can be bought in quantity and so is not so time consuming a dish to prepare. There are many different sorts of *gnocchi*, which are basically dumplings. They can be made, for example, with maize flour and grated parmesan, or with white flour, *ricotta* cheese and chopped spinach.

 Silvana enjoys **Gnocchi di Patate**, with which she has a very light hand. To make the *gnocchi* she first clears and scrubs the kitchen table then dredges a liberal amount of flour onto the clean wood. Meanwhile a large pan of floury potatoes has been boiling on a trivet over a brisk fire. When the potatoes are tender, Silvana drains them and, when they are cool enough to handle, peels them and puts them through the mouli. She makes a mound of potato at one end of the table and sprinkles into it some flour and a little salt, then she mixes the potato and flour thoroughly so each is well and evenly spread through the other. Then with the smallest quantity of water possible or a little beaten egg she forms the mixture into a soft dough. When the dough is just mixed, it must not be worked too hard; she takes a small piece and with the flat of her fingers rolls it into a sausage shape on the floured table. The sausage is about the thickness of a finger. Then she cuts the sausage into small lengths of a little less than an inch. These she rolls again lightly between her fingers and the board, finally making a small dent with the edge of a knife in each *gnoccho*. Silvana is an absolute joy to watch as she makes the *gnocchi* for she works so quickly and skilfully as she caresses the dumplings into shape. To cook the *gnocchi*, Silvana boils up a large quantity of salted water in a big pan. When the water is at a rolling boil she slides in the dumplings a few at a time. They are cooked when they float to the top. As soon as they are floating Silvana fishes them out of the water with a round pierced spoon, making sure that they drain well before putting them into a large warm bowl. Over each layer in the bowl she pours copious spoonfuls of her *ragù* plus a sprinkling of grated *pecorino* cheese. The secret of making light potato *gnocchi* lies in the proportions of the quantity of flour to potato. Too little flour and the dumplings will disintegrate in the boiling water, too much and they will be chewy and heavy. On average you would need 200g or 7oz of flour to every kilo or 2¼ lb of floury potatoes, a little salt and a little water, or beaten egg, with extra flour for the table or pastry board. This is sufficient for three people. You will also need a good meat or a sharp tomato sauce with which to season the *gnocchi*. Some grated Parmesan cheese is also a useful addition.

One of the very basic and essential things that Silvana makes every week is her *ragù*, the meat sauce with which she seasons her dishes of *pasta* and *gnocchi*. As she has a large and very busy household to run Silvana tends to make a big pot of the sauce once or twice a week. She starts the sauce with the basic *battuto*, or *trittata*, chopped ingredients which include celery, carrot and onion. These vegetables, which Silvana always has in her garden, are known as the *odori*: 'the flavourers' might be a rough translation. The *odori* are all chopped finely with a clove of garlic or some parsley then simmered together in good olive oil until they are soft. They must not be allowed to burn. To this mixture Silvana then adds some ground beef, freshly minced, and a little diced fat *prosciutto*, or some of her preserved sausages, crumbled. Occasionally, if she is not planning to make the famous Tuscan *crostini neri*, small appetisers made

with chicken liver, she may add the livers to the sauce. She turns the
meat gently in the pan until it has changed colour. Finally Silvana adds
a spoonful or two of her basic tomato *conserva*, the home-made original
of the tins of *passato di pomodoro* that can be bought in the shops. She
may add a very small amount of white wine to moisten the mixture.
On no account should the sauce be too liquid, and water is almost *never*
added to any pasta sauce in Italy. Sometimes Silvana will flavour the
basic sauce with dried *funghi* instead of meat. To prepare these for the
sauce she lays the aromatic slices in a dish and covers them with a ladleful
of hot water. After a very few minutes the slices will have plumped up.
Silvana then squeezes away the moisture, chops the mushrooms into
pieces with a sharp knife, adds them to the sauce and leaves it to simmer
for about twenty minutes.

 To make Silvana's basic *ragù* you will need one onion, one rib of celery
plus its leaves, one carrot, three sprigs of parsley, 150 g or 5 to 6 oz of
Italian sausages split open, their skins removed and the meat crumbled,
or a mixture of fresh lean minced beef and chopped *prosciutto* or *pancetta*. Also one teacup of tomato *conserva* (see the chapter on August
for an exact description of the different kinds of tomato preserves) or
fresh tomatoes skinned and chopped. Two tablespoons of good olive
oil plus a little more if needed, salt and freshly ground black pepper.
The sauce will be richer if you use a mixture of meats.

Chop the onion, the celery, the carrot and parsley finely. In a small
saucepan heat up the two tablespoons of olive oil, add the *odori* and
allow them to soften. Add the meat, mix everything together and
cook over a gentle flame until the meat has changed colour. Add the
tomato *conserva*. Simmer gently for half an hour and season to taste
with salt and black pepper. If the mixture is too dry add a little more
olive oil or tomato. *Never* add water. Silvana's sauce with *funghi* is
made in exactly the same way but substitutes about 25 g or 1 oz of
dried *porcini* for the meat. Dried *porcini* can be obtained in Italian stores
in England. Both these sauces are excellent with pasta and *polenta* and
delicious in *lasagne*.

Substantial dishes of *cotechino* or *zampone* appear on the Cerottis' table
at this time of year; they may be home-made or bought from the village
shop. They are both boiling sausages – the former a piece of pork skin
sewn into a sausage shape and stuffed, the latter the pig's trotter and
foreleg stuffed with the same mixture of minced pork and spices. *Cote-*

chino can also be obtained in an ordinary sausage skin. Silvana takes the sausage, pricks it all over with a giant darning needle and lays it in a large pan of cold water. She brings the water to a boil, then leaves it to bubble, not boil ferociously, for about two hours for every pound in weight of the sausage. It is served in glistening splendour on a bed of lentils boiled in a little of the sausage broth or with a purée of potatoes. The sausage is cut into slices and the thick skin discarded, but the flavour of the pig's skin permeates the meat and gives it a very rich taste.

 To make *Cotechino con Lenticche* you will need one *cotechino*, 150g or ·5oz of dried lentils soaked overnight in plenty of cold water, one carrot, one rib of celery, one medium onion, three tablespoons of olive oil, two teacups of stock, salt and black pepper.

Take the *cotechino* and prick the skin on all sides with a bodkin. Place the sausage in a large pan of cold water. Bring the water to the boil and boil gently for about 2 hours for every pound in weight of the sausage.

Drain the softened lentils, rinse them, cover with fresh water and cook them until they are soft. Drain them again and put them to one side. Chop the *odori*, that is the carrot, celery, and onion, finely. In a clean saucepan soften the vegetables in the olive oil then add the drained lentils and season with salt and black pepper. After a few minutes of cooking add just enough stock to cover and let the lentils simmer gently until they are very soft and have soaked up the flavour of the stock and the *odori*.

When it is time to serve the *cotechino* first drain the lentils, which by now should have very little liquid left, and make a bed of them on a large oval serving dish. Drain the *cotechino* and slice it into half-inch slices then arrange the meat on top of the lentils. You may also serve a purée of potatoes as an accompaniment to this winter dish. These quantities will serve four people.

Cotechino may be bought in England at Italian food stores. These stores also stock the *zampone*, which is basically the same sausage. The skin of both types of sausages is not eaten and should be left at the side of your plate.

Tuscany is famous for its meat, especially the beef that comes from the Val di Chiana, and this and pork are the meats that Orlando buys when he goes to market. The lamb, rabbit and chicken that they eat are all home-produced and home-killed. The rich meat and vegetable country dishes of France, simmered for hours in tightly covered pots, are not really part of Tuscan or even, it is possible to say, Italian cooking, perhaps because the oven as such is a relative newcomer to the kitchen. There are however a few Tuscan exceptions to this rule: the *stracotto* and the *scottiglia*.

 The **Stracotto** is a beef stew made with wine and herbs and cooked until the meat falls apart, overcooked in fact, which is what *stracotto* means. This excellent winter dish requires three large cloves of garlic, 50g or 2oz of *pancetta* or fat *prosciutto*, a teaspoon of ground black pepper, 1 kg or 2¼ lb of beef, top rump or top side, two tablespoons of olive oil, one onion, one carrot, one rib of celery, salt, one glass of good red wine, 500g or 1lb of chopped ripe tomatoes and stock as needed.

To prepare the beef first you must skin the cloves of garlic and cut them into slivers. Then chop the *pancetta* into dice and mix them with the garlic; sprinkle the mixture liberally with the ground pepper. Next, make small deep cuts all over the piece of beef and insert the pieces of peppered *pancetta* and garlic. If necessary tie the beef around with twine to keep its shape. Then, in a large heavy saucepan heat up the olive oil, add the chopped onion, carrot and celery and let them soften. Put in the piece of beef and turn it to seal on all sides. Sprinkle on a pinch of salt and pour in the glass of red wine. After a few minutes add the tomatoes. Cover the pot and cook extremely slowly for at least four hours; the surface of the liquid in the pan should hardly move. Add stock at intervals if it is needed. The *stracotto* is ready to be eaten when the meat falls apart with just the aid of a fork. To serve the dish carve the beef into slices which will be prettily patterned with the pink prosciutto and white garlic, arrange the meat on an oval dish, reduce the sauce by boiling it briskly and pour a little over the slices of beef.

The *Scottiglia* is made with a mixture of meats cooked with *odori*, carrot, celery, and onion, then served on a slice of bread that has been toasted and rubbed with garlic. The dish originated in harder times when there was not much meat to be eaten and all the neighbours would crowd into one house for the evening, bringing with them whatever piece of meat they could obtain: a piece of rabbit or *prosciutto*, some chicken, a little veal or maybe some tripe, very often game of some description. Then the meat would all be cooked up together in the large cauldron and flavoured with the usual vegetables and wine. The oldest recipes for this dish specify that absolutely no oil was to be used in the preparation of the stew, maybe because the meat was fattier in those days. While the meat was cooking what is known as the *veglia* would take place: the people, usually from a small hamlet like the one Silvana was born in, would sit around the fire and give recitations of Dante and verses that the men had made up themselves. These would very often contain veiled references to the girl who had caught their eye, and in this way the cold evenings passed in a pleasant manner.

Silvana sometimes makes a *Scottiglia* when she has various small pieces of meat that are not enough in themselves to make a meal, and the stew is always served in the same old-fashioned Tuscan way with bread at the bottom of the soup dish.

 To make a *Scottiglia* you would need one large onion, one large rib of celery, one large carrot, a small bunch of parsley, three cloves of garlic, one of which you must reserve, a few sprigs of basil if available, if not, a sprig of rosemary. A half to one *peperoncino* (a small hot red pepper), one glass of olive oil and a total of 1 kg or 2¼ lb of as many different sorts of meat as possible, for example chicken, beef, rabbit, pork, guinea fowl, veal, pheasant; the more types of meat used the better the stew will be. You also require one large glass of rough red wine, 450 g or 14 to 16 oz of canned tomatoes or their equivalent weight in fresh skinned tomatoes, stock as needed, salt and black pepper, and finally four or five slices of stale bread, one for each person.

Clean and chop the onion, the celery and the carrot into small dice. Chop the garlic and the *peperoncino*, tear up the basil but leave the rosemary whole and discard it before serving. In a very large saucepan or large earthenware pot that can be used on a gas ring, heat the olive oil. Add the chopped *odori*, allow them to soften, then add the *peperoncino*, the garlic and the basil or rosemary. Next gradually add all the meat which you have previously trimmed and cut into convenient small pieces. Turn the meat until it is all sealed. Now add the wine, lower your heat and let the wine simmer and evaporate. Next add the tomatoes and a little stock, season and stir well, cover the pan and let it cook on the lowest possible flame for at least two hours. Check frequently that there is enough liquid to just cover the meat and add stock as needed. The *Scottiglia* should cook with hardly any movement to disturb its surface. The dish is ready to be served when the meat comes away from the bones with only the aid of a fork.

When you are ready to serve the stew, lay in each soup dish a piece of toasted bread that has been liberally rubbed with the reserved and halved clove of garlic. On top of the toast ladle some of the liquid from the stew then a helping of the meat.

However, the traditional country way to prepare meat is to grill it over the open wood fire and this remains Silvana's favourite cooking method. Grilled meat flavoured with herbs is one of the most character-istic foods of Tuscany. A meat to be appreciated is a *Lombatina alla Fiorentina*; it is a huge steak weighing at least six or seven *etti* (700 g) taken from the loin of the famous Chianina cattle and flavoured simply with salt and pepper right at the end of the cooking then served with a wedge of lemon. In Italy, beef comes from oxen, not from the *mucha*, the breed of cow seen in England. It is called *vitello* when killed very young at about three weeks having been fed exclusively on milk, and *vitellone* if it comes from older animals that have been allowed to graze but have not been made to work. In this way their meat is flavourful but never tough. *Vitelloni* is slang for idle young men; this is the clue to the famous Fellini film that starred Alberto Sordi. The meat from ani-mals which have been put to work is called *manzo*. Fresh pork is rather less popular in Italy than beef, although the Florentine *arista*, roast loin of pork, is justly famous. Lamb, spring lamb, is considered a great delicacy and is expensive; traditionally it is eaten at Easter time.

 Silvana cooks her **Lombatina alla Fiorentina** over a fire of sweet-smelling wood. She allows the fire to die to red embers then puts a metal rack over it until it is very hot. Then she places the steaks on the grill for three minutes, turns them over and leaves them for another three minutes. Only at the very end of the cooking does she season them with salt and black pepper; to do so before would make the meat tough. Her steaks are dark and well cooked on the outside and soft and rare within. She serves them with a wedge of lemon per person. The meat is cooked in this very simple way to preserve the clarity of its flavour. For four people you would need two large T-bone steaks, salt, pepper and a lemon. The meat can be cooked either over a wood fire in a grill in the garden or under a very hot grill on a normal cooker.

Although Orlando and Silvana derive great satisfaction from this month's tasks, viewing with pride their luscious hams and tasty *salame*, and eagerly welcoming each new-born lamb, their thoughts turn increasingly to the spring months when they can step out into their newly-green fields without fear of the cold. While they sit around the blazing fire at night when the day's work is done Orlando plans which fields he will devote to particular crops and Silvana decides how many rows of tomato plants and *zucchini* she will have this summer.

❧ FEBRUARY

Beside the courtyard of the *fattoria* next to the old domed bread oven lies Silvana's walled kitchen garden. Its walls are topped by wrought-iron fencing which is choked with the tangle of an ancient wisteria. The garden is entered through a high arched iron gate, always kept closed to prevent the hens and rabbits from eating the good vegetables within. These low crumbling walls are lined with rosemary bushes interspersed with sage and marjoram. The woody, oil-laden aromatic rosemary and sage are the herbs she uses most for grilling and roasting her meat and fowl.

Although the farmland is waking from the dreary winter's trance and drifts of violent green appear where the grain sown in November tentatively feathers the fields, Silvana still has little choice of vegetables in the kitchen garden, and the walled area is practically bare. Guido, the blue-eyed blond-haired foreman who lives in a pretty house next to the valley's church, has already dug over the beds for the spring planting. Traditionally the seeds will be sown on Easter Saturday, which coincides with the *luna calante*, the waning paschal moon, the most propitious time for sowing and planting.

The rows of celery plants are just sparse green sprouts but the tops, chopped with a carrot or two, are still the absolutely essential flavouring for *ragù* and *minestrone di verdura*. The black-green cabbages with their plume-like leaves still stand in rows and here and there appears a small cauliflower. The dark-green cabbages are another important ingredient for the *minestrone*, imparting a very distinctive and delicious flavour and texture: the tough leaves remain whole and faintly crisp and will not cook into a mush like the round white cabbage, which is useless for this purpose. Orlando, who likes his food to be rather salty, sometimes takes charge of the cooking pot to make a *minestrone* with the stock that is left after the boiling of a *cotechino*. He adds everything he can lay his hands on to make a big soup, which is what the word *minestrone* actually means. In go the white beans, whole not puréed, *prosciutto*, carrot, celery, potatoes and winter cabbage, while Silvana, eyes raised, murmers about the unseemly extravagance of putting so many ingredients together when a simpler soup is just as nourishing. However, she likes to make the soup later in the year when the *zucchini* are new because she thinks that they are what really makes the *minestrone* good.

 Normally when she makes a **Minestrone di Verdura** Silvana will use approximately these ingredients: one large onion, two large carrots, two ribs of celery plus their leaves, then half a cup of olive oil, 300 g or 10 oz of cooked white beans, the *cannellini* variety, 250 g or 9 oz of *pomodori pelati* (canned peeled tomatoes) or the equivalent weight of peeled and chopped fresh tomatoes, four leaves of the dark Tuscan cabbage (four outer leaves of an English green cabbage), two large peeled potatoes, stock as needed, a small bunch of parsley, salt and freshly ground black pepper.

On her large chopping block Silvana chops the onion, carrots and celery into small dice. In a large saucepan she heats up the olive oil and in it cooks these chopped *odori* until they have softened. Next she adds the white beans, mixing them into the *trittata*, then in go the tomatoes which she breaks up as she stirs them. At this point she may add a little stock if necessary. Next to go into the pot are the diced potatoes and the roughly torn cabbage leaves. Last Silvana adds a ladleful or two of stock and the parsley sprigs, which can be discarded after they have given up their flavour. She seasons the soup and allows the *minestrone* to simmer over a gentle flame until the vegetables are tender. Characteristically minestrone is laden with vegetables; there should only be enough liquid to keep them moving easily in the pot.

When it is time for supper Silvana ladles the soup into deep soup bowls and into each bowl pours a little of her best olive oil. This enriches the soup and the hot liquid releases the fruity perfume of the oil, thus enhancing the flavour of the vegetables.

There are very many different versions of *minestrone* to be found in Italy, using a great variety of fresh vegetables, rice, pasta and herbs in various combinations. However there is one general rule applied to all *minestrone* recipes: the ingredients which take longest to cook go into the pot first. However you may notice that in Silvana's recipe the cooked white beans are added before the raw potato. This is because the beans should be overcooked and somewhat disintegrated to thicken the soup. Indeed many cooks pass the beans through the mouli before adding them to the soup. Silvana and a great many Italian cooks use *dadi* or stock cubes to make up their soups, very often adding them to a light stock that they make out of poultry trimmings, the heads, feet and gizzards. Even Michel Guérard has advocated the use of stock cubes to give a lighter effect to a dish, so there seems no reason to be snobbish and insist upon heavy traditional stocks. However, the large companies such as Knorr and Maggi seem to use different recipes for the cubes that are available on the Continent and these are far more flavourful than those to be commonly obtained in England. It is always a good idea when staying in France or Italy to buy bouillon cubes to take home. Knorr 'Gran Sapore' is particularly good, and they also make a variety flavoured with *porcini* which is useful for a *risotto* of *funghi*.

 Silvana usually makes a great quantity of *minestrone* and what remains after the first meal she combines with bread to make a **Zuppa di Verdura**, an old Tuscan way of using stale bread. To make this she simply toasts a slice of bread for each person, rubs it with a halved clove of garlic, lays one in the bottom of each dish and then pours a ladleful of the soup into each bowl. Most of the old Tuscan peasant meals consisted of bread and a liquid flavouring such as this, using bread instead of rice or pasta and soup or stew instead of a sauce, so giving the characteristic staple of Tuscany. The basic *minestrone* can also be used to make the *Zuppe di Pane* which Silvana used to eat when she was a child.

To make **Zuppa di Pane** you will need soup as in the recipe for *minestrone*, 500g or 15oz of stale bread in slices and a cupful of whole, cooked white beans. In a deep earthenware dish put a layer of sliced stale Tuscan bread. On top of this pour a ladleful of the soup, making sure that the bread is well soaked with the liquid. Then put in another layer of bread, more soup and so on until the bowl is full. Sprinkle the white beans on top of the dish. Reserve some of the liquid from the *minestrone* to top up the bowl as the bread must be well soaked, then put the soup in the oven to warm through. This *Zuppa* was an old country way of making stale bread palatable and it was also an excellent filler for hungry children. Its distinctive flavour depends of course on using excellent bread made from strong flour. If there was any of the *Zuppa* left it could be served again after being recooked over a very low heat. At this stage it is even more delicious when eaten with a thin stream of olive oil poured over it and a couple of spring onions to add sharpness. This **Ribollita**, which means recooked, is served in this way in many a celebrated and expensive Tuscan restaurant.

One vegetable that Silvana does have in her garden at this time of year is the fresh and delicate **Broccoletti di Rape**, Brassica Napus, actually not broccoli as the name implies but a pale grey-green fleshy plant which when in bloom is topped with acid yellow florets. As far as I know it is hardly eaten in England. In fact the tender top branchlets make a delicious vegetable, tasting like something between asparagus and new spring beans. Silvana cooks it in boiling salted water until it is nearly tender, then after draining it thoroughly she chops it up and finishes it in a *tegame*, turning it in olive oil, garlic, salt and black pepper and a small amount of lemon juice. Butter substituted for the olive oil is also delicious. A great many of the green-leafed vegetables are cooked this way in Italy, and Silvana often serves spinach in this manner.

 To serve *Spinaci in Padella,* spinach cooked in the pan, for three people you will need about 1 kg or 2¼ lb of raw spinach, one wine glass of olive oil, two cloves of garlic, salt and freshly ground black pepper. It may be useful to remember when buying spinach that 2 kg or 4½ lb of raw spinach will give you about 500 g or 1 lb 2 oz of cooked spinach.

Wash the spinach carefully and discard any yellowed and damaged leaves. Put the leaves with just the water that clings to them into a very large saucepan and cook them over a very low flame until the spinach has wilted. Remove the spinach from the saucepan and drain the leaves well, squeezing out the excess moisture, then chop it finely. In a flat pan heat the olive oil into which you have put the crushed cloves of garlic to soften. Add the spinach to the oil, mix well and allow to cook until all the oil is absorbed. Season with salt and a generous amount of black pepper.

This dish is delicious too if you substitute a great quantity of butter for the olive oil and at the last moment sprinkle on a very little grated nutmeg.

Bietole, another delicious dark green vegetable which is spinach beet but tastes very different from spinach is something that Silvana cooks regularly. For three to four people she uses about 650g or 1½lb of *bietole,* half a glass of olive oil, one clove of garlic, salt and black pepper and a squeeze of lemon juice. She cooks the *bietole* in exactly the same way as the spinach, but instead of chopping the leaves she squeezes them hard in her hands to extract all the moisture, then in her flat *padella,* a flat shallow-sided frying or sauté pan, she heats the olive oil into which she has crushed a clove or two of garlic. She adds the long *bietole* leaves and stirs them around well so that all the oil is absorbed, then leaves it to cook for a few minutes. Just before serving she seasons it with salt and freshly-ground black pepper and lemon juice. Spinach beet is not I think commonly found in English greengrocers.

 Silvana makes an excellent *Frittata di Bietole,* an Italian omelette flavoured with the spinach beet. To make one of these for four people you would need 400 g or 14 oz of *bietole* prepared as in the first steps of the previous recipe or as in that for spinach, 50 g or 2 oz of *prosciutto* or smoked bacon cut into dice, a scant two tablespoons of olive oil, six eggs, salt and freshly ground black pepper.

In a small pan cook the diced *prosciutto* in its own fat, until it has taken on some colour. Add the cooked and chopped *bietole* and heat it through; you may add a little olive oil if the mixture starts to stick. In a bowl beat up the six eggs and season them with salt and pepper. Tip the *bietole* and *prosciutto* mixture into the bowl of eggs and mix them well together. In a large omelette pan heat some of the olive oil until it is smoking. Tip the egg mixture into the pan and as soon as a crust has formed on the bottom of the eggs lower the heat and allow the eggs to cook through gently. When they are firm but soft slide the *frittata* out onto a plate, then heat the rest of the oil in the omelette pan and replace the *frittata* uncooked side down. Allow the eggs to cook for another few minutes until the bottom has become crusty. To serve the *frittata* tip it out of the pan onto a clean plate and cut it into wedges. It can be served as part of an *antipasto* or, as Silvana does, for a supper dish. The Italian *frittata* differs from a French omelette (heat, speed, golden exterior and melting soft centre) in that the eggs are cooked slowly on a low heat and the finished dish looks rather cake-like and is not folded like its French counterpart. In fact the *frittata* has more in common with the Middle Eastern *Eggah.*

Cicoria is another green-leafed vegetable which is very popular in Tuscany but which I do not believe is commonly grown in England. It is palish green, with long fleshy stalks springing from a central root; the leaves which edge the stalks are narrow and wavy, rather like those of a dandelion. Although it is called *cicoria*, pronounced with the stress on the middle syllable, it has nothing to do with chicory, neither the blue-flowered variety that grows wild, nor the cultivated, tightly-furled white chicon which in Italy is called *endivia del Belgo* and in France *endive*. Nor has it anything to do with *cicoria*, the generic name given by Mrs Grigson in her informative book on vegetables to the *radicchio rosso* which comes from the Veneto area of Italy. In Tuscany, if you ask for a dish of *cicoria* in a restaurant, inevitably a plate of cooked greenery will arrive. If you want a salad of the beautiful red leaves that run from palest pink to deep porphyry then it is safer to ask for an *insalata di radicchio rosso*. However, just to make things more complicated, if you order *radicchio* without qualifying it with the word *rosso*, you will receive yet another cooked green leaf, albeit of the *radicchio* (chicory) family, which is also served as a salad in summer. The delicious green *cicoria* makes another diversion in the confusing question of endive versus chicory. In general if you order a plate of *verdura cotta*, cooked greenstuff, in a Tuscan restaurant, you are likely to receive a portion of one of these many sorts of delicious leaves, proably cooked in the manner I have described.

In Italy, EEC regulations or no, people grow and consume an enormous variety of vegetables and salads that are unknown in England and whose names are often obscure. The aged *contadini* who wheel their little wooden barrows to the country markets, carrying with them small bundles of herbs and salads tied up with green osiers, a few juniper berries and a string of garlic, are not to be regimented by any authority. They will grow what they have always grown and call their produce by their local dialect names.

Country people also like to eat wild salads and vegetables. One of Orlando's favourites is the *luperi*; this is a pretty climbing plant that grows in hedgerows near water. Its top tender leaves and stalk, about the last six inches of the plant, are cooked in similar fashion to the *broccoletti di rape*, and it has a rare and delicate flavour. Orlando is often to be seen in spring gathering *luperi* by the stream and his favourite way of eating it is chopped and stewed with garlic in a little pan, then covered with beaten egg to make a *frittata*. *Luperi* are wild hops and were eaten by the ancient Romans.

Silvana likes to wander in the fields and gather up an *insalata di campo* for supper. This 'field salad' is a selection of young plants to be found on grassy banks and near hedges. Silvana is expert at finding these plants.

Some are like tiny thistle leaves, others are serrated like the dandelion and others look like daisy plants with small white roots that are also edible. They have local names like *ramponcioli, bianchella* and *radagolio.* They make an interesting and unusually textured salad seasoned in the usual way with olive oil, wine vinegar or lemon juice, salt and a little black pepper. It is possible to buy the *insalata di campo,* or *insalata del prato* as it is called in the north, in the shops and it has become very popular on restaurant menus but at a greater price than that of cultivated salads.

Like their neighbours, the Cerottis are starting to feel the approach of spring. Silvana has picked a small bunch of pale primroses to put into the glass pot under the small picture of Christ that hangs over the dining-room door. The cat chases the lizards that have been tempted from their hiding places by the warming sun, their bellies flat and their skins dull after the winter hibernation, and a lone black bee buzzes around the eaves of the *fattoria.*

The most important task of the month for Orlando and his men is to prepare the seed-beds for the new season's crop of tobacco. This lush green valley, although Tuscan, does not have the classic arid Florentine landscape, with its carefully planted cypresses punctuating the cornfields, but is an unique area of Italy, semi-tropical in the summer and abundantly provided with mountain streams to irrigate the tobacco crop which has made the farmers prosper. Tobacco is the main cash crop and the source of security and wealth for the Cerottis and their work force. Between the kitchen garden and the slope up to the shepherd's house there is a flat area of sheltered ground which contains the two long seed-beds and Orlando, followed as usual by his favourite dog, supervises the men as they repair the *ortini.* These long troughs, measuring about two metres by thirty metres, are edged with beautifully cut flagstones stuck vertically into the ground. Every year broken sides must be repaired and the old soil removed. This year Orlando is planning to extend the beds to provide enough plants to fill the extra fields ploughed for the tobacco crop. After the edges have been repaired and the interiors cleaned it is time to fill them with straw and manure from the farmyard midden. Then the men will fetch tractorloads of fine soil from the river's edge. This rich alluvial soil is sieved and raked and sprinkled with fertiliser ready to receive the seeds. They will be sown under the age-old rules of the condition of the moon. Scientists may say that the phases of the moon have only a minute effect upon the growth of plants but Italian farmers still prefer to rely on their own experience and traditions.

The seeds will be planted when the moon is full and about to wane. This year, Orlando has invested part of last year's profits in large semi-circular metal frames, large enough for men to stand under with ease, and a tough canopy to protect the seedlings from bad weather and marauding cats. Under the thick plastic the air is moist and luxuriant, and every day the beds will be carefully watered and weeded. The more love and care that is put into the planting and nurturing of the seedlings the better will be the results.

Silvana, being a good Tuscan, enjoys beans and serves them often, especially during the winter. She grows two varieties in her garden: the *cannellini*, the small white beans, and the *borlotti*, beans which come in the pretty ivory pods that are splashed with sang-de-boeuf. In summer she cooks the beans in their fresh state, often adding them to soups, but she always dries a good supply for the rest of the year and these provide a nourishing tasty vegetable. Her basic way of serving both varieties is to soak them overnight or for at least several hours then to boil them in plenty of water, adding salt towards the end of the cooking. When the beans are tender but still whole she drains them carefully and seasons them with olive oil, salt and freshly ground black pepper. The oil's flavour is enhanced by the hot beans. Sometimes, to make the dish sharper, she will chip small pieces of raw onion into the bowl; the beans are excellent served with sausages grilled over the fire.

 To make *Fagioli Bianchi*, beans flavoured with raw onion, you would need, for four people, 400 g or 14 oz of dried white beans, the type known as *cannellini* in Italy, or the same amount of *borlotti* beans, half a glass of olive oil, salt and black pepper and half a raw onion, the pink variety if possible. Soak the beans overnight in plenty of cold water. Rinse them and put them into a clean pan then cover them with fresh water. Cook them on a medium flame until they are tender, which will take an hour to an hour and a half, depending on the age of the beans. Salt them only during the last fifteen minutes of cooking. Drain them well and tip them into a serving bowl. Pour the olive oil over the beans; the heat of the beans will bring out the scent and flavour of the oil; sprinkle on the chopped onion and plenty of black pepper and serve immediately, perhaps with some grilled Italian sausages and lots of rough red wine.

Silvana cooks her sausages with bay leaves over the fire. To cook them well you must prick the sausages then spear them on metal skewers, alternating the sausages with the bay leaves. Grill them over an open fire or on the charcoal grill in the garden. Turn them frequently so that they are crisp on all sides but still soft within. The cooking time depends on the size of the sausage and the heat of the fire. Excellent Italian sausages are available in England in Italian food stores.

Another typically Tuscan dish is **_Fagioli col Tonno_** and for it Silvana prepares the white beans in the normal manner then after they have been drained and put in a serving bowl she seasons them with the customary oil, salt and pepper and on top arranges pieces of tuna fish which have been preserved in olive oil and which Orlando buys from a vast can at the local store. Silvana also uses ordinary tinned tuna fish, the best of which is called *ventresca*, the belly part of the fish which has the'finest meat.

   The *Fagioli col Tonno* can either be served as a luncheon or supper dish or as a first course and the following quantities for a main dish for four people will serve six at the beginning of a meal. You will need 400 g or 14 oz of dried white beans, half a glass of olive oil, two tins of *tonno in olio di oliva*, if you can find it buy *ventresca*, salt and freshly ground black pepper, half a raw onion, chipped into small pieces, and a small amount of chopped parsley if the colour pleases you.

Prepare and cook the beans as indicated in the previous recipes. Drain the beans well and tip them into a large flat serving dish. Pour the oil over the beans, which incidentally should not be overcooked: they should still retain their shape and have a faint bite. Drain the tuna well and break it into chunks with a fork. Arrange the pieces on top of the beans. Season with ground black pepper and sprinkle on the chips of onion and the parsley if you have a fancy to. This is very good as a first course served with a chilled white wine.

Silvana also likes to cook the white beans with a tomato sauce; this is called *Fagioli all'uccelletto*. To make the dish she first cooks the *cannellini* beans, either fresh ones or the soaked, dry variety. In half a glass of olive oil she colours three crushed cloves of garlic and adds a sprinkling of black pepper and a few sage leaves. These ingredients which serve to give more flavour to the oil must not be permitted to burn. When the garlic has turned colour she adds the beans and some fresh ripe tomatoes which she has first skinned and passed through her food mill. The beans can then be left to stew gently to absorb the flavour of the tomato.

If you would like to make the ***Fagioli all'uccelletto,*** for four people you would need 400 g or 14 oz of dried white *cannellini* beans or 1 kg or 2¼ lb of fresh white beans; two tablespoons of olive oil, three cloves of garlic, four fresh sage leaves, salt and black pepper and 350 g or 12½ oz of chopped and drained tinned peeled tomatoes or peeled and chopped fresh tomatoes. Cook the dried white beans in the manner already indicated or alternatively shell the fresh beans and cook them in slightly salted water until they are tender, for about twenty to thirty minutes. In a large pan heat the olive oil, add the garlic which you may crush, the sage leaves and a little black pepper; it smells wonderful in the hot oil. On no account should the garlic be allowed to become too brown or the sage burn. Add the well drained beans to the flavoured oil then pour in the tomatoes. Allow the beans to cook for about fifteen to twenty minutes on a gentle flame.

· *Uccelletti* are small birds, but the reason for the name of this bean dish remains obscure. Perhaps it is so called because small birds are also often cooked with sage leaves.

These small white beans, the *cannellini* or *toscanelli*, form an important basis for the *minestra* that Silvana makes in the evening for supper. She usually passes the beans through the mouli to make them into a purée to thicken the soup. These *minestre* are usually simple affairs using stock, normally obtained from chicken giblets, beans, a little carrot, celery, a spoonful of tomato concentrate and one or two bouillon cubes. To add interest to the broth Silvana adds some form of small soup pasta, maybe *stelline*, the tiny stars, or sometimes she adds fine spaghetti broken up into very short lengths. Occasionally she will put a piece of beef into the soup, starting with cold liquid so that the flavour of the *brodo* will be stronger and they may eat the boiled beef, or *manzo lesso*, for their main course. Just before she serves the soup Silvana will add a stream of olive oil, which improves the flavour and enriches the soup. This *minestra* is invariably served for *cena*, supper, as Italians tend to eat pasta once a day, at lunchtime. Soup is considered to be lighter and more digestible for an evening meal.

 This recipe is a pleasant version of the ***Minestra di Fagioli,*** the humble bean soup. To make it you will require one onion, one rib of celery, two cloves of garlic, a small bunch of parsley, four fresh basil leaves, 50 g or 2 oz of *pancetta*, three tablespoons of olive oil, 250 g or 9 oz of ripe tomatoes skinned and chopped, 150 g or 5½ oz of cooked white beans, 100 g or 3½ oz of *pasta corta*, short pasta, salt and black pepper, a stock cube or some home-made stock.

First of all chop the onion, the celery, the garlic, the parsley and the *pancetta*. Tear up the basil leaves. In a large saucepan heat up the olive oil, add the chopped ingredients and allow them to soften and the *pancetta* to turn colour. Add the tomatoes, give it all a good stir and let the mixture simmer for ten minutes. Meanwhile put the cooked beans through the mouli to make a coarse purée. Add this to the soup, mix it all well again and let it simmer for a further ten minutes. If the soup is too dense add a little stock or a soup cube dissolved in a small amount of hot water. About twelve to fifteen minutes before you are ready to eat, add the *pasta corta*. This means any sort of small tube-shaped pasta such as *maccheroni rigati*, *rigatoni* or *penne*, but not the very tiny *stelline* and grains which go into a clear *brodo* or broth. This larger pasta adds texture to the bean soup. After twelve to fifteen minutes the pasta should be cooked; it will take longer in a soup than it will when boiled in the regular way. Then serve the soup with grated parmesan or *pecorino* cheese and a spoonful of olive oil.

One very old-fashioned Tuscan method of cooking beans is to cook them in a *fiasco*; this is the round-bottomed chianti bottle without its straw covering. The beans, fresh ones if possible, were put into the bottle then on top was poured a great glass of olive oil and two ladlefuls of water. Some crushed garlic and sage was added too, for flavour. Then the bottle was closed up with a wad of cloth that prevented too much evaporation but allowed some of the steam to escape in case the bottle burst. The cooking was achieved by putting the bottle into hot embers and leaving it for several hours, or by leaving the bottle overnight in the warm wood ashes of the fireplace. Some Tuscan firedogs have their front ends fashioned into cups made up of metal rings in which the *fiaschi* could be balanced in order for them to cook. Finally the beans were poured out of the bottle and seasoned with salt, black pepper and a little more oil. Whole spring onions would be laid on the table for anyone who cared to munch on one, to give a spark to the beans.

It is about a month since the butcher put the four enormous hams into their wooden tubs of salt and garlic. Every day or two Silvana has climbed the wide stone stairs to the rooms under the eaves where the tubs are kept, in order to turn the *prosciutto* so that every part is well and evenly treated with salt. Now she judges that they are in a fit state to be brought down to the kitchen. With Orlando to help her she climbs onto the kitchen table and hangs the *prosciutti* from the beams by the kitchen door using large meat hooks that are pushed through the hocks. There they will remain for another few weeks hanging in the well circulating air, where she can watch their progress as they dry. Drops of salty water will ooze from them and splash onto the tiles. When three weeks or so are up Silvana will take down the hams and wash them well with her own wine vinegar, dry them carefully with clean cloths and cover their entire surfaces with finely ground black pepper. Then they will be ready to hang with the *salame* from the beams over the pantry's huge meat safe.

Depending on the date of Easter, the month of February in Italy, as in much of the rest of Europe, can be devoted to *Carnevale*, the 'farewell to flesh' before the rigours of Lent. *Carnevale* provides an excellent excuse for making different dishes to add spice to the daily diet as well as an opportunity to fill the long winter nights with dancing. Every city town and village organises its *ballo in maschera* or masked ball; from the ornate formal occasions in Venice, where guests wear elaborate costumes and beautiful silk masks still hand-made in the city shops, to the innumerable bucolic village hops. The dances are held every week and towards the end of the month every night. There are processions of masked revellers, floats and streamers, and the streets are covered with drifts of confetti. The ancient purpose of the festival was to vanquish the grey spirits of winter before the coming of spring.

As her contribution to the festivities Silvana is making some of the traditional *castagnole*, fried sweet cakes, for the dance to be held in the next village. Her dark dress covered by a huge white apron, she sets to and scrubs the wooden table in the pantry ready to make the pastry. On the wall over the table are hung in a row her wooden flour scoops and round wooden flour sieves and a large sack of flour stands on a box beside the table. Like other Italian countrywomen, she does not use a bowl to make her pastry in, but uses her board or the table and contains the liquid within the flour. When the table is ready Silvana scoops out a generous heap of flour onto it. Her scoop holds about half a kilo of flour and she uses two scoopsful. Her measuring system, as always, is based on experience and the size of the implements she has to hand. She makes a dip in the centre of the flour into which she cracks six fresh eggs from the white bowl at the end of the table. To these she adds a large tin mug full of melted butter and another of sugar. The eggs go in whole and dexterously with her hands she mixes them and the butter together with the sugared flour, gently pushing the edges of the flour-well towards the centre. To this mixture she adds a pinch of salt and the contents of a small *bustina di lievito*, a pretty little packet of baking powder, and the grated peel of a lemon. Finally she works in a glass of *mistra*, which is a sweet anice-flavoured liqueur much enjoyed by Tuscan country ladies in their cups of black coffee. The men add cognac to their espresso coffee and this is known as a *caffè corretto*, a corrected coffee, and can be asked for at any Italian bar. Next, Silvana kneads the ingredients together into a firm dough, pulling and folding and flattening time after time, her hands working rhythmically and lightly. When she is satisfied that the dough is smooth enough she rolls it into a ball and sets it aside to rest. In the meantime she clears her board and flours her long rolling pin, which is a good metre long and normally used to roll out her home-made pasta. After about fifteen minutes she breaks off small lumps of the dough and rolls them out into long thin strips about two inches or so wide. These she inserts through the rollers of her simple old pasta machine, the one she was given as a wedding present a good few years ago. The pasta machine works like a small mangle and gives the dough the requisite fineness. She lays all the delicate strips side by side on the board then cuts them into diamond shapes with a large old-fashioned fluted pastry wheel.

Meanwhile on the open fire she heats a large pan of sunflower or perhaps arachide, peanut oil. Silvana is quite happy to use these types of oil for these particular cakes, although years ago they too were fried in olive oil. Indeed olive oil was used in their composition before anyone thought of using butter in its place. However arachide oil is light and tasteless and butter makes a delicious substitute for the heavier, richer tasting oil. Arachide is also much less costly to use as a medium for deep frying. She takes a batch of the pastry diamonds into the kitchen and when the oil is bubbling puts them into the pan. Almost immediately they puff up to ten times their original size like small fat cushions; when they are a pretty golden colour she drains them with a pierced spoon and puts them into one of her giant white fluted china bowls. After all the pastry is used and the bowl is heaped with the golden *castagnole* she sprinkles on a quantity of sugar and splashes on a liberal dose of *Alchermes di Siena*, a startlingly pink alcoholic liqueur which is not drunk but used to colour cakes and puddings.

 To make the **Castagnole** you will need 600 g or 1 lb 5 oz of plain flour, 150 g or 5½ oz of sugar, 150 g or 5½ oz of melted butter or olive oil, four eggs, a small glass of anice, cognac or rum, the grated peel of a small lemon, a pinch of salt and 2½ level teaspoons of baking powder.

Put half the flour into a mixing bowl. In another smaller bowl crack the four eggs and beat them as for an omelette then mix in the sugar. Pour this mixture into the flour then add the butter, the grated lemon peel and the salt. Mix all these ingredients together, gradually adding the rest of the flour and the baking powder, then pour in the anice and continue working the dough until the bowl is clean. On a floured board knead your dough until it is smooth and tight. Let it rest for twenty minutes or so. Break off small lumps of the dough and roll them as finely and evenly as you can into long strips, or use a pasta machine like Silvana's if you have one. Cut the pastry strips into diamond shapes about 1½ in long with a wheel or a sharp knife and put them in one layer on a large plate or board ready for frying. When your pan of *fresh* oil is bubbling, put in the diamonds two or three at a time and watch them swell and bob to the surface. When they are a nice golden colour fish them out with a pierced spoon, lay them to drain on kitchen paper and sprinkle them with sugar. They are also delicious served on a small plate two or three to each person and at the last moment covered with thin honey. Country families in Umbria and Tuscany cook numerous batches of these cakes during the carnival season before the beginning of Lent. They are also often offered on the menus of country restaurants and very good they are too.

Most of the Cerotti household are going to the dance, the last *veglione*, a *ballo in maschera*, before the first day of Lent. The wives of Orlando's *contadini* have made piles of cakes too and some are in charge of grilling the sausages for the *pannini*, the rolls that will be served for the late supper. Two of Sauro's cousins, Mariella and Laura, are staying at the *fattoria*. They are Silvana's nieces and come from her native remote village in the mountains, in fact from the house where Silvana was born, which is still lit by oil lamps and candles and where the water is still carried from the spring in the traditionally shaped copper vessels. The *fattoria*, with its television and general bustle, is great fun for them and they are very excited about the dance. Most of the afternoon they have closeted themselves in Silvana's big bedroom trying on their best clothes in front of the looking glass and giggling as they arrange each other's hair.

Silvana herself does not dance any more. After Pietro's death she was naturally in strict mourning for a long period, which of course precludes dancing. At that time and for long after she lost all her desire for life's pleasures and it was only by adhering to a regimen of hard work that she succeeded in subduing her grief. Formal mourning is very much adhered to in the country, and there are set periods of time for different relatives: two years for a parent, a year for an aunt or uncle and so on. Country widows dress in dark clothes, if not the unrelieved black of the southern women, and on Sundays and special occasions wear around their necks, prominently displayed on their usually ample bosoms, a gold locket displaying a photograph of their dear one.

So although Silvana loves to dance, and listening to the old-fashioned dance music remains one of her greatest pleasures, she has got used to just looking on. She says that the dances, too, have changed: when she was seventeen there were schottisches and various formal dances performed in groups and lines, not waltzes and polkas and tangos, which she thinks are faintly scandalous and were invented for lovers. Of course, she says, they flirted and courted too, but after the dances, so they had the best of both worlds. It was at a dance that she and Orlando first met. When she remembers this she chuckles and says: 'I saw him and he saw me and that was that.'

At about nine o'clock everyone is ready to leave for the dance, including Sauro, his hair slicked down and wearing his favourite shirt and new trousers. The men are smart in their Sunday best, their well-laundered shirts gleaming against their wind-reddened faces. Mariella and Laura, their glossy hair fluffed into curly manes, wear the latest fashion in baggy trousers and tucked-in sweaters, and their faces are carefully made up, lips dark and eyes sultry. Just because they live in a remote mountain fastness does not mean that they have escaped the Italian passion for clothes. They all pile into the cars clutching the bowl of *castagnole* and several two-litre bottles of red wine. The affair is to be held in a large barn belonging to a farmer in the next village up the hill.

The barn has been cleared of all its implements and dust and at the rear a rough stage has been constructed on which sit the musicians, on this occasion two very young and solemn men, one playing the drums, the other the piano accordion. They strike up a brisk polka and soon the floor is crowded. Middle-aged men in stiff Sunday suits, some still wearing their felt hats, dance with their wives or neighbours' wives, the women wear flowery dresses and whirls of *felce azzurro*, a much loved and inexpensive scent, fill the air. The event is a *ballo liscio*, literally translated as a 'smooth dance': there will be no rock or disco music, just waltzes, polkas, quicksteps and tangos. It is similar to English ballroom dancing, but performed to a quicker tempo and with more stylized gestures, the dancers upright and formal. During the tango there is a great deal of head jerking and bending backwards. There are no wallflowers or awkward groups of boys standing in rows: everyone dances with everyone, enjoying the music and the movement. The ages range from tiny children solemnly dancing like the adults in one corner to old ladies who sit and gossip and look after the coats. Half way through the evening, the door is flung open and a group of masked costumed figures rushes in. The band strikes up a new tune and the masked dancers form lines and perform a strange dance like a fast minuet. Their faces are covered with veiling pulled tight and they have all manner of odd hats and garments on. There are men wearing sunbonnets and cotton frocks and girls in patched trousers hung with tin cans, but the veils make them all completely anonymous and slightly sinister. The music changes, the formation breaks up, the masqueraders grab at the nearest onlookers and whirl them round in faster and faster circles as the tempo quickens.

Suddenly, at an unheard signal, the music stops and the dancers disappear as quickly as they arrived. It is midnight and time to eat. Trestle tables are pulled out and loaded with the glistening piles of cakes, some drenched with honey, others crisp with sugar. There are fresh fat bread rolls filled with spicy sausages and the dark wine is circulated. As one old lady says: 'We do not put the wine out before midnight or they will all become quite drunk and might forget their manners.' After the supper the dancing recommences, more masqueraders arrive and the floor is strewn with streamers and confetti. Despite their protestations the younger children are taken home to bed, but the music goes on and the dances grow wilder until around four in the morning the exhausted musicians are released and the barn remains silent and empty save for the vine shoots which, propped in a corner, are waiting to be planted.

❧ MARCH

Orlando's fields are for the most part still small, bearing the imprint of ancient farmers, for this is the land of the Etruscans; a small Roman road still penetrates to the very apex of the valley. The edges of the terraced fields are planted with vines and the occasional fig or apple tree, and in some cornfields there remain regularly spaced turkey oaks planted and pollarded to support the vines, a system which was used and called *arbustum* by the ancient Romans. You can even see the ancient *compluvium*, which is a long trellis slung between trees forming a shady pergola for the grapes to hang down from. Unfortunately in many parts of Tuscany this old way of planting, which depends on the corn being reaped by hand, as the spaces between the vines are often too narrow to allow tractors to manoeuvre, has been sacrificed to modern needs. The old supporting trees and the thick gnarled vines have been allowed to fall into decay and new vines have been planted close together, supported by concrete posts and wires. However, Orlando and his men still tend the old vines carefully, but, with an eye to the future, Orlando has set aside a field on the steep southern slope beneath the *fattoria* where he plans to establish a new vineyard. This field must be cleared of stones and ploughed ready for the planting of the new vines.

Armed with secateurs, Guido and his brother Tonio are out in the fields following the lines of old vines, pruning and tying and mending the supports; they have already sown the precious tobacco seeds in the warm frames. Spring is warming the soil, new foliage is forcing its way through and already the days have lost their bitter coldness. Even though it is early in the year the lambs are sufficiently weaned to allow the ewes to be milked for cheese.

Cheesemaking is Silvana's job and she is very skilled at it. Her *pecorino*, hard sheep's-milk cheese, is famous and people come from all over the area to buy it. At about nine o'clock every morning Andrea the shepherd brings the milk to her kitchen in two churns, containing about ten litres each; to make good cheese the milk must be absolutely fresh. He has milked the sheep carefully in the folds, making sure that dirt and droppings do not fall into the pail and spoil the milk. To milk a sheep requires a knack and strong hands, and Silvana ruefully admits that she has never learned how to manage the business. When Andrea is ill they call in a friend of hers, a woman who lives further up the mountain.

Once more the wide hearth plays its vital role in the farm's daily life. Since eight o'clock the large cauldron full of water has been steaming away over a brisk fire. When Andrea appears with the milk, Silvana, her arms straining, empties the cauldron into a large galvanized tin tub standing ready before the fire. Next she strains the twenty litres of milk through a fine strainer to catch any stray pieces of straw or dust and the milk cascades through into a large plastic pail. Her grandmother would probably have used a wooden tub and an earthenware crock for the milk but plastic is lighter and has the same effect, so Silvana has accepted this new aid. She puts the pail of milk into the tub of hot, but not boiling, water and in this simple way she has made something resembling a large *bagno maria*.

The milk needs heat to solidify and separate; but it also needs another ingredient, which is rennet. Originally, when the art of cheesemaking was discovered, rennet was obtained by soaking a small piece of sheep's stomach to extract the necessary substance. The idea may have stemmed from the observation that when a lamb was slaughtered the milky contents of its stomach were found to be curdled. Silvana, however, uses a vegetable substance to produce the same effect, no doubt a discovery of some ancient herbalist. In her garden there are clumps of artichoke plants which are never cut to be eaten. At the end of the summer, after they have flowered and their magnificent purple heads have dried and turned brown, when the moon is in the right phase Silvana picks them and hangs them to dry completely. Then she separates the heads and teases out the stamens until she has a big pile of straw-coloured threads.

She keeps them in a large brown paper bag in a dry place in the pantry. In a discussion on sheep's cheese in the second book of Marcus Terentius Varro's treatise on agriculture the author advocates the use of rennet made from a hare or kid which he says is more efficacious than that obtained from a sheep, but he also goes on to say that some people use the milk of the fig stem plus vinegar or the juice of the fig as a coagulant.

Having put the milk into the *bagno maria*, Silvana takes a handful of the artichoke stamens and lays them in a wide soup bowl. Then she covers them with a ladleful of hot water, allowing them to soak for a few minutes, stirring and poking at them occasionally.

After a moment the water turns a light brown colour. To extract the coagulant fully she rubs the stamens together with both hands rather like the action of rubbing cloth when trying to wash out a stain. When she is sure the juice is strong enough she strains the soup-plate of liquor through the fine wire sieve into the pail of milk, giving the stamens a last rub through the mesh before throwing them away. Occasionally if it is very late (Silvana makes another batch of cheese in the evening after supper) or if she is particularly tired she may use a powdered rennet called *caglio* which is bought from the chemist, but she says the cheese made with the chemical does not turn out so well; it is too industrial a process; besides, if you want to eat genuine food, to make it, you have to work hard.

Next comes a most important action: taking a very long wooden spoon, she stirs the milk thoroughly to mix the rennet well right through the milk to the bottom of the pail. If this step is neglected the milk will only curdle in patches. After giving it a good stir she covers the pail closely with a lid and leaves it to stand in the warm water for at least one hour.

Towards the end of the hour she checks the condition of the milk and when it is the consistency of stiff yoghourt and falls away easily from the side of the pail when tipped, it is ready to be put into the moulds. These are round, about twenty centimetres in diameter, and made of yellow earthenware, their sides and bottoms pierced through with small holes. Each mould stands in a small bowl. Out of the twenty litres of milk she will get three forms of cheese weighing close to a kilo each. A form, or *forma* in Italian, is the name given to a whole cheese.

Next comes the really skilful part of the process and one which is very beautiful to see. Having heaved the pail of solid milk onto the table, the moulds arranged to one side, Silvana crosses her bare arms and dips them to the elbow right into the bottom of the far side of the pail.

She pulls the white curd towards her as if to hug it, then holds the curds in that position, squeezing away the *siero*, whey. Then with a squelching sound she gently starts to break up the curd, gathering a large lump the size of a melon between her hands and squeezing gently. She puts the lump into one of the moulds and pushes it down, using a strange shredding action to break up and distribute the cheese evenly so that there will be no air holes. She fills the three moulds in turn, packing the cheese well down. The extra whey (the liquid left after the curds have separated) trickles from the holes in the moulds into their bowls below. This liquid is reserved and poured back into the shepherd's churns to be used in making *ricotta*. After the bulk of the cheese is in the moulds, she kneads it well down then tips the cheese out of the mould, reverses it and replaces it in the mould. She repeats this operation several times, kneading and turning and kneading again in an hypnotic rhythm. By this time the cheese has a very smooth and rubbery surface. This phase needs patience: the smoother and more tightly packed the cheese is, the better it will be when mature. As the saying goes: 'Cacio serrato e pane bucarellato.' 'Tight textured cheese and open textured bread.'

When Silvana is satisfied with the tightness of the cheeses she takes some coarse salt and rubs it generously on to the top of the forms. This is to draw more moisture out of the cheese. Then she puts the forms, in their moulds and little bowls to catch the drips, into the large deep wooden drawers of the pantry table. There they will remain for twenty-four to thirty-six hours and she will turn and resalt them every night and morning.

Returning to the kitchen, Silvana starts to make some *ricotta*, the soft white cheese which is usually made by the shepherd's wife, who sells it to shops in Cortona. The *ricotta* is made from the whey left over after the first full fat cheese has been extracted. This time, a *bagno maria* is not necessary. Silvana pours all the whey into her large copper cauldron and slings the pot on the hook over the fire which she has made up again. She covers the pot with a lid: many a dish of *ricotta* has been spoiled by soot falling down the chimney at an inopportune moment. She leaves the whey, which is a pale watery yellow colour, until it is at boiling point and the white curds start to float to the top. When the surface is covered with curds she removes the cauldron from the fire. Then, using a flat round perforated spoon with a long handle, she fishes out the *ricotta* and puts it into a fancy round mould which when well drained will be turned out onto one of the best dinner plates.

Ricotta must be eaten at its very freshest, and although there are many recipes for more complicated dishes made with this delicious, delicate cheese Silvana is very fond of the simplest and most homely way to eat it, that is, spread on a slice of fresh Tuscan bread. She simply cuts a slice of bread for each person, heaps on a generous amount of the *ricotta*, then sprinkles on a little salt or sugar according to each person's taste. This is eaten for breakfast or for a *merenda*, a second breakfast or an afternoon treat.

 Ricotta con Caffè is another of the simplest ways to serve the cheese. For two people you would need 200 g or 7 oz of fresh *ricotta*, two tablespoons of strong black coffee and a sprinkling of sugar. To make it you just mix the cheese with the coffee, arrange it in two shallow bowls and sprinkle with a little white sugar. Italians dilute the black espresso coffee made in the little Bialetti coffee machines which are commonly used in Italian homes. They also eat this dish for breakfast or *merenda*. It is rather good eaten as a last course at dinner with perhaps some fruit to follow.

There is a third sort of cheese which is made from the ewe's milk and this is called *ravigiolo*. It is a soft white full-fat cheese and is simply the first stage of the curds before they are kneaded into *pecorino*. To make the *ravigiolo* a pointed oval mould is traditionally used and often a small fern leaf is laid in the bottom of the mould to decorate the cheese. The full-fat curds are simply put into the mould, drained and turned out. It is a rather extravagant soft cheese which must be eaten fresh and is always seasoned with salt, never sugar, which is frequently used with the *ricotta*. Silvana makes it as a special treat. It is the original basis for the filling for *ravioli*, a name often met with in England but rarely in Italy, and which in fact has no semantic connection with *ravigiolo*. *Ravioli* should have a white cheese filling whereas the other filled pastas such as *tortellini* and *capelletti* should have meat-based fillings, although the distinction is now often ignored.

After the cheeses have drained sufficiently to be able to do without their moulds and bowls comes the third stage, the storage of the cheese. In March it is still too cold to put them in the unheated attic, so Silvana has suspended a large board from the pantry beams by a sling. On this the new cheeses are laid in rows. Twice a day she turns them to expose both sides to the air. When the board becomes encrusted with deposits from the skin of the cheese she takes a small iron scraper and cleans it. After a week or so she scrapes the rinds of the cheese too, which have now become a dark yellow colour powdered with a white deposit. The conservation of the cheese is very important as it can quite easily go mouldy. The air in the pantry is very pungent. During the next month, when the frosts have gone, all the cheeses will be taken to their own store-room in the attic. But until then the pantry is full of the pale gold moon-like discs covering the *madia* and the table as well as the swinging boards suspended from the ceiling. The fresh *pecorino* is a creamy yellow colour and has a smooth pliant texture which should not be laced with air holes.

The store-rooms are on the top floor of the *fattoria* and are reached by a wide stone staircase. In two of them the floors are heaped with grain for the winter fodder, sacks of maize kernels, piles of chestnuts gathered from the woods and walnuts and cobnuts from the garden. In other rooms are the tubs in which the hams are cured and two small rooms are reserved for the cheeses. The small square windows of these attic cheese-stores are covered with a fine wire mesh to keep out the flies and other insects and also to allow a good circulation of air. Hanging by ropes from the low-beamed ceiling is a large square board on which the cheese is placed. About a foot from the beams the four ropes are threaded through old saucepan lids, like tin disc-shaped beads in a necklace. Above the lids are arranged branches of sharp thorned twigs and amongst them small mirrors catch the light. A picture of the Blessed Virgin adorns one of the corners, attached to the rope by pale blue ribbon. This odd arrangement has a practical as well as an amulitic purpose. The board swings free of the ground, so there are no table legs for mice to run up. They can, however, scamper up walls and along beams but are prevented from sliding down the ropes onto the table top by the saucepan lids and the twigs. The purpose of the mirrors is more obscure. Perhaps they are put there in the hope that mice may be scared by a sudden glimpse of their own images. The votive picture is a modern equivalent of the Penates, the Roman gods of the store-room. What is certain is that this swinging shelf is a very ancient device: an example of a similar object can be seen painted on the wall of a side chamber of the tomb of Ramesses III in the Valley of the Kings at Thebes in Egypt.

As soon as the frosts permit, Silvana moves all the cheeses up into the attics. Twice daily she climbs the stone stairs morning and evening to add new forms to the store and to turn the cheeses, scraping them and the board regularly and keeping a watch out for any signs of mould. The cheese is a valuable commodity and she makes a modest profit by selling it to neighbours or small tradesmen from the nearest town. Her biggest customer is the man who sells *pannini ripieni*, bread rolls filled with various savoury stuffs, at the Cortona market on Saturday mornings; he also appears at local *festas*.

In a corner of the store-room is an old wooden *bigoncia*, a long cylindrical tub, its neck wider than the base. Originally it was used to carry grapes from the fields to the *cantina* during the *vendemmia*. Now this relic is used to hold the cheeses that are to be kept to mature for a year or more. After that time they will be very hard and piquant and will cost more than twice as much as the ordinary *pecorino*. To keep the cheeses for that length of time Silvana has to treat their rinds. She chooses firm, nicely maturing specimens and anoints them thoroughly with thick olive oil taken from the residue at the bottom of the oil jars and specially kept for this purpose. After giving them a thorough coating of oil she wraps each cheese in several layers of walnut leaves from the tree by the *cantina*, sealing the leaves in place with oil. These dark bundles she lays in the bottom of the wooden tub and leaves them to grow hard, dark and rich. Some people cover their cheeses in a layer of wood ash. The mountain women who make their own cheese all have favourite ways of flavouring the forms. Some rub the outsides with black pepper, ground chili or tomato conserve, some introduce black peppercorns into the forms when they make them, all devices to vary the familiar flavour. When it is ready the specially matured cheese will be stripped of its leaves and the excess deposits scraped away a little from the rind. Then Silvana will use the cheese to grate for various dishes or to eat in thin slivers with fruit at the end of a meal.

 Pere e Pecorino, pears and *pecorino* cheese, is a delightful dish with which to end a supper. There is an old Tuscan saying that you should not tell your *contadini* how good the pears taste when eaten with *pecorino* cheese or you will receive less of both in your share of the produce. To serve this dish fill a bowl with ripe perfect pears, one for each person. On a wooden board place a *stagionato*, seasoned, *pecorino* cheese. This will be hard and piquant-tasting with a deep golden-brown crust. The flavour of the soft juicy pear goes very well with the hard texture and sharp flavour of the cheese.

The familiar name for *pecorino* in Tuscany is *cacio* or *caciotto*. It has become increasingly difficult to find genuine *pecorino* made in the manner in which Silvana makes hers. The cheese stalls in country markets are good places to look as usually they obtain their stock from country women. This lovely cheese, whether bought fresh and soft or seasoned, is an excellent thing to take back home from a Tuscan holiday as it is almost unobtainable outside Italy.

Cheese is one of the most basic ingredients of Italian country cookery. Silvana uses her cheese all the year round in all manner of ways, as a good source of protein, an easy snack to put in a bag with a slice of bread for a *merenda* in the woods, in light and simple dishes for a supper such as *polpette*, croquettes of ground meat, cheese and spices, or the delicious soup, *stracciatella*. Cheese is indispensible too for the *pasta al forno*, and the *melanzane al forno*, the rich dish of aubergine slices fried in olive oil then cooked in layers with parmesan in the oven.

 To make her **Polpette**, which she and Sauro might also eat if they are lunching alone, Silvana uses about 150 g or 5½ oz of boiled potato, 100 g or 3½ oz of cooked breast of chicken, 100 g or 3½ oz of *mortadella* sausage, 50 g or 2 oz of grated *pecorino* or *parmigiano* cheese, one spoonful of finely chopped parsley, one clove of garlic, salt and black pepper, one egg, breadcrumbs and arachide oil for frying.

In a mixing bowl Silvana mashes up the potatoes well, and adds the chicken breast, chopped very finely. Next she adds the *mortadella*, also chopped finely, and then the grated cheese, mixing the ingredients well as she goes. Then she sprinkles in the parsley and finely chopped garlic and seasons the mixture with lots of black pepper and some salt. Finally she binds the paste together with an egg. When all the ingredients are thoroughly mixed she divides the mixture into small balls or sausages, whichever takes her fancy. She rolls the *polpette* in breadcrumbs and fries them a few at a time in a pan of bubbling arachide oil. When the *polpette* are a golden brown she drains them thoroughly and arranges them on a serving dish garnished with wedges of lemon. They make a lovely luncheon dish served with a peppery salad, maybe of rocket, and some cold white wine.

Silvana is fond of serving a *stracciatella* if she has guests for supper. This elegant soup in its simplest form consists of beaten eggs whisked into a steaming well-flavoured clear broth. Try eggs plus grated good parmesan and you have a very distinguished first course. Silvana makes her version with a soft paste made up of beaten eggs, grated *pecorino* and a small amount of soft breadcrumbs. Having made the paste she stirs it into her good stock, made from whatever meat or chicken trimmings she has had at hand that day. This is the sort of dish that really needs a good home-made stock and the *brodo* cubes, although good in their way, can be improved upon for this type of recipe, in which the quality of the broth forms a major part of the dish.

 To make a good broth, **Brodo**, Silvana will use 300 g or 11 oz of beef or chicken, 1½ litres or 2½ pints of water, salt, a stick of celery, a few sprigs of parsley, a carrot, one onion and two teaspoonfuls of tomato concentrate. She puts the cold water into a large pan and salts it, then adds the meat and brings it to a boil slowly over a low flame. When it is at boiling point she adds the *odori* and lets the pot boil gently for three hours or so. Finally she skims off any fat and strains the broth into another pan. This will be the basis of the *stracciatella*. The meat can be eaten as part of the next course.

 To make the **Stracciatella** she takes three eggs, three tablespoons of fine white breadcrumbs, three tablespoons of grated parmesan or *pecorino* cheese, salt and pepper and 1½ litres or 2½ pints of stock. In a bowl she beats up the three eggs, then she mixes in the breadcrumbs and the grated cheese, and seasons the mixture with salt and black pepper. Next Silvana adds a little of the cold stock to the egg mixture, whisking it well with a fork. In a large saucepan she heats up the remaining broth and when it is at boiling point she tips in the egg mixture, gradually whisking it all the while with a long-handled fork. When all the egg is in she lowers the heat under the pan and allows the soup to cook gently for three or four minutes while continuing to stir with the fork.

This month as soon as the first cheese is ready to eat, Silvana will probably make a *Frittata con Pecorino*, a simple dish that really celebrates the arrival of the fresh new cheese. To make this she cuts four slices of cheese, each about quarter of an inch thick, and fries them gently on both sides in a little olive oil. When the cheese is starting to melt and the pan is really hot she pours on four briskly beaten eggs seasoned with salt and black pepper. She lets the eggs cook over a low heat then turns the omelette over in the pan to cook the other side. The Cerottis will probably eat this dish for supper after their evening soup accompanied by *pansanella*, the Tuscan bread salad whose only vegetable ingredients at this time of the year will be onions or maybe a little fresh green garlic. This paucity of greenstuff does not however make for a dull salad. Good bread, good oil, wine vinegar, black pepper, salt and a spicy onion are a marvellous mixture.

 To make the **Frittata con Cacio** for two people you will need two tablespoons of olive oil, four slices of fresh *pecorino* cheese, or otherwise gruyère or possibly sharp real cheddar cheese, four eggs, salt and freshly ground black pepper.

Heat the olive oil in a heavy omelette pan, put in the slices of cheese and cook on each side until they are slightly melted. Beat up the eggs, season them with salt and pepper. Now raise the heat in your pan and pour in the eggs on top of the cheese. Let the eggs set on the bottom of the pan. Lower the heat to a very gentle flame and continue cooking until the eggs are cooked through. Now slide the *frittata* out onto a plate, raise the heat under the pan so that the oil again becomes very hot, then smartly reverse the *frittata* uncooked side down back into the omelette pan. *Coraggio!* It isn't so difficult. Although the Cerottis eat *frittate* as a supper dish, this recipe would make a delicious small lunch with a fresh green salad and a bottle of chilled *verdicchio*, a reliable white wine from the *Marche*.

Pecorino is the cheese that Silvana makes, and therefore uses, most. However she does from time to time buy some good *grana*, a *Grana Padana* or a *Parmigiano Reggiano*. The latter comes from the valley between Parma and Reggio where the cows give a very rich milk from the lush fields in which they graze. *Grana Padana* comes from the areas outside the delimited one in which the cheese is entitled to be called *Parmigiano*. It is a delicious cheese but does not quite have the depth of flavour of a seasoned parmesan. Silvana's criteria of a good parmesan are that it should be a nice yellow, have a crumbly crystalline texture and a nutty flavour. The pale, sawdust-coloured, hard varieties so often seen in English and American stores would not at all meet with her approval. Nor would she approve of the boxes of ready-grated cheese tasting like soap that are offered for sale in place of the real thing. Silvana uses parmesan in the simplest ways so that its special flavour is not confused or drowned by other tastes. Very often she will serve a plain *risotto*, or plain boiled rice, with a good sprinkling of the cheese on top plus a little black pepper, or her home made *tagliatelle* with a piece of saltless butter and again a generous dusting of the freshly grated cheese. Always grate your own cheese at the last possible moment before eating. Silvana rightly considers parmesan to be a special pleasure that should be treated with respect.

For a **Risotto al Parmigiano**, to serve four people you would need two tablespoons of olive oil, one white onion, 400 g or 14 oz of long grained rice, about a litre or 1¾ pints of stock – home-made is best for this dish – four tablespoons of freshly grated parmesan, salt and pepper.

Heat the olive oil in a large heavy saucepan, then add the finely chopped onion. Let the onion become transparent but on no account let it change colour or burn. This would alter the flavour and spoil the appearance of the risotto. Next add the rice and stir it around well until it too has become transparent. Cover the rice with two ladlesful of the stock. Season lightly with salt. Cover the pan and let the rice cook. Check occasionally and add more stock if the rice seems in danger of sticking. When the risotto is cooked to your taste stir in the cheese. Serve in a large bowl and have more grated parmesan and black pepper on the table. Italians like their *risotti* to have a thick and soupy consistency but they also like the grains of rice in this thick soup to remain hard in the centre. For the English taste it is probably better to prolong the cooking until the sauce has evaporated a little and the rice has just cooked through.

This is how Silvana prepares her **Tagliatelle con Parmigiano**, which is her particular favourite dish. To feed four people she will use about 400 g or 14 oz of fresh *tagliatelle*, see the chapter on December for the recipe for this. She has ready four tablespoons of grated parmesan and four walnuts of butter.

Then she brings to a rolling boil an abundant quantity of salted water. It takes at least three litres or five and a quarter pints to cook enough pasta for four people successfully. The ideal amount is one litre to 100 g of pasta. When the water is at a brisk boil Silvana throws in the *tagliatelle*, giving it a good stir around with a long wooden fork to make sure that it is moving freely and has not stuck together in a lump. From the moment that the pasta goes into the water she is aware of the time. At two minutes she lifts out a strand and tests it by biting a strand. When the pasta is *al dente*, cooked through but still retaining a definite bite, she tips it into a colander and drains it thoroughly. When she is making the *tagliatelle* for six or seven Silvana cooks it in the cauldron over the fire. In this case it cannot be tipped out so she uses a pear-shaped pasta strainer. This is often made of cane; its pear-shaped bowl is dipped into the cauldron to scoop out the *tagliatelle*, letting the water drain back into the pot. When the *tagliatelle* is drained Silvana divides it between the dishes, sprinkles on the cheese then places the walnut of butter on top and so to the table, where everyone is sitting waiting for the pasta; the pasta must never wait for the people. Everyone seasons their own plate with black pepper according to taste, although if anyone has been ill or has recently had a child and therefore is eating *in bianco*, nothing but white food, they would naturally forego the black pepper.

❧ APRIL

April brings Easter, the most dramatic festival in Italy. Before the Monday of Holy Week Silvana prepares for a very ancient ceremony, pre-Christian in origin. She cleans her large house from attic to kitchen, sweeping away old cobwebs from the high raftered ceilings, polishing the red-tiled floors and washing the small-paned windows to an unaccustomed glitter. The shutters are flung wide open in all the rooms on the middle floor of the house which are filled with cumbersome country wardrobes and oversized beds with bedsteads of curved decorative metal, painted with panels of violets and pansies, or carved slats of stylised roses. The mattresses of firm horsehair are turned and covered with fresh sheets of heavy cream linen scented with the fields where each week they are hung to dry. Fresh coverlets crocheted in bright wools are laid on each bed.

Next the dining-room table is laid with the best tablecloth and on it Silvana places a large bowl full of new-laid eggs, covered with a white napkin. Fresh lilac is stuffed into the glass pot under the plaster image of Jesus and the house is ready, with Silvana neat in a new headscarf and apron, to receive the visit of the parish priest, Don Franco. He starts his round with the Cerotti house and arrives early in the morning. He dresses in the vestments that Silvana cares for and launders as a service to the little church that lies below the *fattoria* at a small crossroad. It is a simple rural romanesque building. Once in its perfectly proportioned apse hung a painting of the *Madonna in Gloria* by the Siennese painter Martino di Bartolomeo. A picture of a sweet-faced madonna dressed in pink and green surrounded by gold *putti* floating on a scarlet ground, it is now kept in the local museum. The church is denuded of its treasure but mass is said there every Sunday morning for the valley's tiny congregation by the genial priest who drives over the mountain to hold services in this, one of three outlying churches. Only a handful of women besides Silvana, and one or two men, attend the mass and occasionally a local bride is wed in this tiny church, which is a most beautiful and romantic place for a wedding.

When the priest is robed, accompanied by a young server who is also begowned, he walks through the house and sprinkles holy water in each room, blessing the house and the family as he goes. Finally the priest blesses the eggs. The small ceremony pleases Silvana and initiates a fertile new season. The official Roman Catholic attitude to this very old custom is that it reminds the individual of his own baptism and is a renewal of old vows. Years ago the priests went to all houses with their blessing but today they only visit those people who request their presence. After the priest has left on his round of the valley houses, Silvana prepares the lunch for which he will return.

 Today she is cooking *Vitello in Padella*, slices of veal with sage, garlic, olive oil and white wine, cooked gently over the embers. She prepares it in this way, using half a glass of olive oil, two cloves of garlic, five fresh sage leaves, four fillets of *vitello* cut across the grain of the meat, salt and black pepper and one glass of dry white wine. In an old red *padella*, a flat pan, a frying pan is the English equivalent, Silvana heats up the olive oil, then adds the garlic which she has chopped, the whole sage leaves and a small sprinkling of black pepper. She allows the garlic to soften but on no account lets it brown or the sage burn. She is putting these aromatic ingredients into the oil to flavour it; the oil will then coat and flavour the meat. Oil flavoured with burnt garlic and sage is disagreeable. When the garlic is soft Silvana adds the veal, allows it to seal on both sides then pours in a little of the white wine. She lets the fillets cook on a low flame, adding more wine as necessary. The *vitello in padella* does not take a great length of time to cook so Silvana would start the dish near the beginning of the meal. To serve the *vitello* she lays the fillets on a serving dish, then adds a very little more wine to the pan and over a brisk heat mixes it vigorously with the pan juices, then pours this little sauce over the fillets laying a sage leaf on each one.

To start the meal she prepares the customary *crostini*, but as a seasonal change Silvana uses some of the blessed eggs. These are also traditionally eaten hard boiled on Easter Sunday. She hard boils three large eggs and when they are cooked and shelled she chops them very finely with the *mezzaluna* on her big old chopping board. To the eggs she adds a well drained spoonful or two of her own vegetables preserved in wine vinegar, gherkins, carrots, a tiny onion or so, known as *sott'aceto*. These are also chopped very finely before being added to the eggs. Finally, in a bowl she mixes the egg and vegetables with some mayonnaise and a little soft butter into a stiff paste, seasoning it with salt and freshly ground black pepper. She spreads her squares of fresh bread with this mixture to make a substantial appetizer.

 To make **Crostini con Uova** you need three large eggs, two tablespoons of vegetables preserved in wine vinegar, e.g. gherkins, peppers, carrots, celery, cauliflower etc, two tablespoons of mayonnaise, one tablespoon of soft butter, or enough of these two to make a stiff paste, salt and freshly ground black pepper, small squares or rounds of good bread, and one caper for each piece of bread.

Hard boil the eggs and plunge them immediately into cold water to prevent ugly black rings around the yolks. Shell the eggs and chop them finely. Next chop the preserved vegetables finely, drain them well and add them to the egg. Put the egg and vegetables into a bowl and gradually add the mayonnaise and butter to make a stiff smooth paste then season with salt and pepper. Now spread the mixture on the pieces of bread and top each one with a caper.

 For the pasta course Silvana has decided to serve **Pasta e Ceci**, pasta and chick peas, a dish which has more in common with a soup than a conventional dish of pasta. Yesterday evening she put 250 g of *ceci*, chick peas, to soak in a large pan of cold water, then early this morning she drained the softened *ceci*, placed them in fresh, slightly salted water and left them to cook through. When the *ceci* are done Silvana puts two thirds of them plus their cooking water through the mouli, to make them into a pureé. To this pureé she adds the remaining whole chick peas which are left in their whole state to give texture to the dish. Then Silvana heats three tablespoons of olive oil in a large sauce-pan to which she adds two cloves of chopped garlic and a sprig of rosemary. Next she adds a heaped teaspoonful of tomato concentrate mixed into a very small amount of water. When the oil has become flavoured Silvana tips in the chick peas, stirring everything together thoroughly. She brings the pan to the boil then adds 150 g of *tagliatelle* broken up into manageable lengths of about three to four inches; this dish you must remember is to be eaten with a spoon like soup. The *Pasta e Ceci* is ready when the *tagliatelle* is cooked. For four people the quantities are 250 g or 9 oz of dry chick peas, 150 g or 5 oz of *tagliatelle*, three tablespoons of olive oil, two cloves of garlic, a sprig of fresh rosemary (do not use loose leaves of dried rosemary or the dish will be full of the little pungent spikes which will be impossible to remove and not good to eat, whereas the whole sprig can be easily removed from the pan), a heaped teaspoon of tomato concentrate and enough water for cooking the chick peas to give you a thick, well amalgamated soup.

When Don Franco returns at one o'clock everything is ready for lunch. Normally everyone sits down to eat around the kitchen table on two long benches, but for larger parties, Sundays and special occasions the dining room is used. Like the kitchen, this room is mostly filled with a massive table and chairs. In the *tinello*, the sideboard, are kept the biscuits and cakes, one of the few things that are bought, and the li-queurs, *vini santi* and brandies that all Italian country households proudly offer to their guests. *Vin santo* is a strong dessert wine that used to be made in the *cantina* and is used to accompany and soften the hard almond biscuits that are traditionally served with it. The cupboards in the room are filled with the best white gold-trimmed dinner service sufficient for two dozen people, huge tablecloths, piles of snowy napkins and massive china bowls. On the table is a pottery bowl with a twisted basket handle in the egg and spinach splashed glaze of the local ware; it is always filled with fruit or nuts from the orchards. The sideboard is covered with lace mats, family photographs, and favours from the latest wedding in the form of little twists of pink or blue veiling containing sugared almonds, attached with a ribbon to a small dish or trinket.

Today Silvana lays the dining-room table for four: just the three of them and the priest will eat together. The dishes of *crostini* are arranged upon the table, the *ceci* are waiting for the *pasta*, and the *vitello* is absorbing the flavours of sage and garlic. As a *contorno*, the vegetable dish, which will add another dimension to the meal, literally a contour, Silvana has collected a salad from the fields, a bowl of *ramponcioli* and *bianchella*, the local names for these pretty wild plants. The priest, tired after his morning visits, is suitably refreshed by the delicious meal which lasts well into the afternoon by the time that Silvana has served the little cups of strong coffee and Orlando has brought out the *grappa*.

As well as eggs, Easter signifies baby chicks. Silvana takes great delight in the tiny creatures, her *pulcinini*. She keeps the newly-hatched balls of down wrapped up in an ancient sweater in a box under the fireplace. When she fishes out the box to feed the chicks they come tumbling out of the long woolly sleeves. When they are strong enough she entrusts them to the fat old broody hens. And when they are reared and fully grown she will cheerfully dispatch them for roasting. Until then they are allowed to strut and peck in the courtyard and the grassy verges that line the drive. They are fed well on good Indian corn which makes their eggs tasty and the yolks a deep yellow. At the chapel side of the house there are small buildings in which the rabbits have their hutches and the poultry are put to roost at night, when they are well closed in for the woods are full of predatory foxes who lie in wait for the hens even in daylight. Silvana and Nena, the mother of one of Orlando's men, often step outside their kitchens and let out ferocious yells to scare off any foxes that may be lurking. Nena particularly has problems with them because her house is situated far above the *fattoria* right at the forest's edge, which provides handy cover for the wily beasts. On one particular day she lost two of her best hens to the same fox, Her son Menchino, who was working with his *falce*, a small sickle, clearing around some vines near the house, saw the fox creeping up again, intent on stealing the third hen of the day. Menchino, not having a gun to hand, threw his sickle at the fox but missed, with the result that both fox and sickle disappeared into the undergrowth and have never been seen since.

Silvana collects the hens' eggs daily and keeps them in large bowls in the *dispensa*. She uses them of course to make the *frittate*, the flat, almost cake-like Italian omelettes. One of their favourite fillings for *frittate* at this time of the year is *aglio fresco*, fresh garlic, which is sold in Italian markets during the spring. It looks rather like a cross between a spring onion and a very small leek. It is actually the garlic plant picked before the bulb has started to develop. The green part which is long and trailing is also good to eat. Its flavour is excellent, not being particularly hot and garlicky, and it is used a great deal in the *frittate* and instead of an onion in sauces. It unlikely to be found in English vegetable shops, so use small leeks as a substitute.

 To make a *Frittata con Aglio Fresco* for two people you will need two stalks of fresh garlic plus a little of the green part, or one small leek, three tablespoons of olive oil, salt and black pepper and four fresh eggs. Clean and trim the garlic or leek then slice it into rounds. Heat the olive oil in an omelette pan and add the garlic/leek. Let it soften in the oil and turn a pale blonde colour. Meanwhile beat the eggs and season them with the salt and pepper. Raise the heat in the pan and pour in the eggs over the vegetables. You must arrange the vegetables equally over the pan or else one person will get all the garlic and the other none. Let the eggs set on the bottom, then let them solidify over a very low heat. When they have cooked through slide the *frittata* out of the pan onto a hot plate. Re-heat the pan then replace the *frittata* uncooked side down. Allow the eggs to set on the bottom then serve the *frittata* very hot and cut into wedges.

Silvana also makes a very good *frittata* for supper which has a filling of fresh sausages cut into little rounds and cooked until they are practically done before she pours in the eggs to make the *frittate* in the normal way.

 Occasionally for supper Silvana will make *Uova Sode con Aglio*, an egg dish which is extremely simple but also a delight to those who like olive oil and raw garlic. To do this she will boil the freshest eggs, two per person, until they are hard, plunging them immediately they are cooked into cold water to prevent black rings around the yolks which would most certainly spoil the look of this dish. When she has shelled the eggs she cuts them in half lengthways and arranges them on an oval serving dish yolk side up. Next she skins some plump cloves of garlic and chops them into tiny pieces which she sprinkles on top of the eggs. Then she takes a bottle of their own green as green olive oil and pours a thin stream over the eggs, taking care to trickle a good helping over each yolk. A few turns of the pepper mill, a sprinkling of salt and a little chopped parsley complete the dish, whose beauty consists in eating the soft yolks mashed into the fruity olive oil sparked with the throat-burning garlic. This is not a dish for the excessively polite nor is it one which should be attempted if you do not have very fresh eggs, excellent fruity olive oil and a firm plump new season's head of garlic. Soft yellowish rancid garlic is of no use whatsoever for this simple salad.

 Orlando's favourite way with eggs, *Uova in Tegame*, is again very simple and often he will prepare them himself for his Sunday breakfast after mass. He has a tiny frying pan in which he heats up a large quantity of their best olive oil. When it is very hot he breaks in a fresh egg which immediately puffs up in a white ruff. He lets it cook for a few minutes, spooning the oil over the centre of the egg, but before the yolk is set he slides the egg out of the pan and eats it with salt and a piece of Tuscan bread. Again it is the quality of the oil and the freshness of the egg that make this very simple little dish so special.

Out in the fields the cherry, peach and apple trees that stud the edge of Orlando's fields are in full blossom; explosions of pink and white flowers cloud their grey branches. The rows of pollard willows which grow along the pathways and are known as *vincaia* are sprouting their fierce olive-gold osiers. These willows have always been grown and polled especially to provide an essential tool for the care of the vines, pliant, whip-like branches which can be used to tie the new vine shoots to the trellises. Continuing the task that they began in March, Guido and Tonio walk slowly through the fields, strengthening the vine supports where necessary and cutting away all but one or two shoots from each plant so all the strength of the vine will go into producing fine grapes, not excess foliage. They weed the new vineyard, with its lines of as yet naked posts, and check the newly-planted vines for signs of growth. With them they carry clippers and a bundle of osiers, and occasionally they stop to light a small fire from odd bits of wood that are lying around in the fields. They hold the osiers over the flames to soften them and make them more pliable, then they cut off short lengths and with a loop and a twist of the ends the shoots are secured to the supporting wires. The bundles of fresh vegetables and salad that the *contadini* take to market are also lovingly tied up in this fashion.

Easter Saturday is the traditional Tuscan time for sowing vegetable seeds, beans and peas, *zucchini*, carrots, onions, potatoes, parsley and pots of basil. (This custom also holds good in parts of Britain.) At this time the moon is often in the right phase for sowing, the *luna calante*. The walled kitchen garden has been dug and the seedbeds prepared for the

new produce. New garlic is already up and three small peach trees shock
with the vividness of their pink. The sage plant is putting out new leaves
and the rosemary bush is a mass of dull mauve bloom. Although the'
garden here is as yet bare earth, the vegetables that are brought on bright
painted lorries from the south are tender and new. Cerotti brings home
fresh artichokes from his shopping expeditions. There are several varieties sold with their long stalks and ragged leaves still attached. There are
the slim spear-shaped ones with the sharply pointed leaves and the
Roman type that are round and large and are perfect for stuffing. He
brings delicate asparagus, too, grown on the sunnier Umbrian plains,
stiff bundles of the pale green pink-tipped spears and the dark green
slender wild variety which have much more flavour, and which Silvana
remembers picking around her mountain home. Fresh broad beans too,
make an appearance, the small broad beans they eat, served still in their
pods, at the end of a meal as an extra savoury.

Artichokes are very popular in Italy. They are considered to be
health-giving, full of iron, good for the liver and, above all, extremely
delicious. Silvana has numerous recipes for serving them. The blessed
eggs combine well with artichokes to make a very elegant *frittata*. Italian
artichokes, it must be remembered, are picked, bought and eaten when
they are very young and in a fresh and tender state, and Silvana does
not seem to have any problems with tough spiny chokes. For a *frittata*
the small pointed artichokes are more suitable. Silvana uses a short, very
sharp knife to trim the vegetables and a bowl of cold acidulated water
to plunge the cut artichokes into immediately to prevent them discol-
ouring. The water is made acid with a little wine vinegar or a squeeze
of lemon juice. She leaves a two-inch stalk on the artichoke as this is
tender and good to eat, then she peels off the stalk's outer skin and pulls
off all the outer leaves until she is left with the pale tender ones. She
trims off their points too. Then, using the same very sharp knife, she
slices the artichokes lengthways into very thin slices, thin so that they
cook rapidly. The artichoke sections make an interesting decorative pattern. Silvana heats some oil in the frying pan then gently softens the
drained and dried artichoke slices. When they are cooked through but
not browned she adds the beaten eggs seasoned with salt and freshly-
ground black pepper. Then the *frittata* is cooked and turned as already
described. Good variations are to add a little sliced onion to the artichoke, or to soften the artichokes in butter instead of oil and tuck the
filling into a classic French omelette; this makes a splendid luncheon
dish.

To make the *Frittata di Carciofi* for two people you will need one tender young artichoke, three tablespoons of olive oil, four eggs, salt and black pepper. Trim the artichoke of all the tougher outer leaves. With a sharp knife slice the artichoke lengthways into very thin slices. Unless you are going to use the slices immediately put them into acidulated water to prevent them changing colour. Heat the olive oil in the omelette pan and add the slices of artichoke, drained and dried if necessary. Let them cook through slowly. Beat up the eggs and season them with salt and pepper. Arrange the artichokes evenly in the pan, raise the heat under the pan and pour in the beaten egg. Now continue to cook the *frittata* as indicated in previous recipes.

Silvana also likes to serve *carciofi fritti*, which is one of the most popular ways of preparing the vegetable. The artichokes are sliced in the same manner as for the *frittata* then dipped into flour for a light dusting, then into a bowl of beaten egg and lastly plunged into a pan of oil – arachide, not corn or olive oil. The slices must be dipped into the egg and fat individually or the whole thing will coagulate into a mass that will spoil the appearance of the dish. Fried until golden, then served very hot piled on a plate and surrounded by lemon wedges, they are a delightful vegetable with a simple steak.

 To serve *Carciofi Fritti* for four or five people you will need four fresh young spear-shaped artichokes, a plate of seasoned flour, two beaten eggs and a pan of arachide oil for the frying. Trim the artichokes of their tough outer leaves but leave them attached to about 1½ inches of trimmed stalk. With a very sharp knife cut them lengthways into thin slices. Dip each slice into the flour then into the beaten egg and finally plunge it into the bubbling hot oil. Allow them to cook until they are golden brown. As the slices should be very thin they will not take long to cook through. Drain the artichokes on kitchen paper and keep them warm until they are taken to the table. It is a wise precaution to dip each slice into the flour, egg and oil individually and fry them a few at a time otherwise they will coagulate and spoil the appearance of the dish. It is also an absolute essential to have a well sharpened knife to slice the artichokes into fine sections. It is another good idea to err on the ruthless side when discarding the outer leaves of the artichoke: better to throw more leaves away than have a tough stringy *frittata* or vegetable dish.

The round Roman artichokes are best cooked *in umido*, that is, stewed in a pan. Again a little stalk is preserved, the tougher outer leaves dispensed with and the tips cut off. The artichokes must fit tightly into a small pan. After trimming them Silvana enlarges the hole that appears naturally in the top of the round artichokes and stuffs the cavity with a mixture of butter, salt, chopped garlic, parsley and black pepper. Then she places the artichokes stalk side up in the pot, jammed in tightly together to prevent them from falling over during the cooking. If they fall they will not cook through properly. Then she adds a little olive oil and a tablespoon or two of water to the bottom of the pan, covers them closely with a lid lined with greaseproof paper and cooks them gently over a low flame. They are done when a skewer pierces the base easily and the aroma has become too delicious to resist. An alternative and even more delicious stuffing she makes with fine breadcrumbs, grated parmesan, a little chopped chicken or *mortadella*, garlic, parsley, salt and pepper moistened with a little stock or melted butter. This makes a good supper dish on its own, with perhaps a green salad to follow.

 To make *Carciofi in Umido*, stewed artichokes, for four people you will require four round Roman artichokes, young and fresh, 50 g or 2 oz of butter, two large cloves of garlic, two tablespoons of finely chopped parsley, salt and freshly ground black pepper, one tablespoon of olive oil and a little water.

Trim the artichokes of their stalks and the tough outer leaves. With your finger enlarge the round whole that appears naturally at the top of the artichokes where the leaves come together. On a chopping board dice the butter, cold from the fridge. Chop the garlic fairly finely and the parsley finely. Mix these three ingredients into a small heap and liberally season them with salt and black pepper. Put some of your butter stuffing into the cavity of each artichoke. Place the four artichokes stalk side up into a small pan; they must fit in tightly to prevent them falling over during the cooking. Put a very little olive oil and a spoonful of water into the bottom of the pan. Cover the artichokes closely with the saucepan lid lined with greaseproof paper, and steam them over a gentle flame. They are done when the base of the artichoke can be easily pierced with a skewer. Serve with a little of the buttery garlicky sauce which will have collected in the bottom of the pan.

To prepare *Carciofi Ripieni*, stuffed artichokes, for four people you will need four young, fresh round Roman artichokes, 50 g or 2 oz of cooked chicken breast, 50 g or 2 oz of fine white breadcrumbs, 25 g or 1 oz of finely grated parmesan, one tablespoon of finely chopped parsley, one or two cloves of garlic according to taste, a little stock or melted butter to moisten and salt and black pepper.

Trim the artichokes of their stalks and the tough outer leaves. With your finger enlarge the round hole that appears naturally at the top of the artichoke where the leaves come together. Chop the chicken breast finely, put it into a china bowl and add the breadcrumbs, the parmesan, the finely chopped parsley, the garlic which you have also chopped finely and the salt and black pepper. Mix all the ingredients evenly together. When the stuffing is well mixed add little by little either the stock or the melted butter. Use just enough liquid to turn the stuffing into a very stiff paste. Stuff the cavity of each artichoke with some of the mixture. Place the four artichokes stalk side up into a small pan, they must fit tightly to prevent them falling over during the cooking. Put a very small amount of olive oil and a spoonful or so of water into the bottom of the pan. Cover the pan closely by lining its lid with greaseproof paper. Stew the artichokes over a very low flame, checking occasionally to see that there is enough liquid at the bottom of the pan. They are ready to eat when the base of the artichoke can be easily pierced with a skewer.

The great annual drama of death and resurrection starts, of course, on Good Friday. Most towns have large processions, some involving hooded men carrying crosses or statues, some beating drums and singing. Particularly pious country households erect small wooden crosses covered with lights. These are lit up at the traditional time of the Resurrection and Easter Sunday is an occasion of great festivity. Festivity in Italy, as we have already noted, is synonymous with food and plenty of it. In Tuscany, as in other parts of Italy, lamb is the usual Easter speciality. The Cerottis have kept a nice plump young lamb for themselves from the flock that has been sold to local butchers. Andrea slaughters the lamb two or three days before it is required for cooking. Sunday luncheon is the great festive meal and Silvana has planned to make a large dish of *pasta al forno* followed by a leg of lamb which will be accompanied by a dish of *fave al prosciutto*. The meal will end with a walnut and an apple *crostata*. First of course will come the *crostini*, this time of butter softened and mixed with crushed anchovies or anchovy paste to a smooth pomade spread on the rounds of bread and topped with a home-preserved caper.

The proportions of anchovy to butter will depend on how much you like the flavour of the salty fish. The pasta dish *lasagne al forno* she prepares in a large oblong oven dish and cooks in her new electric oven. For the *lasagne* Silvana uses a well flavoured béchamel, her meat and tomato sauce and the large oblong sheets of pasta. She cooks the pasta a few sheets at a time in a very great deal of boiling salted water to stop it sticking together and, when it is just *al dente*, she drains it thoroughly and lays it to rest on a damp tea cloth. The oblong dish is thoroughly oiled and then Silvana starts to put in layers of the various components. First the pasta, then the meat sauce, more pasta, béchamel, until the dish is full. Over the top she sprinkles a generous helping of grated *pecorino*, though, as she says, *parmigiano* would be more flavoursome but she does not always have it to hand. The dish is then put to brown slowly in a medium oven. The great secret of good *lasagne* is to have plenty of creamy béchamel and a sharp fruity sauce, and to balance the ingredients so that there is a definite preponderance of sauce over pasta - like a good sandwich, more filling than bread. For extra richness sprinkle a little parmesan over each layer of the dish.

To make **Lasagne al Forno** for four or five people you will need 400 g or 14 oz of *lasagne* pasta and 500 ml or 1 pint of *ragù*, as given in January's chapter, a thick béchamel made with 50 g or 2 oz butter, 50 g or 2 oz of flour, 500 ml or 1 pint of milk, salt and black pepper, and 100 g or 3½ oz of grated parmesan or *pecorino* cheese, good olive oil as needed. Cook the sheets of pasta a few at a time in abundant boiling salted water. Remove the sheets from the water with a pierced spoon, when they are cooked. Lay the sheets on a clean damp teatowel. Have at hand the hot *ragù*, also have ready and hot the thick béchamel made out of the flour, butter and milk, salt and pepper. In a square straight-sided tin or oven dish which you have liberally oiled with olive oil, place a layer of the cooked pasta. Next spread a layer of *ragù*, then another layer of pasta. Now spread a layer of béchamel, more pasta and so on until the dish is full. You may sprinkle each layer with the cheese, leaving some over for the top. Put the dish into a medium oven to brown for about thirty minutes.

The leg of lamb is cooked over the open fire, but before it is laid over the embers Silvana makes slits in the flesh and fills them with a mixture of chopped garlic, chopped rosemary, coarse salt, black pepper and sometimes a little chopped fat *prosciutto*. Today she omits this last ingredient as the lamb is very young and tender and will not need the added fat. Then she coats the leg well with her good olive oil and puts it in the grilling rack. This is a sort of double-sided metal rack with legs on both sides that hinges to make a sandwich around the meat and is designed to be turned over and so cook both sides of the meat. They are easily and cheaply available in all the Italian weekly street markets and make a good job of cooking small items like sausages, preventing them from rolling around and dropping into the fire. There are all sorts of implements for cooking over the kitchen fire, from elaborate turning spits in decorative wrought iron, powered either by clockwork or electricity, to heavy square iron trivets which are simply placed over the ashes. Even these trivets can be complicated; some are round and rotate so the food nearest the body of the fire can be turned around to the front so that everything cooks evenly. There are also small triangular and circular trivets solely to balance pots and pans upon. Silvana sticks to the simple varieties and has a good selection of small and large trivets around the fireplace.

She watches the progress of the lamb's cooking carefully. First she heaps brightly burning embers under the rack so that the meat is sealed quickly, turning the joint as required, then the embers are left to die down a little to let the lamb cook through. If the fire becomes too dull a small shovel full of fresh embers enlivens it. At the side of the fire she has a saucer of olive oil ready and using a sprig of rosemary as a brush she bastes the leg frequently. After the meat has sealed she sprinkles on more coarse salt and once or twice a few drops of wine vinegar. This she is convinced gives flavour and makes the meat tender. Tuscans like their meat highly seasoned, highly salted and well cooked, preferring a rich salty crust to the moist pink flesh that is preferred in France.

 To prepare an **Arrosto di Agnello**, or roast leg of lamb, you will require two sprigs of fresh rosemary, three cloves of garlic, 75 g or 2½ oz of *pancetta* or fat bacon (this may be omitted if the lamb is very young and tender), coarse salt, coarsely ground black pepper, one leg of lamb, olive oil and a few drops of wine vinegar.

Strip the leaves from the sprigs of rosemary. On your chopping board chop them, the garlic and the *pancetta* into small pieces, combining the three ingredients. Mix a good pinch of salt and black pepper into your heap of stuffing. Make cuts here and there over the leg of lamb and stuff into them this *pancetta* and garlic mixture. Anoint the joint well with good olive oil and sprinkle on more coarse salt and pepper. Put the lamb on a rack in your roasting tin and place it in a hot oven to seal the meat, then lower the heat to cook the lamb through. Baste occasionally with olive oil which you can brush on with a sprig of rosemary and once or twice sprinkle on a few drops of wine vinegar. If your oven has a revolving spit then use that instead of the rack and tin.

Country Tuscans like their lamb to be well cooked with a crusty salty exterior. They do not carve the joint into slices but break it into large chunks. The Tuscan cooking times are therefore much longer than French cooking times. As long as the exterior of the leg is well cooked, the degree of pinkness of the inside of the joint and the way it is carved should be a matter for the personal taste of the cook and those who will eat the lamb.

To serve with the lamb Silvana decides upon *fave con prosciutto*, young tender broad beans cooked with olive oil, garlic, sage, *prosciutto* and stock. To make this she softens the garlic and colours the *prosciutto* (cut into small dice) in the olive oil, adding a leaf or two of fresh sage for flavour. These ingredients she does not allow to brown, especially the sage. Next she adds the shelled beans and turns them in the oil and *prosciutto* mixture. Finally she adds a rich stock to cover and allows them to simmer away until tender. Silvana usually has a pot of stock bubbling over the fire. In her busy farmhouse there are always chicken legs and gizzards available and she extracts the goodness from them with the addition of a carrot or two and some celery leaves and a few herbs. She does not keep stock but makes it freshly whenever she needs it.

 To make **Fave al Prosciutto**, broad beans with ham, for two people you will need 1 kg or 2¼ lbs of broad beans, two tablespoons of olive oil, 30 g or 1½ oz of *pancetta* or bacon, two cloves of garlic, three fresh sage leaves and stock as needed. Salt and pepper.

First shell the beans. In a large saucepan heat up the olive oil and add the chopped garlic, the *pancetta* cut into dice and the sage leaves. Allow these to cook gently until the *pancetta* has taken on colour and the garlic has softened. Do not brown or burn them. Add the shelled beans and turn in the oil until they are all coated. Next add hot stock to just cover the beans. Season with black pepper, but taste carefully before adding salt as there will be some in the *pancetta*. Allow to simmer gently until the beans are tender. Drain and serve with a little of the juice.

Right at the beginning of the broad bean season, when the beans are small and tender, they are often served raw and in their shells. They are simply put in a basket and left on the table so that those who want to can help themselves, shell them and eat them with absolutely no additions. They may be eaten at the beginning or the end of the meal, and their bitter, tender flavour is delightful.

In the square dining-room the table is laid for the Easter meal with the best gold and white china on a green checked cloth; large matching checked napkins lie on each plate. Flasks of red and white wine stand at each end of the table and on the *tinello* there are bottles of *spumante*, sparkling dessert wine and a large *colomba*, a dove-shaped *panettone*. This is the yeast-lightened sponge sold at Easter and Christmas time which comes in several varieties, though the traditional sort is of the lightest sponge imaginable covered with veiling sugar. All Italians buy several *panettone* at every festive opportunity and enjoy them with a glass of sparkling wine. The ones sold at Easter time are in the shape of doves or lambs; those at Christmas look rather as if they have been cooked in old-fashioned jelly moulds. As well as the *panettone* there are dishes of almond macaroons, a gift from a sister-in-law, and a large bowl of fruit. Apart from these things Silvana has made the traditional Sunday *crostata*; most Tuscan country households round off their large Sunday lunches with this solid dessert. The *crostata* is a sort of tart, the base and the covering latticework made of soft rich pastry bordering almost upon cake, and the filling is sometimes jam or in this case home-grown walnuts crushed and mixed with honey into a paste. Silvana has also made one with a filling of soft apple slices.

The guests arrive and group admiringly around the succulent lamb sizzling gently over its bed of embers. The air is full of the scent of young beans, sharp and appetizing. Soon the signal 'a tavola' is given and everybody sits down to enjoy their Easter lunch, from the piquant anchovy *crostini* to the last wine-soaked macaroon.

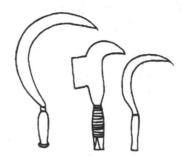

❦ MAY

In this month of May the really hard summer's work begins, and it is time to hire extra hands, men and women. Cerotti telephones around to his regular people to let them know when, weather permitting, the planting out of the tobacco will begin. The young plants in their humid hot *serre* are sturdy and large enough now to be transplanted. Orlando's workforce consists of several local men who, being without much land, hire themselves out on a daily basis when required; they are complemented by a group of village women who have worked in the fields since their girlhood. The actual labour of planting, although now done with the aid of a machine, and especially the work of hoeing, are extremely hard and tiring. The hoe, *zappa*, is in itself remarkably heavy, with a short stout wooden handle and solid blade. But the women are extremely tough. Mostly of short stature and robust shape, not by any stretch of the imagination of fashionable or athletic build, they are nevertheless made of solid muscle, and brown as berries. Their heads shaded by floppy straw hats, they work with engine-like steadiness through the long hot days. The day's work starts at seven-thirty and often goes on until eight in the evening. As with all farming it is the weather which dictates the long hours worked. Once the plants have been taken out of the *serre* they must all go in before by ill chance a storm breaks. Their breaks consist of an hour or so for lunch and various stops for a *merenda* in the morning and afternoon. Lying in the shade of nearby trees or hanging from a branch there is always a satchel full of two-litre wine flasks, and they quench their thirsts liberally throughout the day. The men, as well as planting and helping with the *zappatura*, the weeding of the tobacco plants, carry the very heavy wooden boxes of plants and lift and arrange the large pipes that bring water from the river to irrigate the fields.

All day their chatter and laughter echoes around the valley which May has transformed. The blossoms have been chased from the trees by the tender new leaves and suddenly everything has become green. The hedgerows where they sit to eat the *merende* are studded with the white flowers of wild strawberries, and only the roses and irises around the *fattoria* add a note of colour. The winter wheat has reached its full height and the fields undulate in the fresh winds. It is easy now to discern which fields have been sown by hand, as a pattern of faintly curved ripples shows the uneven trajectory of the sower's cast. These small meadows are usually those sown by Menchino and the crop is for his family's use. At the corner of each field he has planted a slender cross made from two reeds, to act as a talisman. The vines are putting out healthy new leaves and tendrils and Guido and Tonio must spray them with a virulent green copper solution to protect them from blight.

The Cerottis, having been brought up in the old tradition, assume the responsibility of feeding their workers. A guiding and much quoted principle of country life is that those who work eat. So they all sit down together round the vast dining table to enjoy their food. Silvana says she has heard that in foreign places the workers are not fed at the expense of the employers and she thinks that is a scandalous state of affairs. The seasonal increase in mouths to feed, usually sixteen to twenty-four per day, of course creates an enormous amount of extra work which she does by herself. Only when there is a special *festa* with more than one main course to prepare does a niece or a sister come over the hill from the old family home to help.

All Italians are very conscious of food, almost, one might say, obsessed with the table and the quality of cooking, and the subject of food is never very far from the lips of men or women. I once overheard a conversation in an Italian train between two businessmen who were strangers to each other. For the entire two-hour journey they discussed with passion their particular way of making *Spaghetti alla Carbonara* and other pasta sauces, behaviour which would appear distinctly odd in an English railway carriage but is very normal in Italy. So, Silvana in this remote valley is daily preparing food for critics and what is more for critics who, although bucolic, know what they are talking about.

The midday meal, *pranzo*, which in Italy is the main meal of the day, takes the traditional form. On workdays there is a first course called *primo* which is also referred to as *minestra* and consists of pasta dishes, *risotti*, polenta dishes or various small *pastina* in *brodo*. Next comes the *secondo*, a meat or fish course and an accompanying vegetable or salad dish, the *contorno*. Finally there comes fruit or cheese and coffee: *frutta, formaggio e caffè*. The *caffè* is always an *espresso*, a tiny cup of very strong black coffee. No Italian would ever ask for a *cappuccino*, or worse, a *caffè latte*, to end a meal. Who would want to consume a great milky drink after eating a carefully chosen and balanced meal? On Sundays and special occasions there will be an *antipasto* before the pasta course, which is of course what the word actually means, and maybe two or three different *secondi* and *contorni* and a dessert. Wine and *acqua minerale* are drunk as a matter of course with the meal. The Cerottis do not need bottles of commercial water as they have their own excellent spring water.

As well as providing this fare every day, Silvana must make sure that there is variety in the food: meat one day, fish or fowl the next, differing vegetables and so on. She balances her meals beautifully, serving a plain salad or bland vegetable with a main course that has a rich sauce, an interestingly garnished vegetable with plainly cooked meat; no conflicting strong flavours are served together, and the weight of the three courses is considered.

The art of balancing a meal is one which the Italians know well and this, plus the basic structure of the Italian meal, is something that many foreign visitors to Italy might study with profit. It is so easy for the uninitiated to order the wrong sort of dishes in the wrong sequence in a restaurant and sadly end up with an unbalanced and disappointing meal.

Silvana generally starts the workday *pranzo* with a pasta, preferring to leave rice and *brodo* dishes for the evening meal, the *cena*. Pasta in its basic form as a filling dish for poor and numerous families does not figure very largely in the old traditional repertoire of Tuscan recipes. Its place in Tuscany was always filled by bread-based dishes such as the *zuppe di pane* and *ribollita*. However the southern Italians when they migrated to the industrial north of Italy in search of work took their staple with them and now *pastasciutta* is a daily dish all over Italy. The sophistication achieved in its preparation has to be tasted to be believed.

Firstly there is the incredible variety of pasta shapes, from the tiniest grains and stars, *semine* and *stelline* for putting into soups, to the giant *cannelloni*, running the gamut of many thicknesses of spaghetti and spaghettini, all numbered to avoid confusion, the barley sugar twists, *fusilli*, the bows or butterflies, *farfalle*, the *vermicelli*, the list is endless. These all fall in the category of *pasta secche*, that is pasta made from durum wheat and water. *Pasta all 'uovo*, pasta made with the addition of egg, has another range of shapes: *tagliatelle*, *taglialine*, *fettucine*, *lasagne*, *lasagnette* and so on. Each shape is suitable for a particular sauce, for instance *spaghetti alla carbonara* (*spaghetti* with a sauce of *pancetta*, parmesan, *pecorino* and eggs) is invariably *spaghetti* not *rigatoni* or *bavette* or *tagliatelle*. This is because the textures of the sauce and the pasta marry well together. Then the sauces themselves are extremely numerous, ranging from the simplest and cheapest (at least in Italy where the ingredients are easily available) and also one of the most delicious, olive oil, garlic and hot pepper (*olio, aglio e peperoncino*), to clever concoctions using for example cream and truffles or a pureé of black olives. Then apart from the plain pastas there are the filled ones, which, traditionally, are served on festive days.

For her work-a-day first course Silvana favours *pasta corto*, short medium-width pasta such as *rigatoni*, *tortiglione* or *penne*. The *rigatoni* are short ribbed tubes and the *penne* are the same shape but smooth and cut to a point diagonally at each end like a quill pen, from which their name is taken; *penne* are feathers. They are often served 'all' *arrabiata*', angry, which means with a tomato sauce well spiced with chili, but this is a southern dish and besides Silvana thinks *peperoncini* are too fierce for the digestion. Tuscan men think they are an aphrodisiac. One wonders what their reaction would be to an Indian meal *á la Inghilterra*. Silvana has two basic sauces, one made solely of tomatoes and olive oil on a basic *soffrito* of carrot and celery, and the other, already described, is essentially the same with the addition of meat, either crumbled Tuscan sausages, some chicken livers or *carne macinato*, minced beef. The meat she uses for the sauces is always fresh, never gruesome leftovers.

 To make a dish of **Pasta Corta al Ragù** for four people, you will require 400 g or 14 oz of *penne*. Do not waste your time or money on buying pasta that is not Italian, cook something else. Those made by Buitoni or Barilla are excellent. You also need half a pint or 250 ml of *ragù* as given in January's chapter and some grated parmesan or *pecorino*.

Never buy boxes of ready grated parmesan, as they bear little relation to real parmesan. It is much better not to use the cheese at all if you cannot obtain the real thing.

Bring a large saucepan of salted water to the boil. You need one litre or 1¾ pints of water to cook 100 g or 3½ oz of dry pasta properly. When the water is at a strong rolling boil tip in the *penne*, stirring them around with a long-handled wooden fork to make sure they have separated and are moving freely. The water will have gone off the boil when you introduced the pasta, so put on the lid until the water has regained boiling point then remove it again. From the moment the pasta goes into the water time it; this is easiest with a little timer. At the seventh minute, test a piece of the pasta by biting it, do so again at the eighth minute and so on until the pasta is cooked but still resists the teeth. At that point, swiftly tip the pan into a colander and drain the *penne* thoroughly; they should make a slithery sound as you shake them in the colander and have a shine to their surface. If they look at all floury then they are overcooked and there is nothing to be done with them. The purpose of draining the pasta absolutely throughly is to remove all drops of water which would only serve to dilute the good sauce. This sauce you will have had simmering on the stove ready for the moment when you spoon it onto the *penne*. You may serve the *penne* in two different ways. Either in single pasta bowls with a tablespoon or so of sauce on top of each bowl, so that everyone can mix his own. Or in a large bowl, in which case you can put a small layer of *penne* in the bottom of the bowl, then some sauce and so on until each is used up, then mix all together. This ensures that each piece of pasta has its just coat.

A great deal is written about the method of cooking the pasta itself, but very little is said on the subject of the relationship of the pasta to its sauce. There should not be so much sauce as to drown the pasta, nor should there be so little as to be meagre. The sauce should have a definite oil base so that it clings to the pasta and there must be no watery pools at the bottom of the bowl. And it should have a rich concentrated flavour so that a moderate amount will go a long way. In my opinion the just balance is achieved only with years of experience and a sharp idea of how the dish should be. And the only way to understand the precise quality that makes a dish of pasta excellent is to eat one prepared by an Italian cook in Italy, which is as good an excuse as any for a visit. This may seem a long digression on the preparation of a humble staple, but the simplest things are often the most difficult, difficult but not impossible if you employ care, concentration and the best ingredients.

One of the problems of feeding such a large group of people over several weeks is to achieve variety in the dishes. The structure of the meal is rigid so the changes must come in different ingredients and textures. Although this particular area of Italy is a good distance from the sea, fish still plays a part in the weekly menus. Fish shops as such are not common in inland towns, although overlooking the main *piazza* in Cortona there is an ancient open-air fish market equipped with small marble slabs and running water. However the fish still sold there on market day comes not from the sea but from the Lago di Trasimeno. It is therefore freshwater fish and of the carp, pike and eel variety. Silvana is rather fastidious about these lake fish and will not serve many of them; she distrusts their eating habits and dislikes their flavour. *Lumache*, snails, which are quite popular in the mountain district, also meet with her disapproval. Some people, she says darkly, enjoy them but they are not to her taste.

The one freshwater fish that the family does enjoy is trout. They are plentiful in the small river that borders part of Orlando's domain. Sauro, when he returns from school on the country bus, often spends the hot afternoons fishing in the tree-shadowed pools and Silvana is always delighted when he comes rushing in to bang down a tin full of shiny trout on the bright oil-cloth covered table. Silvana has several ways of preparing the trout but one of her favourites is to cook it *in umido* with fresh tomatoes and basil. This is a perfect summer dish, using the freshest firm fish, sweet summery tomatoes and cool green perfumed *basilico*, which has a natural affinity with tomatoes. After cleaning the fish Silvana puts them in a large *tegame* in which she has heated some olive oil and a very little chopped garlic. After turning the fish once she adds the pulp of two or three tomatoes, a sprinkling of salt and some freshly ground black pepper. Lastly she spreads on top five large basil leaves, torn, not cut with a knife. There is a local superstition that basil must never be cut with a blade but always torn with the fingers; this precaution ensures protection from snake bites. It is also far pleasanter and more aesthetic to tear the soft perfumed leaves. The large, flat red-enamelled pan is then partially covered and left to simmer over a low flame until the trout is cooked, the sweet peppery scent filling the cool dark kitchen. The basil grows in three big acanthus-decorated terracotta pots grouped around the little fountain in the kitchen garden. The seeds, planted at Easter-time, have now formed sturdy small plants which will thrive in their hot moist position. Basil needs sun and copious moisture to flourish and rewards the gardener with waves of delightful sweet scent when it is watered.

To prepare a dish of **Trote al Pomodoro e Basilico** for two people you need two nice fresh trout, two tablespoons of olive oil, one small clove of garlic, the pulp of a large marmande tomato or the pulp of three or four fresh, preferably home-grown, small tomatoes, salt and black pepper and four or five basil leaves. Basil plants can be found in many greengrocers and are a pleasure to have on the kitchen windowsill.

First clean the trout, rinse them, drain them well and dry them on kitchen paper. In a large frying pan big enough to take the trout comfortably, heat the olive oil in which you have put the finely chopped garlic. When the garlic has softened but not turned colour put in your trout and turn them once in the hot oil. Next add the fresh tomato pulp, spreading it around the trout, sprinkle on some salt and black pepper and lastly tear up the basil leaves and spread them on top of the pan. Cover the pan with a lid almost completely and simmer over a low flame until the fish is cooked.

To compliment this dish with its insistent though subtle flavour Silvana might prepare some plain boiled potatoes. To give them their typical Tuscan flavour she will drain them well and pour over them a measure of her fruity olive oil. The heat of the potatoes releases the scent and flavour of the oil and turns a humble staple into something exquisite. Try this with tiny new potatoes in their skins.

Silvana also serves the trout fried. She dips the cleaned fish into a heap of flour seasoned with salt and black pepper then plunges them into bubbling hot oil until they are crisp and golden on the outside and a soft cream colour within. The fish are then piled onto an oval white china dish and served with pieces of lemon as a garnish. Larger trout can be split and stuffed with a mixture of fine breadcrumbs, finely chopped garlic, salt and pepper and a sprig of rosemary or parsley then grilled over the open fire and regularly basted with olive oil and sprinkled with coarse salt. When served they should be opened to reveal the stuffing then sprinkled with more olive oil and a squeeze of lemon juice. Here again the olive oil, warmed by the heat of the fish, releases its savour and enhances the flavour of the fish.

 To serve **Trote alla Griglia** to two people you will need two large trout, two slices of good white bread, two tablespoons of very finely chopped parsley, one large clove of garlic, salt and freshly ground black pepper, olive oil and coarse salt. First clean, rinse, drain and thoroughly dry the trout. Soak the bread in cold water then squeeze all the moisture away. Crumble the damp bread into soft crumbs and leave in a small heap on your chopping block. Next chop the parsley very very fine with your *mezzaluna* and chop the garlic too. Combine the parsley and garlic with the heap of breadcrumbs, mix them well together and season with salt and black pepper. This filling should have the consistency of a paste rather than a crumbly stuffing. It should also be green rather than white, which means there should be more parsley than bread. Stuff the trouts' stomach cavities with this mixture and close the slits with toothpicks. Anoint the fish with a little olive oil, sprinkle them with a little coarse salt and grill them on the barbecue, basting them with more oil as necessary.

When trout is not available another favourite fish is the dried salt cod called *baccalà* in Italy or *morue* in southern France. *Baccalà* should not be confused with *stoccafissa*, stock fish, which is a similar North Sea cod but is preserved by being air dried without the aid of salt – the pieces are wrapped around poles to dry, hence the name. Before reaching a fit state for cooking it must be beaten thoroughly with a wooden mallet and soaked in cold water for three to four days, the water being changed three or four times a day. These preliminary steps must not be neglected because if the *stoccafissa* is insufficiently softened no amount of cooking will improve it. This tediously long preparation is probably the reason why *baccalà* is more popular, even though it too needs to soak before cooking. This very traditional fish, the *baccalà*, is sold in most of the small Italian grocer shops and can be seen in large salt-encrusted barrels. The fish seen hanging in stiff greyish-white triangular shapes from hooks in the shop ceilings is usually *stoccafissa*. Salting is one of the oldest methods of conserving fish and meat and was one way in which Italians living far from lakes and the sea were able to have a year-round supply of fish to eat on Fridays.

Orlando brings the *baccalà* from the village shop. Before it can be eaten it must be soaked for twenty-four hours to rid it of excess salt. Silvana puts it in a large bowl full of clean cold water then places the bowl under the tap in her kitchen sink. The bowl is brimming with water and the tap is left to run slowly into it so that it overflows slightly, thus ensuring that the water is constantly changed. After twenty-four hours the fish should be ready to be cooked. Silvana dries and cuts the large fillets into convenient pieces about two inches by three, then she has a choice of ways in which to prepare it. It can be cooked like trout, *in umido* with a tomato sauce. To do this Silvana puts some olive oil in the large *tegame* together with several cloves of garlic; this stronger-flavoured fish will take more than the delicate trout. She dips the pieces of fish into seasoned flour and fries them gently in the hot oil. When they are a pretty golden colour she adds the pulp of four to five ripe tomatoes, some chopped parsley, salt and black pepper. Then the fish is left to cook through thoroughly. In winter, when fresh tomatoes are not available, she uses a mixture of her tomato conserve and some home-bottled tomatoes from the store cupboard. The fish when cooked has a subtle creamy taste and a firm, slightly chewy texture, but not the unpleasant salty or fishy flavour that one might expect. It has, however, a totally different quality from fresh fish. With it she may serve a dish of *fagiolini verdi*, tiny tender green beans lightly cooked in boiling salted water then drained and turned in the pan with olive oil and served with slices of lemon. *Baccalà*, too, can be simply dipped in flour and fried in hot oil as is the trout but ideally it requires a more interesting treatment to enliven the rather solid quality of the flesh.

To make a dish of *baccalà* in any of its varied guises you must first rid it of the large amount of salt that it has absorbed during the curing process. An efficient way to do this is, as Silvana does, to put the fish to soak in a large bowl full of water with a slightly running tap feeding the bowl continually to keep the water changing. After at least eighteen hours of this treatment, twenty-four is better, you may then put the fish into a bowl of hot water for half an hour to complete the process. If the fish is not thoroughly soaked it will be inedible. Once the soaking is completed it is time to trim the fish and take off any skin.

 To prepare *Baccalà in Umido* for six people you will require 1 kg or 2¼ lbs of the soaked and trimmed fish, a plate of flour, three cloves of garlic, four tablespoons of olive oil, the pulp of four or five ripe tomatoes or a tin of peeled tomatoes drained and mixed with a little *passato di pomodoro*, maybe a very little salt, black pepper and a handful of coarsely chopped parsley.

First of all cut the fish into convenient pieces about two inches by three and dip each piece into the flour to coat it. Chop the garlic up roughly. In a large flat pan heat up the olive oil and in it allow the garlic to become a pale blonde colour but do not let it burn. Next put in the pieces of fish and allow them to brown on both sides. When they are a pretty golden colour add the tomato pulp to the pan, spreading it around the fish. Sprinkle with black pepper and throw in the handful of parsley. It is better to reserve any salt that may be necessary until near the end of the cooking time, as the fish will

probably be salty enough on its own account. Now lower the flame
and let the fish cook through well for at least an hour.

With this rich fish dish you might like to serve **Fagiolini Verdi** as
Silvana sometimes does. For six people you will need 1 kg or about
2¼ lbs of fresh small green beans, a little olive oil, lemon juice, salt and
black pepper. Plunge the beans into a pan of salted boiling water and
let them cook until they are tender but have not lost all their crispness.
Drain them well; in a small pan warm up a little olive oil, don't cook
it, put the beans into the oil and toss them around, squeeze on some
lemon juice and sprinkle with salt and black pepper. The scent of a
newly-cut fresh lemon is one of the delights of the kitchen; do not be
tempted to use any shrivelled specimens that may lurk in the bottom
of the fruit bowl for this bean dish.

Perhaps Silvana's favourite way of preparing *baccalà* is with parsley and
potatoes. She fills a deep pan with layers of thinly-sliced potatoes, generous layers of chopped parsley, the fish, more potatoes and so on until
the dish is full. She adds a little olive oil to each layer and finally some
water, then covers and simmers the dish slowly. The flavours of the fish
and parsley permeate the potatoes beautifully. This dish can also be made
in the oven with the addition of layers of chopped onion and tomato,
more oil but no water.

 To make Silvana's **Baccalà al Prezzemolo** for six people you will need
1 kg or 2¼ lbs of soaked and trimmed *baccalà*, 500 g or 1 lb 2 ozs of
potatoes, peeled and sliced into thin slices, a large tuft of parsley, olive
oil, salt and black pepper and a little water.

Spread a little olive oil on the bottom of a very heavy and shallow
saucepan, then on the oil arrange a layer of potato slices, season them
and trickle on a little more oil. Next sprinkle on an even dusting of
chopped parsley, then a layer of *baccalà* cut into small pieces. Drizzle
the oil over the fish, then more parsley and another layer of potato
and so on until the pan is full. Add a little water to prevent the fish
from sticking to the pan. Let it cook over a very low flame for at least
an hour until the potatoes are tender and the fish cooked through; add
more liquid if the dish seems to be catching. This dish can also be
cooked successfully and more simply in the oven where it will just
require olive oil for moisture. To vary the flavour you may put a layer
of thin pieces of onion on top of the potato and a layer of tomato
slices on top of the fish.

One of the meat dishes that Silvana occasionally serves to the work-force is her version of *Osso Bucco*. This differs from the classic Milanese dish in that she uses olive oil instead of butter to cook the meat and right at the end of the cooking she adds a zest of chopped capers. The classic *gremolata* with which the Milanese enliven the dish consists of finely chopped garlic, parsley and lemon peel. This fresh mixture, which is barely heated through, gives a delicious spice to the rich meat.

To cook Silvana's **Osso Bucco** for four people you will need four slices of shin of veal cut about one inch thick, two tablespoons of olive oil, two cloves of garlic, one glass of white wine, two tablespoons of *passato di pomodoro*, salt and freshly ground black pepper and a few plump capers.

In a large flat heavy-bottomed pan soften the sliced garlic in the olive oil. Then brown the slices of shin on both sides. The pan should be large enough to hold all the slices of shin side by side in one layer. Next add the glass of wine and the tomato conserve and season with the salt and pepper. Allow the meat to cook very slowly until it is tender. Three or four minutes from the end of cooking sprinkle the capers on top of the meat. If the dish shows any signs of sticking during the cooking time moisten it with more wine and tomato.

In Italy there are always fresh peas in their pods to be bought in the markets in season. Silvana always grows rows of peas in her *orto* and this is her favourite way of cooking the delicious sweet vegetable, **Piselli con Prosciutto**. The fresher and tinier the peas, the better this dish will be. For three people you will need 1 kg or 2¼ lbs of fresh peas, two tablespoons of olive oil, 30 g or 1½ oz of *pancetta* or bacon cut into dice, two chopped cloves of garlic, three fresh sage leaves, black pepper, salt and a little stock as needed.

First shell the peas. Then heat up the olive oil in a large saucepan. To the hot oil add the chopped garlic, the *pancetta* cut into dice, and the sage leaves and a small sprinkling of black pepper; this mixture will smell delicious. Allow it to cook gently until the *pancetta* has taken on a little colour and the garlic has softened. Do not allow it to burn as this will make the flavour bitter; the whole idea of the dish is to emphasise the sweetness of the peas. When the garlic has softened tip the shelled peas into the saucepan and turn them in the perfumed oil until they are all coated, then add as little stock as possible and season with a scrap of salt; but be careful with this as the *prosciutto* will be salty too. Allow the peas to cook on a gentle flame until they are tender, adding a little more stock if they seem to be drying out. Cook the first peas of the season like this or with some butter instead of olive oil and eat them on their own with fresh bread.

Whatever Silvana decides to serve for a *secondo* during these busy summer months, the meal invariably ends with fruit, maybe ripe yellow peaches, apples, sweet red water melon or cherries. Finally she serves tiny cups of strong black coffee to wake everyone up. When everyone has eaten and returned to the hot fields Silvana is left in the suddenly silent kitchen to tackle the vast pile of plates and glasses; but she is at least sheltered from the burning sun.

Later in the afternoon Silvana will go out into her garden and do a little work there; she may potter in the small corner set aside for the flowers, mostly dahlias, Sweet William, snapdragons and Michaelmas daisies planted amongst sage bushes and hydrangeas. She goes into the vegetable garden to pick vegetables or salad for supper, and to see what is ripe and what is coming up; the cool late afternoon is also the time when she does her watering. Sometimes she picks up an old sack and a small sharp sickle and wanders off into the fields to pick specially planted vetches' to feed her rabbits; they will enjoy the herbiage and ultimately the family will enjoy the well fed rabbits. Occasionally she will take a kitchen chair out into the courtyard and sit in the shade of the house, her hands busy with a pile of mending, while the hens scratch about by the doorway and the old black sheep dog sits companionably by her side.

❦ JUNE

During this beautiful month of June, when the corn is ripening to a pale greeny gold, and scarlet poppies spread across the roadsides and meadows, an important event is taking place in the Cerotti family; one of Orlando's nephews is getting married to a young girl from a neighbouring village. The village, however, is over the border and the girl is Umbrian.

There is a great deal of usually good-natured rivalry between Tuscans and Umbrians, especially when it comes to the question of food. The Tuscans chide the Umbrians for being too hedonistic, drinking too much wine and not taking life seriously enough, and they distrust the richer Umbrian cooking. The Umbrians, on the other hand, maintain that the Tuscans have no sense of humour, are too severe and prone to keeping their money well tucked away under the mattress; they deride the plainness of Tuscan cooking. Where a Tuscan uses just toasted bread, olive oil, salt and garlic to make the delicious *Bruschetto*, an Umbrian will add a few slices of truffle to his if at all possible. However this regional rivalry which makes Italy the fascinating mixture that it is should not be exaggerated and both families are delighted with the forthcoming wedding.

Weddings in Italy are tremendously important and invariably lavish affairs. Engagements are long and the wedding date is usually set by the bride's father; it probably very much depends on the state of the family finances. The guest list can run into hundreds – on this occasion there will be three hundred people, the entire population of at least three villages – and everyone of course expects a gargantuan feast. On the wedding day, a beautiful clear June morning, with the hills covered in brilliant yellow *ginestra* whose heavy scent fills the air and wafts down into the valley, the guests of the bride's family all assemble at her home at about eleven o'clock in the morning, wearing their best dresses and suits; they crowd around the house and chat. The large double front doors are wide open and in the huge hallway at the foot of the stairs which lead to the main part of the house a buffet is laid. The festivities commence before anyone has set foot in the church. Two long trestle tables are laid with damask cloths and are loaded with all sorts of savouries and sweet cakes. There are soft rolls filled with *prosciutto* and *salame*, open sandwiches of hard boiled egg and mayonnaise topped with stuffed olives, rolls filled with slices of herb-filled *frittata*, plates piled with home-baked cakes and of course huge flasks of wine. There is also beer, and orangeade for the children. The bride's brothers and sisters ply the guests with food but only the occasional privileged elderly guest is allowed upstairs to greet the bride. Eventually she is ready and comes down the wide staircase on the arm of her father. Already the photographer is snapping away. Italian girls are usually lovely; their wedding days are something that they treasure and their dresses are often amazingly beautiful. Brunella's is no exception and she stuns the eager crowd with her voile gown with its long pleated train. Framing her face she wears white silk flowers in her hair that cascade to her shoulders. Her father Alberto, the stocky strong village blacksmith, is very elegant in his dark serge suit. They are both rather stiff and nervous.

The tiny church where the marriage is to take place is only a few steps away from the house so everyone sets out on foot in a procession, the bride and her father leading, followed by her mother and grandmother and the rest of the numerous family and friends. At the church the groom and his family and guests are waiting; a young cousin of the bride's had been delegated to watch for his arrival. The couple are married by the bride's uncle, Don Luigi. During the ceremony Brunella's sister sings the *Ave Maria* and a very young guest has to be persuaded that it is not a good idea for him to hold the bride's hand. Afterwards everyone has their photograph taken with the new couple.

Silvana enjoyed the wedding service and sat in the congregation with her sisters-in-law. Orlando, however, preferred to stand outside in the sun with some of his cronies and chat about farming and such matters. As there are so many guests the wedding reception is to be held in a nearby country restaurant which can provide for up to five hundred people.

After all the photographs have been taken and everyone has piled into the cars there follows a hair-raising drive, a seemingly endless procession of Fiats, from the humble *cinque cento* to something far grander, careering around the twisting country road all intent on reaching the feast as soon as possible and making an uproarious din with their horns all the way. At the pretty country inn an *al fresco* bar is arranged on a large lawn where *aperitivi*, wine and small salted biscuits and nuts are served. Eventually everyone in the huge crowd settles down at the long white-clothed tables. Since Orlando is an important uncle, he and Silvana sit at the top table with the bride and groom and the close family. There is a promising array of knives and forks and already the tables are laden with quantities of wine. Before each place there is a menu, showing in all eleven courses.

To begin there are the *antipasti*. The band of waiters bring round vast silver platters containing tiny pizzas filled with mushrooms and tomato, canapés of smoked salmon and stuffed olives, not those that appear in jars for cocktails, but large green *ascolano* olives which are stoned, stuffed with a delicate forcemeat then rolled in fine breadcrumbs and deep fried. There are also tiny veal sausages wrapped in silver foil, *crostini* of chicken liver paté, piquant tomato *crostini* with liberal doses of chili, the thinnest slices of parma ham and stuffed eggs flavoured with anchovy and capers. The waiters go round the tables several times, bringing the hot *antipasti* first then the cold. The guests are encouraged to help themselves to wine and there are already calls for the bottles to be replenished. After the *antipasti* it is the turn of the *pasta*. This comes in three separate courses: first the restaurant's own *tagliatelle* with a rich *ragù*, then *cannelloni*, the large round tubes filled with meat and tomato covered in béchamel and parmesan and baked in the oven, lastly *tagliatelle verde*, *tagliatelle* made with the addition of finely pounded spinach to give a delightful green colour; this is served with a sauce of cream and *prosciutto cotto*. Silvana, although faintly scandalised by the extravagance of the dishes, is thoroughly enjoying herself. Good food cooked by somebody else is a real treat for her. Orlando is swapping jokes with his brothers and making short work of the excellent Umbrian wine.

Everyone having done justice to the pasta, the waiters bring the first main course which is *Piccione in Salmi*, pigeons roasted briefly then finished in a rich sauce based on brandy, *soffrito* of carrots, onions and celery, enriched with concentrated stock from the crushed pigeon bones, then thickened with butter and flour. Great dishes of *fagiolini verdi* and potatoes roasted with meat juices, whole cloves of garlic and rosemary are passed around with the pigeons. Then comes aromatic roast lamb and roast pork; these are served with *sformati* of *piselli* and *carciofi*, pureés of peas and artichokes mixed with eggs and grated parmesan and baked in moulds in the oven. After the lamb and pork come large dishes of spit-roasted duck, guinea fowl and chicken and with them a refreshing green salad. All through the meal guests propose toasts to the bride and groom or their parents, and the chant of 'bacio, *bacio*, *bacio*' goes round the room, everyone insisting that the groom should kiss his bride. In the interval between the main courses and the *dolci* the young parish priest and his choir sing a cheeky song that they have composed all about Alberto and his family, who are very popular in their village. There are no stilted formal speeches.

The wedding cake is carried in to loud applause and there is a fusillade of spumante corks flying through the air. As well as the wedding cake there is a great iced chocolate cake with *vin santo* to go with it. Finally baskets of fruit are circulated, then coffee and much-needed *digestivi* or brandy. The feast has been going on for five hours and the end is signalled by the bringing in of decorative baskets of *confetti*, small mementoes of the day, one for each guest. Brunella has chosen miniature straw hats trimmed with flowers which are attached to wisps of veiling holding sugared almonds and a little card inscribed with the names of the bridal couple.

After the majority of the guests have taken their leave the hard core of revellers, mainly from the close family, set off in procession in their cars to install the bride in her new home. The line of cars, now much smaller, drives up through the mountains and branching off onto tiny unmade roads the procession eventually arrives at the groom's home, a rambling grey stone farm house with an old-fashioned *torre* or tower for drying chestnuts. The new couple will live with the groom's parents, who are farmers in a small way. Brunella will help her mother-in-law in the house and Fabio will continue to work on the farm, a traditional arrangement. Girls move to their in-laws' house when they marry but the eldest son at least remains in the family home with his wife. Very many of these old farmhouses are rambling structures because they consist of many stages of building; for each new bride at least one room is added on to the house. However this way of life is on the decline as most modern Italian girls want homes of their own with central heating and all the trimmings.

The cheerful party arrives at the house and there is yet more wine, liqueurs and sweet cake to be consumed. Brunella's new room has been furnished with great care. She had chosen traditional country furniture and the vast *letto matrimoniale* has an elaborate bedstead of curved brass with a lacquered plaque at the head decorated with flowers. The coverlet is made of exquisite hand-made cream lace; these lovely covers are still to be found in some country markets. The photographer is still of the party and takes pictures of the pretty room in all its new splendour. Later the couple will have a lavish memento of their wedding day in the shape of an enormous album packed with hundreds of excellent colour prints. The album itself is magnificent. It is shaped like a beech leaf and the cover is of hand-worked pewter, the veins of the leaf carefully formed in the metal. The lining of the cover is made of heavy watered silk and is the colour of the inside of a cobnut shell. It is hard to believe that such workmanship still exists in this century.

Orlando and Silvana return to the *fattoria* towards evening in time to chase the hens into the *pollaio* and feed the rabbits. Supper will be a very sparse affair after the day's indulgences. Silvana particularly enjoyed the dishes in the wedding feast that she herself seldom or never makes. She was also interested in the differences between her cooking and that of the Umbrians. This recipe for *ragù* which they ate with their *tagliatelle* points out the differing styles of Tuscan and Umbrian cooking if you contrast it with Silvana's recipe for the same sauce.

 For an Umbrian *Ragù* for six people to season 600 g of pasta you will need 300 g or 10½ oz of a mixture of lean veal, pork and chicken, 50 g or 2 oz of fat *prosciutto*, 30 g or just over 1 oz of butter, a rib of celery, one carrot and a small onion, a little white wine, salt and black pepper, 300 g or 10½ oz of ripe tomatoes and a teaspoon of tomato concentrate. These ingredients are for the first stages of the sauce and so far the *ragù* is fairly similar to Silvana's. Next you will need 20 g or 1 oz of *rigagli di pollo*, chicken giblets cut into small dice, 20 g or just under 1 oz of dried *funghi*, 50 g or 2 oz of butter, three tablespoons of thick cream, a small black truffle cut into thin slices and a pinch of nutmeg.

Mince the meat together with the *prosciutto*. In a large heavy pan melt 30 g or about 1½ oz of butter and add the minced meat and the *odori*, that is the celery, onion and carrot kept whole or cut in half. Let the meat just change colour over a gentle heat, it must remain soft, then sprinkle the meat with two or three tablespoons of white wine and allow the wine to evaporate. Then add the tomatoes deprived of their skins and chopped and the tomato concentrate, mix all the ingredients together and let the *ragù* cook gently for an hour, checking occasionally to see that it is not too dry; if it is, add a very little stock. Meanwhile, soak the dried *funghi* in a little hot water, squeeze them dry and chop them into small pieces; cook the *funghi* gently in a little butter. Similarly chop the giblets into small pieces and cook them gently in the rest of the butter. When the *ragù* has cooked for one hour, remove the *odori* from the pan. Then add the giblets and the *funghi*, mix them all together and let them cook for a few minutes. Finally just before serving turn the heat down as far as possible and stir the cream into the sauce, then sprinkle on the pinch of nutmeg and finally the sliced truffle. These must be stirred in very gently and not allowed to cook; the flavour of the truffle will be stronger in this way. Serve with perfectly cooked fresh *tagliatelle*.

 A dish that Silvana particularly enjoyed was the **Sformato di Piselli** which with the sweet peas of June was especially delicious. To make it you will need for four people, 800 g or about 2 lb of shelled fresh peas, 100 g or 4 oz of butter, a wine glass of stock, 50 g or 2 oz of grated parmesan, 40 g or about 1½ oz of flour, a teacup of milk and a pinch of salt, 100 g or 3½ oz of lean *prosciutto* cut into small dice and four eggs.

First shell the peas. In a large pan melt half the butter, add the peas and the glass of stock and let the peas cook in the covered pan on a gentle flame until they are done. Meanwhile make a *besciamella* with the rest of the butter, the flour and the milk. Separate the eggs, mix the yolks and beat up the whites until they are fluffy. Have ready and buttered a tall-sided mould, a pan of fairly hot water and a hot oven. As soon as the peas are tender (there should be very little liquid left) add the parmesan to them and mix them lightly together. Add the *besciamella*, the diced *prosciutto* and the egg yolks to the peas, mix them well then fold in the egg white. Pour the mixture into the tall mould and place it in the pan of water; finally put them into the hot oven for twenty-five minutes. Tip the *Sformato* out of the mould onto a serving dish and take to the table immediately.

Silvana makes a similar dish but she would pureé the peas, leave out the *prosciutto* and leave the egg whites unbeaten. She also makes a wonderful dish called *Purée di Fave*, which is an excellent way of serving the vegetable when the broad beans are no longer small and tender enough to be eaten raw as a *stuzzichino*, an appetite provoker at the beginning of the meal. She shells the beans, discarding the outer shells for the benefit of the rabbits, then also shells each individual bean of its tough outer coat. After this she makes a pureé of the beans with milk and butter and black pepper. It is a dish of which she is particularly fond and which, she says, sits in its dish and says '*mangimi, mangimi*' – 'eat me, eat me!'.

 To make *Purée di Fave* for two people you will need 500 g or about 1 lb of shelled broad beans, 50 g or 2 oz of butter, a small amount of full cream milk, salt and black pepper. Deprive the beans of their outer skins then cook them in a little salted boiling water until they are tender. When they are done pass them through the mouli. In a clean pan melt a little of the butter, add the bean purée and little by little the milk, mixing all together into a smooth stiff cream, season with salt and pepper and add the rest of the butter, stirring until it melts. When you have achieved a smooth purée serve it hot, perhaps with *Petti di Pollo alla Griglia*, grilled chicken breast, or a *Frittata di Cacio*, or any delicate dish.

Orlando and his men and women work on steadily through the month at the *zappatura*, which is essential if tobacco plants are to grow tall and strong; they are already springing up out of the ground. Guido still attends to the vine-spraying, especially after heavy showers of rain, and the hay is ripe enough to be cut and made into the pretty circular hay ricks that decorate the *contadinis'* farmyards.

The cherry trees are full of glossy red cherries which vibrate with the buzzing of beautiful irridescent green scarab beetles, attracted by the ripe fruit. This month, Silvana has the enjoyable task of preserving those cherries that are not eaten up for dessert. The crooked old wooden ladder made from a slender tree trunk split down the middle, which explains its crooked shape, is propped against the cherry trees and on the kitchen table there is a battered twig basket full of the dark red fruit. Silvana preserves the cherries in brandy or a cherry-flavoured spirit sold expecially for the purpose, called *ciliegin*. It comes in two-litre bottles. To make the brandied cherries Silvana washes and dries the fruit carefully, discarding any that are not perfect. She leaves on the stalk but trims it off about a quarter of an inch away from the fruit: then she places the fruit in scrupulously clean seal-topped jars and pours in the brandy or *ciliegin*. The jars are then sealed and dated and put away in the dark pantry to mature. The cherries are best kept for at least a year and improve with age. They are delicious served in tiny bowls with a little of their liquid at the end of a meal.

Strawberries, both cultivated and wild ones, are another delight this month. A traditional Italian way of serving *fragalone*, the large strawberries, is to drown them in red wine in which a few cloves have been steeped. This brings out the strawberry flavour in a surprising way. Alternatively they can be cut into pieces and sprinkled with sifted sugar and lemon juice, then left to marinate for an hour or two before eating. The lemon and strawberry meld together in a delicious way. The little *fragolini*, or wild strawberries do not need these accompaniments as their flavour is in itself so rare that it is a shame to mask it. Silvana loves *fragolini* but finds it difficult in the course of her crowded days to devote enough time to picking and hulling them.

At the front of the Cerotti *fattoria* bordering the rose-lined drive there are large beds given over to medicinal herbs. In June the *camomilla* is in full bloom and ready for picking. Camomile is a very pretty daisy-like flower with a large almost oval yellow centre, delicate white petals and feathery leaves. There are two sorts; *camomillone*, which is the large variety, and then a daintier version, which Silvana prefers. The scent of the *camomilla* is strong and sweet, almost fruity, and its properties are of the sleep-inducing kind. Silvana is careful to pick the flowers and leaves at the right phase of the moon so that the herb will be at its strongest. She gathers great armfulls of the flowers and lays them carefully on sheets of cardboard to dry in the sun. With the small delicate *camomilla*, she says it is not necessary to separate the heads from the stems as the dried greenery will do no harm in an infusion. When the flowers are well withered and dry Silvana shakes them all into large paper bags which she hangs on strings from the pantry beams. Late at night, when she has finished the last batch of cheese, and especially if she has had a difficult day, she will make a *tisane* to calm and relax herself. She puts about two teaspoonsful of the dried flowers in a cup and adds some boiling water in which they will steep. After the herb has given up its strength and the water is a clear pale yellow colour, she strains the *tisane* into a glass and flavours it with a squeeze of lemon juice and sometimes a spoonful of sugar or honey. This infusion she swears sends her into a swift dreamless sleep; the ritual is pleasant and the sweet-smelling *tisane* is delicious. Silvana gives this camomile *tisane* with a slice of lemon to Orlando when he is suffering from gout, a remedy which was also prescribed by Nicholas Culpeper in his collection of herbal remedies.

Silvana also has *malva*, mallow, growing in the garden. It has large five-petalled cold pink flowers, the long scalloped-ended petals streaked with a deeper lilac. Its leaves are shaped like miniature maple leaves. Silvana gathers these fresh and infuses the leaves and stalks in boiling water. She keeps the limpid pale green liquid in a glass bottle. The *malva* water can be used in several ways: as an aid to digestion, as a remedy for coughs and chest colds, and as a vaginal douche it is mildly cleansing and soothing. Mallow is thus indicated for these conditions in many herbal treatises. Silvana also uses what she calls *agramina*, a rough grass, in the same way for much the same complaints. It does not look in the least like *agrimonia* or sticklewort and I am unable to identify the plant. The violet is another plant that provides a remedy, this time for bronchial troubles. Nena, who suffers from a weak chest, is particularly keen on an infusion of violets to provide relief from bronchitis. However, although Silvana will resort first to these herbal remedies when there is a slight illness to be cured, anything more serious or persistent merits a visit to the doctor and the most modern medicines available.

When Silvana was a girl, she says the *anziani*, the old people, were very skilled in the use of herbs and nearly all the common plants had some application or other. To be at their strongest and most efficacious they had to be picked at the right phase of the moon, and this rule also applied to all the activities of the farm and household. Everything has its proper season. Even the preparing of wooden posts had to be done at the right phase of the moon so that the wood would have the best chance of remaining solid and not rotting in the ground. At the right time the seasoned poles were stripped of their bark, the ends sharpened into a point with an adze, then they were singed over a fire and finally planted in position. Orlando used this same method when setting out his new vineyard. The *luna calante*, the waning moon just after the full moon, was the right time for planting and moving wine and the rising half moon was the most propitious time for the hatching of eggs as this was thought to influence the eggs to break in their centres and make the chicks' entrance into the world easier.

There were also a few taboos to be observed involving women during their monthly courses. Surprisingly these did not include the one preventing women from handling hams at this time, which is well known in France as well as in some parts of England. In Tuscany menstruating women were not allowed to touch wine vinegar in case it turned to water, or to handle flowers and plants lest they wither and die.

Silvana learnt the uses of various herbs from her mother and grand-mother. Years ago, when her family lived on an extremely remote mountain in a tiny group of houses, there was no orthodox medical aid available in the near vicinity. They treated all ailments and injuries as best they could at home. Silvana's grandmother and her mother gave birth to their numerous children (Silvana was the youngest of eleven) alone, without the aid of a doctor or indeed of a midwife, the *levatrice*. Silvana's first son was born in hospital, but for Sauro's birth she returned to the family home, to the same room and bed that she herself had been born in. She says that she vividly remembers the bitter January night, with its fierce wind that rattled the old shutters and scattered the sparks in the wide-chimneyed hearth. For hours she paced around and leant on the massive kitchen table until the birth was imminent and her sisters helped her into bed. After the birth, in keeping with tradition, she ate only '*in bianco*'. All her dishes were white, consisting mainly of rice and pasta with grated *pecorino* to flavour it, and the fresh *ricotta* or *ravigiolo* that they made at home.

❧ JULY

All the hard work of the year is coming to fruition. The tobacco plants stand tall and triumphant in the fields and the corn is ripe. The apple and pear trees are loaded with maturing fruit and Orlando's vines have put out bunches of bitter green grapes which will expand and sweeten in the high summer sun. The magnolia tree that grows beside the *fattoria* has its full complement of waxy white flowers and the doves flutter around their nesting boxes amongst them. Bees lurch noisily through the warm air as they ravage the wild flowers and return heavy with pollen to their wooden beehives on the terraces above the *fattoria*. The hives are shaped like small square houses made of wooden slats, each crowned with a pitched roof. The once bright orange and leaf-green paint on them has now faded to a comfortable peach and soft almond. On the façade of each hive, painted in black and yellow, is a crude drawing of a bee in flight. Crickets sing incessantly and at night the meadows' darkness is pricked by the floating, pulsing light of fireflies.

Early every morning the farm hums into life and tractors hauling racks of freshly-picked tobacco leaves rattle along the pathways. The drying kilns are operating day and night. Years ago the tobacco was dried in towers especially built for this purpose. They were tall narrow brick buildings equipped with a fireplace and several chimneys which were used for ventilation and which were opened and closed by means of metal flaps attached to long dangling wires. The tobacco was hung in bunches clipped between split wooden poles suspended by wires from the roof. The fire was kept burning day and night, the heat conducted through the tower by a system of pipes. This old method depended on the *contadini* keeping a watch all night over the fire to keep it alight. The modern electric and oil-fired kilns make this night vigil unnecessary and are clean and efficient, though the fuel bills are enormous. When the tobacco is dried to a pale gold colour it is compressed into bales of a quintale in weight or 100 kilograms. Then Cerotti and his men stack the bales in the attic storerooms. When the harvest is good the little chapel is also piled high with fragrant bundles. Later, in the autumn, a buyer from the government will arrive to assess the quality and offer a price for the tobacco.

The inconstant weather is the only thing that really preoccupies Cerotti. July is an uncertain month. The blazing sun beating onto the fields and burning out the bright meadows can disappear behind sullen clouds, and a suffocating humid heat plays upon the nerves. Thunder grumbles threateningly in the distance, lightning jabs at the hills and eventually the black skies release torrents of cool rain that soaks into the sandy lanes, fills the empty streams and beats into the standing corn. The tobacco plants are bent by the wind, but this is not their worst enemy. The freak hailstorms that occasionally occur are to be more dreaded, as the ice cruelly tears the tender tobacco leaves and makes them valueless. The only creatures who enjoy these storms are the frogs who live by the valley's streams and the ducks. Silvana also likes the freshness in the air that comes after the storm.

Towards the middle of the month the beautiful beige corn is ripe for cutting. The larger fields are sheared by machine but those surrounding the house of Menchino and his mother Nena are narrow terraces and have to be reaped by hand, since the spaces between the vine-supporting oaks and the olive trees are too small for the machines to turn in. These small fields illustrate well the essence of the beauty and economy of Tuscan peasant life. The terraces were hard won, carved by hand out of the steep hillside. They were planted with economy, lines of olive trees alternating with the lines of pollard turkey oaks which support the vines. Around the trees the land is sown with corn, ploughed with ancient ploughs drawn by white oxen and reaped by hand. Not a centimetre of the earth's potential is wasted. The produce is the backbone of Tuscan peasant food. Good bread from the corn, olive oil for savour and wine to drink. Vineyards and olive groves lying in the sun are always beautiful and when growing amongst poppy-sprinkled corn provide a classic image of the southern country idyll. Menchino, who in November sowed the corn, now sharpens his sickle and in the bright heat, to the sound of the crickets, he methodically severs the long stalks, which neighbours help to tie into stooks. These they arrange into pyramids of three at regular intervals across the fields.

All *contadini* houses have in their near vicinity a threshing floor where the corn used to be flailed by hand, each household helping their neighbours until everyone's corn was safely in and threshed. Under Mussolini communal threshing machines were introduced which were hauled into the town piazzas, and the corn was brought into the cities for the *cittadini* to thresh for their own bread. There are many photographic records of threshing taking place in the centres of Rome and Milan.

The *battuto* machine is owned by one family in Orlando's part of the world and circulates all the farmers who have grain to thresh. The farmers pay for the hire of the machine and the operator goes merrily from one harvest home to another for the week or two that his machine is in demand. Orlando's threshing ground is situated just below the shepherd's house and is surrounded by large ricks, convenient for the sheep pens. On threshing day all his men and also cousins and brothers from other valleys group around the giant orange machine which has laboriously been dragged on its metal wheels across the mountain. Some take turns to fork the corn into the mouth of the machine, which is driven by two long belts. Others watch the sacks as the grain pours in, halting the machine and changing the bags as needed. Others toss the discarded straw and start to build the ricks. Smaller farmyards like Menchino's have circular ricks built up around a tall pole stuck in the ground. When completed they look like small circus tents, but are narrow at the ground level. The hay is sliced off with a razor-sharp tool.

Meanwhile, Silvana is caught up with the harvest feast. Today, because there are so many people to cook for, she has some help: a sister, her niece, a sister-in-law and the shepherd's wife, who, being Sicilian, will add a quite different flavour to the dishes that she cooks. Under the magnolia tree the women set up long trestle tables and cover them with bright blue and white checked cloths. It is seven thirty and already the sun is hot. The men have started to thresh the corn and the roar of the machine rattles the window panes. The first break for refreshment will come at nine and a *merenda* for twenty-five must be prepared. For this breakfast, nothing has to be cooked; Silvana will rely on the contents of her pantry and fresh produce from the kitchen garden. She and her friends go into the walled enclosure and set about choosing some ripe melons, picking those with the ripest, strongest scent. They select large green water melons and golden yellow cantaloups. Silvana also stops to gather a big bunch of the flat-leafed Mediterranean parsley, some sage leaves and several large sprigs of rosemary. They lay the melons on the kitchen table and one of them slits the smooth skins to test their choice of fruit; with their combined experience they have chosen the ripest and most juice filled. Silvana's sister starts to carve the melons into slices and arrange them on large oval white dishes. The bright red water melon is placed separate from the yellow cantaloups. While they are thus occupied the baker's van drives into the courtyard. The scent of newly-baked bread floats out as the van doors are opened. Today Silvana will need far more of the two-pound loaves than she normally buys. The baker's boy counts out fifteen of the large, flat oval loaves and puts them into a paper sack. In the wicker baskets in the back of the van he also has some *schiacciata*, the round flat breads which are best eaten hot straight from the fire or oven. This soft pizza-like bread is ideal for the breakfast that Silvana has planned for the harvesters. Normally she makes the *schiacciata* herself but today there are too many other jobs to see to. She picks up two of the golden-brown cartwheels and carries them into the kitchen. The baker's boy is pressed to some wine and a slice of melon which he eats while waiting for Silvana to find her purse and pay him.

Next the *prosciutto* must be brought out from the pantry, and *salame* and some brawn cut down from their beam in the pantry. It needs skill and a long sharp knife to carve slices from the ham which Silvana cured herself during the cold month of January. She props the ham on a wooden support which is shaped in a right angle, the vertical slat being carved into a v shape at the top to hold the hock end of the *prosciutto*. Excess fat is trimmed off, then thin slices are carved across the narrow edge of the ham parallel to the bone. The trick is to cut each slice as thin as possible and to keep the slice large. Commercial *prosciutto* is often boned, which makes the shopkeeper's job much easier as the ham can then be cut on a bacon slicer into paper-thin slices. It is this finely-sliced, rosy meat that is served up with delicately pared melon or fresh figs in restaurants as an *antipasto* to lunch or dinner. In country households *prosciutto* and fruit are invariably served for a *merenda* or breakfast. Silvana fills a plate with the ham and the other women slice up the big *salame* which are seasoned with garlic, black pepper and sometimes cinnamon. At about ten to nine the women carry out the dishes of ham and sausage, the melons and piles of white plates. They fill the tables

with the food; the bright colours of the melons look appetizing against
the sky-blue cloths. Glasses are placed by each plate and the two-litre
flasks of red and white wine which have been cooling in the pantry are
placed all along the table. Finally Silvana brings out the fresh bread and
starts to slice the *schiacciata* into triangular slices. The threshing machine
ceases its buzz and the men troop into the courtyard, stopping first to
splash their hot faces and wash their hands in the stone sink by the
chapel. Silvana has hung a variety of linen hand towels there for them
to use. They all find places around the long table and settle in the kind
shade of the magnolia to enjoy their first break of the day. The women
stand behind the chairs and pass the dishes, watch to see if more of
anything is required and indulge in verbal battles with the men, all
conducted in the best of humour. Under the tables the dogs devour
dropped scraps and the hens peck at the melon rinds.

Although country people like the Cerottis eat *prosciutto con melone* for
breakfast, in Italy it is usually served as an *antipasto* to lunch or dinner.
Occasionally in the height of summer it appears on restaurant menus as
a main course; in this case the portion served is a more generous one
and it does make a delicious light course when a heavier meat dish is
not suitable.

 To serve **Prosciutto con Melone** you will need four slices of Parma
ham cut in the thinnest slices and three small segments of ripe honey-
dew melon per person. Slice the melon into narrow segments, discard
the seeds and pare off the rind. Arrange the fruit on small plates beside
the ham. **Prosciutto** is also delicious when accompanied by fresh figs,
Fichi Freschi. Prepare the figs by trimming off the stem and make
four incisions from the stem to the base of the fruit. Then carefully peel
back the skin to form four petals. Place the peeled figs with their petals
spread around them on one side of each plate and on the other side lay
the pieces of *prosciutto*. Three or four slices of ham and two figs are
sufficient for one person. When there is no fresh fruit available you
may also serve *prosciutto* with pieces of fresh unsalted butter.

While the breakfast preparations have been going on, one of the
women has been in charge of preparing the stone bread-oven in the
courtyard to cook some meat dishes for the harvest lunch. Years ago this
domed oven would have been lit on one day every week to bake the
family bread. Some *contadini* families still make their own bread out of

good strong flour, water and yeast. The saltless Tuscan bread makes the perfect background for the salty hams and *salame* and a good sop for tasty sauces and fresh green olive oil. Today, however, the oven is needed to cook the assortment of meat and poultry that is to be served for the harvest lunch. The oven is dome-shaped, with one central chimney and a small door at about waist height. The floor of the oven, also at waist height, is made of one large flat stone. It must be thoroughly swept of old ashes, then a fire constructed with some kindling and two large logs is lit. The door is closed firmly and the brick walls left to become as hot as is possible. In a hot country an outdoor oven is excellent for summer time when the kitchen becomes unbearable when the wood stove is lit.

Meanwhile Silvana and her friends start to prepare the meats. There are several plump chickens, ducks, young rabbits just right for roasting, a few kilos of pork loin, which will be cooked *in umido*, and a whole lamb. Silvana fetches the lamb carcass and starts to split it up into leg, shoulder and saddle parts. She uses a curious chopper made for her by the village blacksmith, shaped in one piece with a curved blade and a long handle. Within reach on the table is her large chopping-block, worn to a hollow in the centre from years of pounding garlic and chopping herbs. To season the lamb she makes a mound of chopped garlic, diced fat *prosciutto*, the rosemary picked that morning, coarse salt and a good deal of ground black pepper. Her pepper mill resembles an old-fashioned coffee mill: she pours in the whole berries at the top, turns the handle and the ground pepper falls into a little drawer at the bottom of the apparatus. With the quantities of pepper that she uses she needs a larger machine than the normal variety which is only ample when a couple of turns of the mill are all that is required. Silvana makes small pockets in the flesh of the cuts of lamb and stuffs them with the piquant mixture. Finally she dribbles olive oil over the joints, rubbing it well into the surface with her hands, and sprinkles on more salt. This lamb, born months after the spring lambs, will have an excellent flavour but not quite the delicate one of those born in February and killed younger. When the lamb and the rabbits are ready, having made sure that the flames have died in the oven and the stones are extremely hot, the women will carry the meat to the oven, put it inside and again close the doors closely. The accumulated heat will cook the lamb to the degree they prefer.

Meanwhile, the shepherd's wife has busied herself with the preparation of the rabbits. She has five carcasses which have had their heads removed

and their interiors thoroughly cleaned, and she is equipped with a large
bodkin and some coarse thread. On the table amongst the jumble of
spices, bottles and glasses there is a pile of heads of garlic, whose cloves
are plump and white. She breaks off about half a dozen cloves per rabbit
and loosens their thin papery skins with the flat of the knife, then she
bruises the cloves slightly to make their juices run but does not break
them up entirely. She too has a small heap of finely ground pepper and
salt mixed up together and, taking pinches of this mixture, she rubs the
condiments well into the interior of the rabbit and also over the outside.
Next she places the bruised cloves of garlic into the body cavities. The
herb that will give the rabbits their most distinctive flavour comes next:
on the table are bunches of drying fennel stalks and flowers which are
commonly to be found in the valleys hedgerows. For each rabbit she
chooses a bunch of fennel stalks and flowers, placing the bouquet along
the length of the rabbit's interior over the garlic. Finally she adds a good
Tuscan sausage made of pure pork, crushed garlic, black pepper and salt.
Each rabbit is then neatly and firmly sewn up to enclose the stuffing
whose scent in the oven's heat will penetrate the flesh, perfuming it
exquisitely. Finally she drapes some thin slices of *pancetta* over the rabbits,
tying them into place with twine, then anoints them all with olive oil
and they are ready for the oven.

 If you wish to roast a rabbit in this manner, **Coniglio al Forno,** to
serve four people you will need one young whole rabbit, skinned and
cleaned, with the head and forelegs removed, a tablespoon of salt and
finely ground black pepper mixed together, the mixture should have
more pepper than salt in it, six cloves of garlic, a bunch of dried fennel
stalks plus their heads, one large Tuscan sausage and six or seven slices
of *pancetta* or bacon.

Take pinches from your heap of salt and pepper and rub them well
into the flesh of the rabbit, inside and out. Next skin the cloves of
garlic and bruise them slightly with a knife but do not break them up.
Place the garlic inside the carcass, spreading the cloves evenly through
the cavity. Take a small bunch of the dried fennel of the right length
to lie inside the length of the carcass and lay on top of the garlic.
Finally put in the sausage which you have pierced here and there with
a fork. With a bodkin and some fine twine sew up the rabbit so that
its stuffing is firmly enclosed. Finally cover the outside with the slices
of bacon and secure them with more twine. Anoint the carcass with
olive oil and cook it in the oven, using a rotisserie if you have one.

Silvana's sister-in-law has been preparing the ducks, which will be cooked in a vast *padella* on the stove. She will flavour them with *prosciutto*, tomatoes and sage and they will be served in this tasty sauce.

 To make *Anatra in Padella,* for four people you will need one plump young duck, three tablespoons of olive oil, one onion, one carrot, one rib of celery, four fresh sage leaves, 150 g or 5½ oz of *prosciutto*, salt and black pepper, a glass of dry white wine and 600 g or 1 lb 5 oz of fresh tomatoes that have been skinned and chopped.

Wash the duck, dry it well and cut it into pieces. Chop the *odori*, that is the onion, carrot and celery, into dice. In a large flat pan heat up the olive oil and in it allow the chopped vegetables to soften. Add the *prosciutto* cut into dice and let it change colour, then add the four sage leaves. Put in your pieces of duck and let them take on colour on all sides. Pour in the white wine and allow it to evaporate. Then add the tomato and season with salt and black pepper. Let the duck cook gently for about an hour and a half. If it shows signs of drying up moisten it with a little stock. To serve arrange the duck pieces on a flat dish and pour a little of the sauce over them.

The chickens, they all decide, should be cooked *al diavolo*, that is split open, flattened, anointed with lemon juice, olive oil, *peperoncini*, salt and pepper and grilled over the open fire. From time to time the chickens will be basted with more oil and lemon to keep them moist.

 Pollo al Diavolo is a very good dish to cook on a garden barbecue over a wood fire. For four people you will need one chicken, which must be split through the breast bone then pressed open and flattened, so that you will have two flattened halves of the chicken joined down the back. Into a large dish pour a glass of olive oil and the juice of a large lemon. Into this put a good sprinkling of ground up *peperoncini*, about two of the little hot red peppers ground up in a mortar or chopped very fine with a sharp knife. Then add a sprinkling of salt and pepper. When you have mixed the sauce a little, put in your chicken to marinade for half an hour on one side and half an hour on the other. Finally grill the chicken over your wood fire for about twenty minutes a side, basting it occasionally with the remains of the marinade.

In spite of the hot day, the fire has been burning brightly to heat the water up in the vast blackened cauldron suspended by a chain from a bar that swings out from the wall at the back of the fireplace. The water will be needed to cook the pasta without which any respectable Italian lunch is incomplete.

 While the lamb and rabbits are roasting Silvana starts to prepare the fillets of pork which will be cooked *in padella*. She trims the meat of fat and sinew, then in a large flat pan she warms some oil, several chopped cloves of garlic and a few fresh sage leaves. When the garlic is about to turn colour, but well before it is burnt, she puts in the meat, turning it to seal, then she lowers the flame and allows the pork to cook through gently. When the pan juices threaten to dry up she dashes on a little white wine to make a small sauce. Salt and pepper are added when the meat has sealed. To cook this dish for two people you would need two fillets of pork, two tablespoons of olive oil, two cloves of garlic, four fresh sage leaves, salt and black pepper and about half a glass of dry white wine. Serve the fillets on a plate with the little sauce made of the pan juices and the wine poured over them; place a sage leaf on each fillet.

Tuscan chickens are famous for their flavourful meat which is the result of their being fed on good Indian corn and allowed the run of the farmyards to peck and scratch as they will. They are very popular fowls as a main course for the large Sunday lunch, and their delicately flavoured livers also go into making the savoury *antipasti*. There are several ways of making liver *crostini* but today Silvana uses a recipe that adds a little zest to the rich livers. She peels and chops very finely two white onions and sautés them very gently in some olive oil until they are transparent but not brown. Then she chops up the poached livers into very small pieces and adds them to the onion mixture, allowing them to cook gently. Finally she adds some slivers of lemon peel, a little lemon juice and a very few of her home-preserved capers, salt and pepper. A sprinkling of very finely chopped parsley adds another note of colour. While she is thus occupied her niece is preparing the bread. In most restaurants the bread for *crostini* is lightly toasted, but in country households this step is often omitted. Instead the small squares and rectangles of bread cut from the rough country loaves are dipped on one of their surfaces into a bowl of warm stock; this is to soften the bread to aid the spreading of the savoury paste and keep it moist. Finally the chicken liver mixture, which should have the consistency of granular porridge, is spread and the slices arranged on a big flat dish.

 To make Silvana's **Crostini di Fegatini** to serve to five or six people you will need five chicken livers, one onion, two tablespoons of olive oil, a small piece of lemon peel, half a teaspoon of lemon juice, three or four capers, salt and freshly ground black pepper.

First clean the chicken livers, making sure there are no traces of the green bile duct upon them. Chop the onion very finely and set it to soften very gently in the olive oil. It should become transparent but never brown. Add the whole livers to the pan and cook them gently until they are nearly done. Remove the livers from the pan and chop them finely then return them to the onions. Next add the lemon peel cut into tiny splinters and the lemon juice, chop the capers and add them too; season with the salt and pepper. Let the mixture cook gently for a few minutes; if it becomes too dry add a little white wine. Take small rounds of bread, maybe cut from a small baguette, dip one face into warm stock just to moisten the surface, then spread the paté onto the bread. Serve on a large dish with *crostini* of other flavours for contrast.

The shepherd's wife convinces them all that it would be a good idea to make some spicier *crostini* to add interest and colour to the first course. She fills a saucepan full of *pomodori passati*, that is a thick purée of tomato pulp without either seeds or skin. To season the sauce she adds salt and black pepper and two dried red *peperoncini* whose fierceness she can vouch for as they come from her home in Sicily. While the sauce is simmering they gather around the fire and toast some slices of bread; the toasting is necessary for this type of *crostini*. When the toast is ready it is rubbed on one side with a clove of garlic cut through the middle; this gives a sharp pungent scent to the bread. Finally spoonfuls of the hot sauce are placed on each piece of toast. These *crostini* should be made only a short time before they are served as they can become soggy if left to stand for too long a time. They are even better when made of bread fried in olive oil, topped with chopped fresh tomato and sprinkled with a small amount of ground *peperoncini*.

To accompany the meat courses they must have at least two dishes of vegetables and the women are all of the opinion that the simpler and fresher the better for this particular meal. So the youngest cook is dispatched to the kitchen garden to pick armfuls of fresh salad. She chooses several large escarole lettuces, as she likes them for their pretty pale greeny yellow curls and their bitter taste. To these she adds some dark, long-leafed *radicchio* (not to be confused with the red *radicchio* from Treviso which is still a relative newcomer to Tuscany but is fast becoming a great favourite because of its immense versatility. It can be grilled to make an unusual, subtly flavoured vegetable and also produces pasta sauces of surprising elegance. It is also of course very pretty, with its rose to purple colours. Silvana has already planted some seeds but it will be a good while before she is tempted to put the plants to their more sophisticated uses.) As well as the great bowls of salad, which are carefully washed by Silvana's niece, the women have picked a quantity of new French beans, or *fagioli verdi*. These they will prepare simply by boiling them in salted water, draining them well and when hot seasoning them with good olive oil, the juice of a lemon and of course salt and black pepper. Mediterranean people do not labour under the terrible delusion that all food must be so hot that it scorches the mouth or else be rigid with the tasteless iciness of the refrigerator. Olive oil poured over a hot vegetable gives up its fruity flavour in the gentle heat, and the dish is best eaten when it has cooled off just a little. Then the true flavour is strongest.

With all the meats coming to perfection, the salad awaiting its seasoning (this step must of course come just before serving) and the *crostini* ready, they now have only to think of the table and the pasta, which waits for no one. As the sun is now at its hottest they decide instead to eat inside in the cool of the dining room. Two of them lay crisp clean cloths and put out the plates and pasta bowls, cutlery and glasses, plus more large flasks of wine. On the *tinello*, sideboard, there are bowls of peaches and early apples. They lay the plates of *crostini* down the table, alternating the bright red spicy ones with those of the rich pink-brown liver.

 The sauce for the pasta is simmering away on the stove. Today it is *Sugo di Pomodoro*, a fresh tomato sauce which will be lighter than a meat sauce on this hot day. To make it, Silvana uses onion, carrot, celery, olive oil, fresh basil and either fresh or bottled tomatoes. For four people you will need one onion, one carrot, one rib of celery, three tablespoons of olive oil, five basil leaves, 350 g or about 12 oz of fresh ripe tomatoes, skinned and chopped, or the equivalent weight of well-drained bottled or canned tomatoes. Chop the *odori* finely and in a saucepan let them soften in the olive oil. Add the basil leaves then the tomato, and season to taste with salt and black pepper. Let the sauce cook for about half an hour. If it is too dry add some olive oil, but do not add water. To be effective this simple sauce must be made with the best ingredients, that is *olio extra vergine d'oliva*, ripe marmande tomatoes and fresh basil.

Water is bubbling and spitting into the fire, the sauce is ready and there is a large mound of grated *pecorino* in a bowl. Silvana calls the men to wash, and as they troop in through the busy kitchen and take their places at the long table she plunges the pasta into the boiling salted water, giving it a good stir to spread it around the cauldron. She has chosen a short pasta as it is rather easier to handle in such large quantities. It will take about eight to twelve minutes to cook and must be checked at the eighth minute to see its progress and then every minute or so until *al dente*. Meanwhile the men are devouring the tasty *crostini* and slaking their thirsts with white wine. When the pasta is at the right point of tenderness Silvana plunges the pear shaped wicker strainer into the cauldron and fishes out the pasta, draining it thoroughly. She puts a layer of it into the bottom of one of the big bowls, then one of her helpers sprinkles on a layer of sauce, then more well drained pasta and so on until the bowl is full, in this way the sauce is spread evenly through the large bowl and each piece of pasta has its just coat. The men are again served by the women who stand behind chairs and pass the bowls and dishes of cheese. While they are all engaged in enjoying the pasta, Silvana and her sister go outside to the oven to fetch the lamb and the rabbits, whose spicy, herby scent is overpowering. They carry the aromatic meat across the courtyard and then, using knives and poultry clippers, they cut the joints and rabbits into portions. The garlic, fennel and sausage inside the rabbits smells the sweetest. They pile the dishes high with the lamb and rabbit and carry it into the dining room; with it they pass the giant bowl of salad which has just been dressed with a lot of olive oil, a little wine vinegar, salt and pepper. Next they carve up the chickens, arrange the duck on a plate and put the sage-flavoured pork into a shallow dish with a little of its sauce. These are taken in next, accompanied by the *fagioli verdi*. It is at this point during the meal that the men start to drink the red wine. Normally they drink whatever they prefer but during special meals Italians tend to drink white wine with the pasta courses and red with the heavier meat courses. The really heavy rich reds like a good Barolo, a Vin Nobile di Montepulciano or the splendid ageless Brunello di Montalcino are only drunk with rich roasts and game. They are wines to be respected. However these expensive perfumed wines do not concern the Cerottis at their harvest meal; here they will drink their own good wine. By now the lunch party has become very noisy; the women are getting a little tired and are very hungry. They clear the plates and set out the fruit, some matured *pecorino* cheese and the bottles of home-distilled *grappa*. This will keep the men busy until coffee is called for. Meanwhile Silvana's sister has cleared the kitchen table and laid a clean cloth. Finally they all sit down and enjoy the food that they have kept back for themselves, which includes it may be said all the tenderest parts of the chicken and their favourite cuts of lamb. They end their meal with strong coffee and some elegant little chocolates that someone had the foresight to bring.

Well into the cooling afternoon the men stumble out of the dark house into the bright courtyard. They now have to finish their work here then move on to the next threshing ground. This time it will be Menchino's corn that must be threshed. The lumbering machine will be pulled up the hill, past the small cornfields, now bare except for the shiny stubble. Tonight Menchino's mother will provide the harvest supper and Silvana and her friends will cheerfully go up the hill to her aid.

❧ AUGUST

The corn that was harvested during the month of July lies piled in its sacks and represents one of the fundamental and most characteristic staples of Tuscan cooking. The country people know how to use bread to its greatest advantage. The old peasants who baked their loaves only once a week became adept at using the stale bread in ways that made their meals both appetizing and economical. Their dishes of *zuppe*, *ribolliti* and *cacciucco*, a fish stew, were all based on thick slices of the rough saltless bread, which has the nutty flavour of real unrefined flour. Silvana has learnt these lessons well and makes many dishes based on bread. One of her favourite supper dishes is *acquacotta*, which literally means 'cooked water', and signifies a poor man's dish made out of absolutely nothing. It is a very ancient recipe, that comes partly from the charcoal burners who lived deep in the Tuscan forests and are traditionally among the poorest of people. In actual fact *acquacotta*, which has many variations, is an absolutely exquisite dish fit for the most fastidious food lover. One version uses pieces of the *funghi porcini* which in France are called *cêpes*. The *funghi* are cooked gently in a pan with olive oil, salt and pepper and some *mentuccia*, the small-leafed wild mint that grows in the fields. When the *funghi* have given up their juices a little tomato *conserva* is added, and a ladle of water for each person. The mixture is then left to simmer gently. Whilst the *funghi* simmer, a lidded soup dish must be prepared. In it should be one raw egg per person beaten up together with a generous handful of parmesan cheese. When the *funghi* broth is ready it must be tipped into the soup dish and stirred into the eggs and cheese. The dish is then covered and left to stew for a few minutes. It should be eaten hot, but not too hot; again, as we have observed before, to bring out the flavour. To serve it one must place a good slice of hot toasted bread in each soup plate and pour over a ladleful of the *acquacotta*.

 To make *Acquacotta con Funghi* for four people you will need 400 g or 14 oz of fresh *porcini*, three tablespoons of olive oil, two cloves of garlic, a sprig of *mentuccia*, wild mint, salt and black pepper, two teaspoons of tomato *conserva*, a scarce litre or just under 1¾ pints of stock or water, four eggs, four tablespoons of grated parmesan and four slices of good bread.

Clean the *porcini* carefully and cut them into pieces. In a large saucepan heat up the olive oil then add the cloves of garlic which must be chopped, the leaves from the sprig of *mentuccia*, wild mint, and a sprinkle of black pepper. Let the garlic soften but on no account let it burn or even turn brown. Next add the *funghi* and turn them in the oil over a very low heat; after a while the mushrooms will start to give up their juice. At this point add the very small amount of tomato, season with salt and pour in the stock. Cover the pan and let it simmer for twenty minutes. Meanwhile beat up the eggs with the parmesan cheese in the bottom of a lidded soup bowl. When the *porcini* broth is ready and brought to boiling point pour it into the soup bowl and stir it into the egg and cheese mixture; the boiling broth will cook the egg. Put the lid on the dish and leave it for a few minutes. Now toast your bread and lay a hot slice in each soup bowl. Ladle the soup on top of the toast, making sure that everyone has their fair share of *porcini*. The whole object of this *zuppa* is to savour the perfume and taste of the *porcini*. This very delicious mushroom has a most particular rich flavour and there are no substitutes for it. The *mentuccia* also has a different quality of flavour to garden mint. However you can make a tasty but quite different soup using cultivated mushrooms and substituting parsley for the *mentuccia* or savory. This might be a good opportunity to use a *porcini*-flavoured bouillon cube or a few dried *porcini* to give a hint of the true flavour to the stock. But do not use dried *porcini* for the bulk of the mushrooms as they have a very different texture to fresh mushrooms, being small and relatively chewy, not plump and soft.

Silvana is also fond of this dish in its other varieties. When the *peperoni* are ripe in the vegetable garden they make an excellent variation to the soup. To prepare this she cuts the pepper, a red or yellow one if possible, into strips, pausing of course to remove the seeds and membranes. Then she heats some olive oil and chopped garlic in a pan. When the garlic starts to turn colour she adds a finely chopped onion, some celery and finally the small strips of pepper. After the vegetables have softened she adds the pulp of a fresh tomato or so and some water or chicken stock. Then she leaves the pan to cook for about twenty minutes on a gentle flame. While the soup cooks she toasts some slices of bread over the fire. Finally the toast, one slice per person, and it must be hot toast to absorb the broth better, is placed in the soup bowls and she ladles on the soup to cover the bread. Orlando, who likes cheese very much, sprinkles a handful over his bowl; then there is silence as conversation is forgotten over the good food.

 To make *Acquacotta con Peperoni* for four people you will need two red peppers, one onion, a rib of celery, two cloves of garlic, the pulp of a large marmande tomato, half a litre or less than a pint of stock, salt and black pepper, as needed, four slices of bread and one more clove of garlic cut in half.

Clean the peppers, remove the seeds and membranes and cut the flesh into short strips. Chop the onion, garlic and celery finely. In a large pan heat up the olive oil, add the garlic and let it flavour the oil, then add the onion and celery; do not let either the garlic or the onion burn. Next add the peppers and turn them in the oil until they begin to soften. At this point add the tomato pulp and a little of the stock, season and leave the soup to simmer for twenty to thirty minutes. Add more stock if the tomatoes do not have a great deal of juice in them. Toast the four slices of good bread and rub one surface with the cut clove of garlic. Put each slice in the bottom of a soup dish and pour the soup on top.

These dishes were invented to utilize stale bread and make it palatable. Shepherds and woodcutters and those who by nature of their employment were away from their homes for long periods of time would carry loaves with them that became harder and harder as the days wore on. They also carried a little salt cod and maybe some pieces of *pancetta*. At the end of the day they would make small stews consisting of an onion or so, some wild herbs for flavour, the *pancetta* and tiny pieces of the cod. Then they would pour the savoury mess over a hunk of their dry bread. Before the latter decades of the nineteenth century tomatoes were not commonly used all over Italy and the shepherds may have carried with them a small bottle sealed with wax that contained *agresto*, or the juice of half-ripened sour grapes. They would pick the grapes in August, squeeze them, and keep the liquid to flavour their food with a fruity taste which the tomato has now replaced.

Many of Silvana's dishes derive from this old way of making bread more interesting. Today she often turns her *minestrone* into a *Zuppa di Verdura* simply by lessening the amount of liquid in the soup and pouring it over a slice of toast. *Zuppe* of whatever type must have a slice of bread in the bottom. Tuscan *contadini* children were fed the nourishing *Pappa al Olio* or *al Pomodoro*, which was simply a pap made, in the first case, of garlic, olive oil and water in which were boiled small pieces of bread until it was amalgamated into a thick porridge. For a tomato *pappa* the bread was cooked in a sauce of fresh tomato, oil, a little garlic, perhaps some basil and of course salt and black pepper. These were simple and delicious suppers for very young children and also for the very old and toothless.

 To make **Pappa al Pomodoro** for four people you need 600 g or 1 lb 5 oz of ripe tomatoes, the marmande variety or garden tomatoes, 200 g or 7 oz of Tuscan bread, two cloves of garlic, a small bunch of basil, a little stock, three tablespoons of olive oil, salt and freshly ground black pepper.

Deprive the tomatoes of their skins and cut them into small pieces. Put them into a thick saucepan with the bread which you may tear into pieces, the two cloves of garlic which must be bruised and the sprigs of basil. Over a very gentle flame stir the mixture; the bread will gradually disintegrate and meld into the tomatoes. At this point add the olive oil and a very little stock if needed, season with salt and a lot of black pepper. Let the *pappa* cook gently, stirring occasionally to make sure that the texture is becoming even. The dish should be evenly thick with no lumps but definitely not of a watery consistency. To serve the *pappa*, which must be very hot, pour it into individual bowls and add a trickle of olive oil and another spray of black pepper. This simple country dish of course depends completely on the pure flavours of the very best fruity olive oil, flavourful firm tomatoes and bread that has texture and the taste of good flour. The basil adds its own particular scent. It makes a very nice first course for a simple dinner.

Silvana uses bread in other ways too, and one of the nicest is in stuffings for various vegetables. One of the most unusual pretty and delicious dishes she makes is *Fiori di Zucchini Ripieni*, stuffed courgette flowers. Early in the morning she goes to the kitchen garden and picks a small bunch of the fresh yellow *zucchini* flowers. To make their stuffing she soaks a slice or two of bread in some water, then squeezes the moisture away thoroughly. To flavour the stuffing she grates some *pecorino*, or *parmigiano* if there is any in the *dispensa*, finely chops some garlic and a few sprigs of parsley, then adds a small amount of *mortadella* which she chops into tiny pieces. Then she kneads the ingredients, plus salt and black pepper, with the bread into a fine paste. She inserts spoonfuls of the paste carefully into the bell of the flowers, being careful not to split the petal. When it is time for lunch she has ready a dish of beaten egg and plate of sieved flour. She dips the stuffed flowers into the flour and then rolls them briefly in the egg. Finally she plunges them into a pan of bubbling oil. When they are a light golden colour she drains them well and serves them. She often makes the dish when she has very few people to lunch or perhaps when Orlando is away from the house. Silvana is quite pleased not to eat meat every day and the stuffed flowers are quite sufficient for a light lunch. When she wants to use the flowers as a *contorno* to accompany meat she will often simply omit the stuffing and fry the empty flowers after their coating of egg and flour. They make a delicious and decorative dish.

 To make the stuffing for the **Fiori di Zucchini Ripieni** to serve twelve flowers as a *contorno* for six people you will need about two slices of good bread, four thin slices of *mortadella*, two if the slices come from a very large *mortadella*, a clove of garlic, a few sprigs of parsley, two tablespoons of grated parmesan, salt and white pepper and a little olive oil.

Soak the bread in water and squeeze it dry, then crumble it into fine crumbs. Chop the *mortadella* very finely then chop the garlic and parsley together, also very finely. Combine all these ingredients in a bowl and add the grated cheese to them; season the stuffing with salt and white pepper. Finally make the mixture into a dry paste with the help of a few drops of olive oil. Carefully insert spoonfuls of the mixture into the bell of each flower. Dip the blossom briefly into flour then into beaten egg and so to the bubbling pan of arachide oil which will brown the flowers very quickly. Serve the flowers with a light meat dish, perhaps a fillet of veal cooked simply with white wine. The stuffed flowers can also be served as part of a main course together with other stuffed vegetables, maybe the *zucchini* themselves or tomatoes.

Perhaps the way that Silvana most likes to use extra bread is in the old-fashioned Tuscan bread salad, *Pansanella*, which appears on her table all year round. During the grey months, as we have already seen, it contains little more than a sharp onion. Now, however, at the height of summer its list of fresh ingredients and colours expands. To make the salad she soaks half a loaf of bread in cold water then squeezes out the excess moisture and flakes it into small crumbs in a large deep salad bowl. Into the bowl she tears about ten large fresh basil leaves. Fresh scented tomatoes go well with basil, so with a sharp knife she cuts small pieces off the tomatoes straight into the bowl. It is worth mentioning at this point that I have never seen Silvana or any other country cook chop tomatoes or any other sort of vegetable on their wooden chopping boards. These boards they seem to reserve for garlic and herbs. Invariably Silvana cuts vegetables straight into a bowl. After the sweet tomatoes she adds the short dark-skinned cucumber. To prepare this she peels off the dark green skin entirely, as it is usually too tough to eat. Then she makes a series of deep cuts lengthways into the cucumber, then turning it round she makes another series of cuts across the first incisions, so ending up with a chequered pattern of squares about a quarter of an inch square. Finally she slices the cucumber across every quarter of an inch and the cubes fall freely into the salad. In this way she has neatly diced the cucumber without the aid of a chopping board. She prepares the salad immediately before eating so there is no need to drain the cucumber for fear that its liquid dilutes the dressing. To this green basil, red tomato and pale almond cucumber she adds a pretty pink onion, peeling it and then chipping small pieces into the salad with her sharp knife.

Now using her chopping block she finely chops a sprig or two of parsley and two fat cloves of garlic and sprinkles them into the salad bowl. Finally after mixing the fresh ingredients evenly through the bread she is ready to add the dressing. Another particular habit of Italians is the manner in which they dress their salads. They are very puzzled by the French method of mixing a dressing in the bowl, and I suspect that they find this perverse. With enormous brio and confidence, they dress their salads directly in the following way. First they sprinkle a good pinch of salt into the salad-filled bowl then they dash in a very little wine vinegar. After the vinegar they pour in the olive oil, using a circular movement around the bowl and finally they add a grind or so of black pepper. After all the dressing is in, they turn the salad well with a fork and spoon. Silvana uses exactly this method when dressing her *Pansanella* and amazingly every time there is just enough to cover the salad nicely, never too much acid vinegar and no pools of dressing at the bottom of the bowl.

The *Pansanella* is of course delicious, with a wonderful texture and flavour. Its very simplicity demonstrates again the basis of Tuscan cooking: the freshest, best ingredients used in the simplest manner to retain their natural flavours. This salad depends on the bread being made with good nutty flour that has not been refined into tastelessness, and produce that is fresh from the garden. The tomatoes are not watery and the onion is sharp and new. The basil permeates it with its peppery perfume, the sweet oil adds richness.

 The quantities that you will need to prepare a **Pansanella** for three or four people are roughly these: four thick slices of good white bread that is not too fresh, half a cucumber, two firm, sweet tomatoes, one onion, the pink variety is pretty, a small bunch of parsley, more if you do not have several leaves of fresh basil, one or two cloves of garlic according to your taste, half a teacup of olive oil, two teaspoons of wine vinegar, salt and black pepper.

Soak the bread briefly in water then squeeze it dry and crumble it into a large salad bowl. Peel the cucumber and dice it into the bowl, then chop the tomatoes into small pieces and add them. Next chop the onion into small dice and chop the garlic with the parsley finely. If you have basil leaves tear them into pieces and put them into the bowl. Mix all the ingredients so they are well distributed through the dish. Then either dress the salad in the Italian way by just pouring the seasonings into the salad or mix them in a cup and taste before dressing the *Pansanella*. The *Pansanella* should be served cool; in the old days in *contadini* houses it was left in an airy place to cool and for the bread to become flavoured with the oil before being served. This does not mean, as some recent writers on Italian food have suggested, putting the *Pansanella* in the refrigerator, which will only serve to rob it of all its flavour. Older versions of the recipe do not use cucumber but include wild greenery and rocket. The *Pansanella* is correctly eaten as a *primo piatto*. In the old days the *contadini* did not drink wine with it as this might conflict with the vinegar in the dressing. Instead they drank *acquarello* or *mezzone*, which was grape juice before it had fermented and the sugar had turned into alcohol. Very often nowadays *Pansanella* is served as part of the *antipasti* in Tuscan restaurants and Silvana enjoys it as a supper dish.

During this month of August the hot sun burns up the landscape and bleaches the green meadows. The maize is ripening and Orlando's workers still sweat at their toil in the tobacco fields. In the vineyards the grapes are large and sweetening and the pergolas of dessert grapes near the house are already bearing ripe fruit. The air around the fig trees is full of the hot sweet scent of ripe figs and the edges of the fields have fringes of sallow green anice-flavoured fennel. Silvana's vegetable garden is bright and full of burgeoning tomato plants, *zucchini* which must be cut every day and aubergines, lying fat and black in the shadows.

 The *zucchini*, courgettes, are picked when they are young and tender and Silvana sometimes serves them stuffed with a mixture similar to the one she uses to fill the *zucchini* flowers. She chooses larger specimens of the vegetable and, trimming the top and bottom, she parboils them whole in boiling salted water. When the *zucchini* are partially cooked but still very firm she drains them and leaves them to cool. Then with a tool like a potato knife she hollows out the middles of each *zucchino*. This pulp she then mashes in a bowl with a little ground veal, garlic, chopped parsley, parmesan cheese, salt and pepper. Then she fills the *zucchini* with the mixture and sets them to cook in an oiled dish in a medium oven. Silvana also likes to serve *Zucchini Fritti*. To make this dish she slices the vegetables into small thin rounds and dries them with a cloth. On the stove she has a pan liberally filled with a glass of olive oil which she brings to a high heat and in this the *zucchini* are cooked until they brown. She serves them with a good sprinkling of chopped parsley.

To many people, the tomato is the most characteristic ingredient in Italian cooking. They are I think labouring under a delusion that is fostered by Italianate restaurants in Britain and America that are staffed by Neapolitans. The tomato admittedly does play a great part in sauces, but in most restaurants in the greater part of Italy the menus contain a majority of dishes prepared without tomatoes. Certainly not all pasta sauces contain tomato and most meat dishes are not cooked with them. A few of the most delicious pizzas are quite innocent of the cheery red sauce. The tomato was relatively unknown in Tuscany until the middle of the last century, when Garibaldi and his men brought it back with them from Sicily and introduced it to the new Italy. However Tuscans did come to know and love the newcomer and have incorporated the flavour into their oldest recipes, as we have seen with the *acquacotta*. In late August, Silvana's kitchen garden is full to bursting with ripe tomatoes. She plants at least two varieties: the southern plum-shape ones that have a very particular flavour, and the larger round misshapen sort called marmande which are at their peak for salads when they have achieved that strange pinky-green colour. The family cannot possibly consume so many fresh tomatoes, so it is time to fetch out the big copper preserving pan and the glass jars and bottles. Tomatoes are usually preserved in three different forms, each of which has its particular uses. First there are the ordinary tinned or bottled whole tomatoes, *pomodori pelati*, which contain a high percentage of liquid and are best used for dishes that require a tomato base but need a long cooking time. Secondly there is the purée, *passato di pomodoro*, which is a much thicker reduction of tomatoes, sometimes flavoured with celery, onion, carrot and basil, then called *pomaruola* or *conserva*. This is ideal for sauces which need a rich body of tomato. Thirdly there is the tomato concentrate, *concentrato di pomodoro*, which is the tomato reduced to a very strong paste and flavour and is useful for colour and flavour in a dish where bulk tomato is not required. Silvana usually uses a purée of tomatoes for her sauces so she prefers to make a rich thick *conserva* or *passato* of tomatoes. She also likes to utilize her fresh basil while she has it and preserves her tomatoes with a base of the flavoursome carrot, celery and onion.

At the very end of August Silvana can be seen in the *orto* filling her twig baskets with ripe whole tomatoes. She is very careful to select perfect specimens with no trace of damage or decay. The kitchen table is spread with the lovely fruit and at the end of the table is a bunch of green basil and a few onions, the yellow variety, a carrot or so and some ribs of celery. To make the *conserva* Silvana cuts the tomatoes into four and puts the pieces into a very large pan together with some salt, pieces of carrot, celery and a roughly chopped onion. Then she leaves the pan to simmer very gently on a low flame until the tomatoes dissolve into a soft red mass. When the tomatoes have reduced, the vegetables softened and the excess liquid has cooked away, she forces the mixture through a fine sieve to eliminate the skins and seeds. The purée is left overnight in a large pottery bowl. Around Naples, where the southern gardeners and cooks really prize their tomatoes, they put their tomato conserve in large shallow pottery bowls called *scaffaria*. The conserve is reduced to a very thick and jam-like consistency and on the firm surface they spread a thick layer of coarse sea salt which covers the tomato completely. The salt attracts moisture from the tomatoes to make a dense concentrate. Then the bowls are left out in the sun for several days. The resulting *conserva* has a wonderful consistency and a rich, sweet flavour.

Silvana does not follow this southern custom but she does add salt to aid the conservation process. Then comes the time to put the thick scarlet conserve into pots. Silvana uses glass jars with patent metal tops like jam-pot lids. The jars are thoroughly scalded and dried, then she spoons in the conserve to the top of the pot. Some conserves and pickles are put under a layer of olive oil but in these types of jars the oil eats away the linings of the lids. Instead Silvana puts a layer of ground black pepper right over the surface of the conserve. The lids are then screwed on extremely firmly. When the time comes to open the jars Silvana breaks the vacuum with a coin, listening carefully for the sound of the breaking seal to be sure that the jar has been properly closed. Badly sealed tomatoes can provoke serious stomach upsets.

As well as the delicately-flavoured *conserva*, Silvana also bottles whole plum tomatoes. To do this she peels the tomatoes by plunging them for a few moments into boiling water, which effectively loosens the skins. Then she packs the naked raw tomatoes into large glass preserving jars and on top of each jar she lays a large basil leaf or two to lend its distinctive flavour. Every year she buys new rubber rings for her jars and is careful to screw down the tops meticulously. Even in August the fire must burn brightly for the next step of the ritual. She places as many of the large jars as will fit tightly and upright into her cauldron, first wrapping the jars well in thick paper to prevent them from rattling. Then she pours in water that must come well over the tops of the jars; she is most insistent about this point. Finally the cauldron with its load of fruit is swung over the bright flames and the pot is left to boil for thirty-five minutes. The jars must on no account be touched or interfered with during this process as dire explosions of flying glass will occur if the bottles are moved. After the statutory thirty-five minutes of boiling the fire is left to die down and the bottles are left overnight in the cauldron to cool down to a safe temperature for handling. Silvana is more stern and strict, and sensibly so, in her admonitions over bottling than in most of her other preserving methods.

After the warm red crop has been preserved in these diverse ways Silvana dusts down the glass-fronted dresser in the pantry. She lines the shelves with fresh white paper then proudly arranges the new bottles and jars in rows. They gleam like jewels in the dark pantry and make a perfect illustration of old-fashioned peace and plenty. The Cerottis are aware that it may be more economical to buy preserves in bulk at the local shop than to sow seed and wait for the harvest. But they are also aware that there is more pleasure and satisfaction and better eating to be had from their own good home-grown and home-prepared produce.

 Naturally Silvana likes to use her tomatoes fresh while she has them and one of her favourite suppers is a dish of deep fried tomatoes, **Pomodori Fritti,** a homely and delicious dish. To make it she chooses firm, hardly ripe tomatoes of the marmande type and cuts them into small pieces the shape of half moons, small enough to cook through with some speed. Then she rolls the tomato pieces in either some of her good home-grown flour, ground at a local mill from their own grain, or alternatively in some fine maize flour, the sort that usually she keeps for *polenta*. The *polenta* flour, besides being a pretty yellow colour, gives a very crisp *croccante* finish to the dish. If she is feeling extravagant she will cook the tomatoes in boiling olive oil, but usually she contents herself with arachide oil, which is lighter, cheaper and tasteless. She plunges the tomato pieces into smoking oil and cooks them quickly until the surface is a light golden colour. The resulting flavour is an enhancement of the sweet raw taste of the perfect tomato. Imagine the combination of these with a few slices of cool fresh mozzarella strewn with basil leaves.

The ripe young tomatoes come into their own again to make the simplest and yet most subtle spaghetti sauce. To make this delight Silvana picks small, hardly ripe marmande tomatoes, and cuts them into thickish slices over a bowl so as not to lose any of the juice. She does not place them into boiling water to skin them as this would in some measure alter the flavour by cooking the tomatoes slightly. Then she covers the tomatoes with her own green olive oil. Into the bowl she places some bruised cloves of garlic and several torn leaves of basil. This delicious mixture is left to marinate on the pantry table. The sauce lacks only black pepper and salt, which she will add just before serving. When the spaghetti is *al dente* and well drained, Silvana fills up a large china bowl with the hot pasta then pours the raw sauce on top. She mixes the sauce gently into the spaghetti, whose heat permeates the oil and basil and exaggerates their scent and flavour. This is a simple dish, needing the minimum of last-minute cooking and fuss, but redolent of the pleasures of the summer garden.

 If you would like to make **Spaghetti al Salsa di Pomodoro Crudo** to serve four people you will need 400 g or 14 oz of medium-thickness spaghetti such as Barilla no. 5, eight small tomatoes, golden, fresh and sweet smelling, preferably home grown; old mushy flavourless tomatoes will not do. Then one teacup of the best green olive oil, no other sort of oil can be used, a small bunch of fresh basil, one or two cloves of garlic and freshly-milled black pepper and salt.

On the day that you plan to eat this dish for your supper, in the morning take the small tomatoes and skin them with a sharp knife. You can if pressed for time omit this step; what you must not do is put the tomatoes in boiling water to loosen the skins, as this will start to cook them and so change their flavour. Cut up the tomatoes roughly and put the pieces in a pottery bowl. Add two well-bruised cloves of garlic and the basil leaves torn up. Finally pour the green olive oil into the bowl and mix it through the tomatoes. Leave the bowl of oil-covered tomatoes to marinate for the day in a cool place, but *not* in the refrigerator. You want to develop the flavour, not kill it..

In the evening cook your spaghetti in the manner described in May's chapter. Tip the well-drained pasta into a serving bowl and pour on your sauce which you have salted and sprinkled with black pepper; you have also removed the cloves of garlic. Serve the spaghetti immediately and taste how good the flavoured oil is when warmed by the heat of the pasta. If you do not have the correct ingredients or the time to concentrate on this dish do not attempt it. As ever, its success depends on the best, freshest, yet simplest ingredients, and care.

Silvana learnt to cook solely from the example of her mother and aunts, and maybe her grandmother. The recipes were handed down by word of mouth and by demonstration. Different female relatives have their own particular specialities and skills; one of Silvana's cousins is famous in the family for her extra-delicious cakes and biscuits. Silvana is always pleased to taste the fruits of other people's labour and she is, although thoroughly versed in a great variety of the traditional Tuscan dishes, always delighted to learn new dishes from friends from other regions of Italy.

One such friend is Signora Rosa. She and her Tuscan-born husband are an elderly couple from Rome, who come to the valley with their son to spend an occasional summer week in a small cottage they have purchased from Orlando. In fact Signora Rosa spends most of her holiday with Silvana and together they enjoy themselves chatting and cooking new dishes, each learning from the other. Rosa is responsible for the sleek black aubergines lying in the sunny garden. A few years ago she introduced Silvana to a dish of *melanzane* in the Roman style. Silvana was so pleased with the new dish that she has grown the vegetables ever since. The two women sit together at the kitchen table and talk as they slice up the aubergines into rounds. They sprinkle each slice with salt and place it in a colander to drain. When the last slice is in place Silvana weighs down the *melanzane* with an old weight from her cheese balance to encourage the bitter juices to run away. Rosa says that the *melanzane* will soak up less oil when treated in this manner, an idea of which the ever-economical Silvana heartily approves. While the *melanzane* are draining Signora Rosa makes a béchamel sauce with the butter, flour and milk that Silvana produces from the *dispensa*. Silvana grates up a large chunk of the best parmesan into a heap of golden grains. The oven is set and a large shallow dish well greased with olive oil. When all is ready Silvana rinses the aubergine, which is now floppy and slightly brown, pats the circles dry and hands them to Rosa, who fries them lightly in some olive oil. Finally they take turns to arrange the slices which have been drained of excess oil in a thin layer over the bottom of the dish. When they are all arranged in a neat overlapping pattern like tiles on a roof Rosa pours on the béchamel and spreads it evenly over the aubergine. Next Silvana sprinkles on a thick layer of the parmesan. A sprinkle of salt, a few turns of the pepper-mill, and the dish is ready for the oven. It will be done when the top is a beautiful crisp gold.

From this first lesson Silvana has enthusiastically added her own touches to the new dish. As well as the béchamel she adds a layer of her tomato conserve to the aubergine, building up the dish like a *lasagne* but replacing the pasta with slices of aubergine. More often than not she will use grated *pecorino* instead of parmesan. She successfully cooks it on a trivet over the open fire, covering the dish with an old tin saucepan lid. Onto the lid she heaps burning embers and in this way she concocts a very primitive oven. The heat penetrates the lid and browns the surface of the dish beautifully. It is almost like using a salamander, that very ancient kitchen utensil named after a lizard that was supposed to be able to walk over live coals. The salamander, a large flat-bottomed vessel with a handle, was filled with burning embers and held over a dish of food to brown the surface without cooking the interior, in fact an archaic grill.

Late August sometimes sees the beginning of the hunting season; occasionally the opening date comes in September, an event looked forward to by all the men in Cerotti's employ and also enjoyed by their wives, as the beginning of the *caccia* means pheasants and all manner of small birds for the table. The hunting season extends for a few months and the rules governing the hunt are strict. No-one is permitted to shoot two days in a row, and the days for shooting are laid out in a calendar. The types of gun used are also strictly controlled. So on the appointed day the valley is full of the sound of shots. Men from the local towns prowl around the hillsides wearing smart hunting gear, whilst their valley counterparts, though less magnificently clad, bag most of the game. The beginning of the hunting season in Italy is an important event. It is announced on the evening TV programme, and the newspapers are full of stories of hunting accidents, said by some to be not so much accidents as the settling of old scores. The *macelleria* are full of plump pheasant, thrushes, quails, ortolans, snipe and woodcock. Mediterranean people have no qualms about consigning song birds to the pot. It may however be a comfort to remember that these birds have enjoyed a free natural life, and that only a percentage of them are shot as game, a clean, swift death. On the whole it is a much more satisfactory mode of existence than that of the poor creatures reared in factory conditions to face the terrors of the slaughterhouse.

❧ SEPTEMBER

On early September mornings the *fattoria* is wreathed in clouds, banks of mist that float through the valley exposing just the tips of the hills and the valley floor. The morning air is cool. Later in the day the sun becomes hot, hot enough to burn away the cloud, and the days have a curious technicolour depth and brilliance about them. The colours of the landscape are deeper and richer. In Orlando's meadows the sheep graze upon a new growth of herbage brought up by the gentler sun and soft rain; in fact a sort of mini-spring has occurred. The tobacco fields are now crowded with the giant-leafed plants, each topped by a cluster of sticky pink or white flowers. Their lower stalks are bare, the leaves having been stripped away by the bands of workers. The kilns are burning day and night; the workers come to the fields, pick enough leaves to fill the kilns, then remain idle until the tobacco is dried and the kilns are empty and ready for another load. Orlando plans to install a new kiln next spring with the profits that he is sure to make from this season's crop.

On the arbours of turkey oaks, the vines are heavy with black grapes, veiled with purple bloom, and the green grapes shine like polished jade. The sun has been strong enough to make them sweet and there has been sufficient water to make them plump and juicy. However they are not yet ripe enough for the *vendemmia*, which will come in October. High on the slopes behind the *fattoria* the olive trees are the last to emerge from the morning mists. They are full of glossy berries which will not be picked until very late in November or early December.

The *caccia*, the hunting season, always starts on a Sunday and all the men in the valley are well prepared for it. They all have their licences, which are fairly difficult to obtain, they must demonstrate that they are reasonable shots, and are able to recognize various species. They have all been busily cleaning their guns for weeks. On the Sunday morning in question, usually in late August or early September, the *caccia* begins early and the sound of firing echoes around the valley. The men keep to the fields and the forest's edge as the higher slopes are still covered with mist, making visibility poor. Orlando moves quietly through his fields, dressed in dull khaki green trousers which are lined with water-proofing and an old khaki jacket, with a leather bandolier strung over his shoulders and around his portly waist. He is after pheasant. These he puts down in the forest so that he may enjoy the sport, and he becomes very annoyed if foreign hunters, those Umbrians, come and bag his game. In Italy unless one fences the land and puts up notices forbidding hunting there is no way in which it is possible to stop hunters coming on to one's land and shooting. However, they must not shoot within 150 metres of a dwelling, for obvious reasons. Unhappily they do not always obey this rule if they know a house is empty, or suspect that it is. They also do not confine their attentions to birds but also pick figs, apples, mushrooms and anything else that takes their fancy. Naturally this type of rogue always comes from afar. The valley men are far too well brought-up to indulge in such antics. They also have far too much respect for hard work to trample through the tobacco fields in search of their prey. Many are the times that the valley has been filled with the sounds of Orlando's infuriated shouts when he spies hunters in his fields. His rage is awe-inspiring and the hunters who have come from nearby towns usually do not return to the valley.

Today he bags a brace of pheasant and some *tordi*, the fat speckled thrushes. Silvana will be pleased. She looks forward to the hunting season for the different flavoured meat it will provide. Wild birds and animals obviously have very different diets to the domesticated fowls and animals. It is this difference in their diet that gives their flesh its particular taste. The *tordi* for instance live on distinctly flavoured berries and this gives them their special perfumed flavour which is much sought after in Italy. In the same way the Tuscan chickens and their eggs have a particularly rich colour and taste because they are usually fed upon home-grown Indian corn. Pigs fed partly on fruit give excellent pork. The flesh of animals and fowl fed on industrial prepared foods will never have their full flavour, especially those fed on fish. Who can enjoy a chicken that tastes of fish? Sadly, in this last case, it is inevitable that these animals are what they eat.

Silvana likes to have pheasant for her Sunday lunch, and this means that Orlando must go hunting on a Thursday. Unlike other countries where pheasant is hung for a long period of time to achieve the characteristic gamey flavour, in Italy they are inclined to shorten this period to a very few days. Silvana thinks that two to three days is sufficient; she also plucks and cleans the birds a day after they are shot. In other areas of Italy the birds are not cleaned until they are to be cooked. Although it is realized that a fresh pheasant has no very special flavour, a great many Italians are not prepared to risk to any great degree the mortification that brings the flavour.

Hen pheasant are much to be preferred to the male bird as they are fatter and have less tendency to dry out in the cooking. Silvana rarely roasts pheasant for this reason. It may also be that as the birds are cooked very soon after being killed the flesh has a tendency to be tough. To combat these problems Silvana stews the pheasants very slowly. She cuts the bird into convenient pieces with her sharp poultry shears and puts them in a deepish flat *tegame* to brown slightly in olive oil, then adds more olive oil and some water, the latter a very unusual addition, as any liquid she uses usually comes in the form of stock or wine. She stews the pieces very, very slowly in this mixture so that the flesh may remain soft and moist. In another pan she prepares some *odori*; she chops up some onion, carrot, a small amount of celery and a bay leaf or two which she picks fresh from the large bay tree near the hen coops. These she allows to brown gently in olive oil and she seasons them with salt and black pepper. When the vegetables are softened she adds the mixture to the pheasant, which has been cooking gently for some time so that the oil and water have partially evaporated. The resulting dish is tender and flavoursome and much appreciated by Orlando, whose skill has provided the main ingredient. As an alternative Silvana may use this same recipe with the addition of a little tomato concentrate for added colour and sweet flavour. This is a good example of the use of a tomato concentrate where a bulk of tomato is not required. To accompany the pheasant with its sauce she will serve a very plain *contorno*, maybe some grilled *polenta* or possibly some fresh *cannellini* beans. These are the white beans which when new are a strange waxy greenish-white colour and come in the pretty long pods that are the colour of ivory. Silvana always has these beans in the garden and most of them she dries for bean dishes through the winter. Sometimes, as in this case, she cooks them in their tender new state, and they are very good as a vegetable or on their own with a little raw onion, olive oil and black pepper.

To make a **Fagiano in Salmi**, for four people, you will need one hen pheasant, one onion, one carrot, one rib of celery, two bay leaves, four tablespoons of olive oil, one chicken liver, a dessert spoon of tomato concentrate and about a glass of red wine. You may also use this recipe for *faraona*, guinea fowl, or a *gallina*, a hen.

Cut the pheasant or guinea fowl into several pieces and chop the onion, carrot and celery. In a heavy bottomed pan heat the olive oil, add the *odori* and let them soften, then add the pieces of the fowl and let them brown, seasoning them with salt and pepper. Add some of the red wine and the cleaned chicken liver; leave the pan to simmer until the chicken liver is cooked through. Remove the liver and chop it into small pieces; mix these with the tomato concentrate and a little wine and return it to the pan; stir it well into the vegetables. Cover the pan and let it cook gently until the bird is tender, adding more wine if necessary. To serve, put the pieces of fowl on a plate and pour a little of the sauce around them. Silvana would have cooked the pheasant first with olive oil and water to make the bird more tender but in the recipe above this step is omitted, as elsewhere pheasant is usually hung for a greater period of time.

Orlando likes to eat the fat dark-speckled thrushes or *tordi*, with their dark perfumed flesh. There are plenty in the meadows and on the edges of the forests, as there are plenty of the plump blackbirds, *merli*, which Orlando also enjoys. Probably the only small bird likely to escape Silvana's pot is the robin as it has a disagreeable flavour. The next recipes are given solely for interest, though, the *tordi* may easily be replaced by quail or pigeon.

To cook her **Tordi**, Silvana plucks them, first dipping them in very hot water to make the task easier, then she removes the head and legs, opens the back with scissors and cleans the insides thoroughly, rinsing them and drying them carefully with a clean cloth. Next she fetches a large flat pan and in it heats some olive oil and some diced fat *prosciutto* which she has cut off the ham hanging in the larder. When this has changed colour she adds the cleaned birds and on a brisk heat browns them on every side; at this point she adds a little chopped onion. When the thrushes are a lovely golden brown she bathes them in some white wine and allows them to cook until the wine has evaporated. Afterwards she adds a quantity of stock almost enough to half cover the birds and lets them cook gently in this liquid for about a quarter of an hour. She cooks most other small birds in this manner, sometimes in a pan held on a trivet over the open fire, first browning them then cooking them *in umido* with stock and white wine. Occasionally she may add fresh sage leaves, or some parsley. These small birds can be prepared to advantage on a spit over the fire, but Silvana takes care to anoint them well with oil to prevent them drying out. With the spit-roasted birds she serves a slice of *polenta* which she heats to a crackling gold over the fire.

 Another extremely delicious method of serving the **Tordi** is with crushed juniper berries, which compliment the flavour of these berry-eating birds. In half a wine glass of olive oil Silvana browns three whole cloves of garlic, two bay leaves and two or three crushed juniper berries, which she picks every other year from the juniper bushes growing in the woods. The thrushes, which she has plucked, cleaned and thoroughly drained without removing their heads, are now put into the flavoured oil and when she has turned them several times in the oil she sprinkles them with salt and pepper and bathes them with a glass of red wine. She leaves the birds to cook for about twenty-five minutes, moistening them occasionally with some hot stock. After this time she removes the birds from the pan, takes off their heads and necks and grinds these finely in her wooden pestle and mortar. The resulting paste she adds to the sauce in the *tegame* together with a ladleful of stock if the mixture has become too dry. When the sauce has begun to boil she replaces the birds, to be immersed in this rich new sauce for about ten minutes. When the dish is ready for the table she puts out three large soup plates and into each puts a large slice of bread, moistened with stock, onto which she ladles the sauce to form a bed for the *tordi*. Here again is the typical Tuscan use of bread to act as a sop for the rich flavoured sauce, whose depth of flavour has been provided by the addition of the ground-up bones of the bird. When making a *salmi* of this sort many Tuscan women add chopped-up chicken livers or the liver of the particular fowl that is being cooked to add a special richness to the sauce.

Silvana's methods of cooking this sort of small game are very simple and learnt, as always, from her mother and grandmother. There are many more luxurious recipes that come from other areas and towns of Italy: pheasant cooked with cream and seasoned with truffles, bathed with cognac, or served with sauces of *porcini*, wonderful special dishes for the most sophisticated table. But here we are concerned with Silvana's brand of Tuscan country cooking and so have concentrated on the methods of the huntsman's wife. There are also many more game birds eaten in Italy but they do not flourish in Orlando's valley so Silvana does not have the opportunity to cook them.

September is usually a good month for that most treasured of Italian occupations, which is in fact almost a national sport: the gathering of wild mushrooms. There is no subject of conversation other than football more likely to bring a gleam to an Italian eye than that of *funghi*. It will provoke a stream of reminiscences of the best and biggest *fungo*, the best place to hunt for them and the most delicious way to cook them. After a heavy rain and seven days of strong sunshine, a combination likely to produce the subtle atmosphere necessary for the growth of the *funghi*, the countryside teams with *funghi* hunters. There are generally two sorts: the country people, usually old ladies and gentlemen clutching home-made twig baskets and stout sticks, who have been collecting in secret hidden places for time immemorial, and the enthusiasts from the town who have driven out in search of fresh air and free mushrooms. They usually carry the ubiquitous plastic bag. *Cognoscenti* know however that *funghi* do not take well to plastic: the substances in the plastic provoke a chemical reaction in the *funghi* and if they are not removed from the bags very soon they will become a disintegrating unappetising mess. The closed bag also prevents spores from the *funghi* from escaping and forming new colonies as the collector moves around the forest.

The *funghi* season starts in the summer, as soon as the weather is warm, and extends until the first frosts inhibit the spores. However the *funghi* are fugitive uncertain things and are not always to be found. They are uncultivatable on an organized scale; they can only be encouraged. Some years there are very, very few and sometimes none at all, which of course adds enormously to their value, especially in restaurants. Other years there is an abundance of them, plenty to be eaten fresh and plenty left over for drying. Orlando always keeps his eyes open and a small cotton sack handy when he makes the rounds of his fields, and he is a good *funghi* spotter. He likes them so much he has even bought a piece of land which, having a mixture of chestnuts and pines, is very suitable, and is in fact famous for its *funghi*. The problem is that it is too famous, and he must be sure to be up early before the rival *funghi* hunters. In years when the mushrooms are scarce, and also in years of plenty, there are strict laws enforced by the forest rangers. No-one may pick more than two kilos and *funghi* under a certain size may not be taken.

There are centres in various towns where people are encouraged to take their mushrooms for inspection, as some varieties are horribly and invariably fatally poisonous. Every few years there are sad little items of news in the local papers, which tell of deaths from imprudent *funghi* eating. However these grim thoughts need not detract from the pleasures of *funghi* hunting and eating if a few essential rules are followed. *Never eat any mushroom unless you are absolutely sure from past experience, and knowledge learnt from an expert, what it is*; if in any doubt throw them out, well away from domestic animals and poultry. Any specimens about which there is any doubt must never be allowed to come into contact with recognized *funghi*, they should be placed in a separate container. The terrible *Amanita Phalloides* if allowed to lie in a basket of edible *funghi* can leave enough poison to pollute and kill.

Silvana and other countrywomen like her have obviously received a thorough education from their mothers and grandmothers and grand-fathers, or whichever *anziana* in their family was the *funghi* collector. Interestingly, some families will eat certain varieties that other families are convinced are inedible. There are *funghi* which are uneatable, being very tough or evil-tasting and some poisonous types are not fatally poisonous; some sorts can have their poison dispersed by long and careful cooking. These latter may well have been eaten by country people in times of hardship, but today it is not very likely that anyone other than a total enthusiast would willingly go to such trouble and risk. Silvana and Orlando always argue over one type of white mushroom that they call *Prugnolo* (*Clitopilus Prunulus*) which is a large white trumpet-shaped mushroom. Silvana is convinced it is not good to eat, but Orlando insists that it is and picks them specially for himself. Silvana cooks them in a separate pan and turns her nose up at the dish which Orlando enjoys. It is a matter of family custom and habit; the *funghi* are clearly not poison-ous, but Silvana will not eat them and they are, to be truthful, rather tasteless.

One of Silvana's greatest pleasures is to go hunting for *funghi*. She sets off carrying a small prettily shaped twig basket and a stout stick with which to despatch any vipers that she may by ill-chance discover on her hunt. She is usually dressed, as are most countrywomen, in a dark

long-sleeved overall; hers is of deep indigo cotton printed with tiny
sprigs of coloured flowers. These overalls are invariably covered with a
large apron, again of a dark colour relieved maybe with a tiny white
leaf or spot pattern, the sort of apron that is to be seen hanging from
the umbrellas over the market stalls in the country towns. Her apron
has a capacious pocket to hold fruit or odds and ends that may be picked
up on a walk through the fields and gardens. A pale scarf covers her
head and is knotted at the back under the combs. This cotton scarf is
again a part of the traditional Tuscan country woman's attire, without
which they feel incompletely dressed, like nuns without their coifs. Her
firm shapely legs are clad in patterned lisle stockings held neatly just
above the knees with garters and her shoes are tough leather boots laced
to the ankles. In wet weather she wears gum boots, and would not
dream of venturing into the undergrowth without protective footwear,
again as an insurance against the much-feared vipers. When Silvana
ventures out unencumbered with her basket she often carries a spindle
and spins the rough white sheep's wool as she walks; she spins a coarse
yarn with which to knit heavy winter socks to keep their feet warm in
the bitterly cold winter months. Occasionally she carries her knitting and
walks along head down, her needles held low in the continental fashion.

Of the 230 or so varieties of *funghi* which may be seen in the famous
free *funghi* market of Trento (other Italian markets are subject to controls
by the local commune and usually are confined to selling about fifteen
of the most recognized and safe varieties), Silvana will gather about six
or seven varieties which she knows and which grow in the particular
landscape around the Cerotti household. Probably the most sought-after
and enjoyed of the *funghi* that grow well in Orlando's forests are the
porcini, known in France as *cèpes*. There are several varieties of this splendid mushroom, but in Orlando's area probably the *Boletus Edulis*, *Boletus
Pinicola* and *Boleteus Aereus* are the most common. Not that the Cerottis
use or are aware of these Latin names; to them they are plain *funghi
porcini*; the *Boletus Pinicola* is a *pinaroli* and the *Aereus* a *porcino nero*, but
porcini all the same. They grow well in Orlando's woods which are a
mixture of pines, fir trees, oak and chestnuts. The ground around the
trees is rich with a mulch of fallen leaves and in a good *funghi* year the
forests are a mass of the yellow gold of *chanterelles* growing on grassy
banks, and plump reddish bronze and chocolate capped *porcini*. Other
less inviting *funghi* light up the woods too, some with eerie luminous
green and blue flesh; there are even the classic red-and-white spotted
toadstools of fairy tale fame. Occasionally Silvana will find some *ovole*,

Amanita Ceasaria, which are rather rare, have a gentle taste and are extremely expensive. They are of the same family as the deadly *Amanita Phalloides,* so care must be taken in their recognition. These mushrooms grow in the woods. There are others which prefer the meadows such as the Parasol Mushroom, which Silvana calls *scaroche,* whose Latin name is *Lepiota Procera,* and of course the humble field mushroom, the *pratolino.* Silvana will only gather these if they are tiny and pink centred; when they have become large with velvety brown gills she discards them, I think because of the black liquid they release in the pan, which she finds disconcerting. Another favourite, that grows on fallen trees, is the *Armillariella Mellea* which Silvana calls *famigliola* and which is also known commonly as *chiodino.* These are pretty cinnamon-coloured small round-topped mushrooms that grow in bunches off the old wood. Silvana also enjoys a kind of *funghi* which looks like a *Russula Vesca* and which she calls *biete.* It ranges in colour from a subtle purple pink to a clear pale persimmon and has a distinctive, rather bitter taste. I have been unable to exactly distinguish the species.

The names the country people give to the various species are a source of great confusion to a stranger. The same mushroom can have several different dialect names within the space of a mile or two. In the valley the beautiful apricot-scented *Cantherellus Cibarius, chanterelle,* are called *guatelli;* across the hill they are called *gallinacci,* which is a commoner name. It is also known as *galletto, gialletto* and *finferlo* in different parts of the country, and these are a few of the commoner names. Mushrooms of the same family which look very similar such as the *pinaroli* and the *porcini neri* are not usually distinguished by the country people; they all go in the basket together under the general heading of *porcini.* The dark, drier specimens are however preferred to the softer bronze-headed *edulis* variety, whose spores become a soft spongy olive green with age. This is because the darker variety are harder and less likely to be attacked by grubs.

Silvana is delighted to be able to fill her basket with six or seven large *porcini,* a treasure certainly worth the hour or so she has spent wandering through the woods, turning over leaves with her stick and hunting under bushes. The *porcino* has such a solid firm flesh that it is more often than not served as a meat course. Some country people say that it is better than any piece of meat, and Silvana is inclined to agree. Her favourite way of cooking a firm fresh large *porcino* is on the grill over the wood fire. To do this she first cleans the *porcino* of any moss or dirt if possible without immersing it in water. She cuts off the stem close to the cap and lays the *fungo* in a shallow dish. The herb most suited to the *porcino*, and its natural ally, is *mentuccia*, which is a small-leafed plant of the mint family that grows wild in the fields all over Tuscany; it has an oily aromatic minty flavour. *Nepitella, satureia calamintha,* a wild savory, is also often used with *porcini*. To season the *porcino* Silvana chops a generous pinch of these small leaves into tiny pieces, then cleans one or two cloves of garlic and splits the cloves into long slivers. She makes a small heap of salt mixed with ground black pepper. The *porcino* is lying in the dish with its red-brown smooth skin upwards. Silvana studs the mushroom with the slivers of garlic, pressing them down through the skin into the firm nut-white flesh below. Then she reverses the mushroom, presses in a few more slivers of garlic and sprinkles the *mentuccia* and the salt and pepper over the pale yellow-green gills. Finally she pours on a generous measure of olive oil, pouring slowly so that the oil is well absorbed into the mushroom, then leaves it to marinate for ten minutes or so, so that the oil may penetrate well. After this preparation the *fungo* is ready to be cooked over a slow fire. It must be turned occasionally and anointed with more oil. It is ready when the flesh has shrunk and the top is a little wrinkled. The flavour is exquisite, strong and rich and impossible to describe, as it resembles nothing else particularly closely. As with a fresh white truffle, the flavour must be experienced to be understood. The Cerottis are especially content when these wonderful mushrooms can be served in this manner at their supper table. They eat them without any accompaniments so as not to distract from the flavour and they mop up the juices with the plain saltless Tuscan bread.

 Large firm *porcini* are exceptional mushrooms and there is no substitute for them. However you can grill large cultivated or field mushrooms in this way, but they will of course have an entirely different flavour. To serve **Porcini alla Griglia** for four people you will need four large or eight smaller fleshy mushrooms, the *porcini* if you have them or, if not, cultivated or field mushrooms, four large cloves of garlic, a handful of mint or parsley or savory, salt and freshly ground black pepper and about a glassful of olive oil. Clean the *funghi* and cut off the stalk close to the cap, then skin the garlic and cut the cloves into slivers. Pierce the caps of all the *funghi* with the slivers of garlic, pushing them here and there into the flesh. Chop the mint, parsley or savory, and to this little mound of herb add a pinch or so of salt and a pinch of black pepper. Mix this seasoning together well, then turn over the mushrooms and sprinkle it into the gills of the mushrooms, pressing it well in. Finally lay the *funghi* on a dish and pour the olive oil over every mushroom, making sure that each has a sufficient quantity of oil to moisten and flavour the flesh. After about fifteen minutes, grill the mushrooms, if possible over a wood fire, turn them twice and anoint them with more olive oil as they cook.

Grilling is not the only way to prepare the *porcini*. Silvana also prepares them *in umido*. To do this she again cleans the mushrooms carefully and slices them up into segments. This dish also utilises the stalks, which were not used on the grilled dish. In a flat *tegame* she heats some pieces of garlic in about half a glass of olive oil. When the garlic is just turning colour, it must never be allowed to burn as this would ruin the flavour of the oil, she adds the *funghi* and stirs them around in the pan. At this point she adds either the *mentuccia* or a small amount of chopped Mediterranean parsley, a little salt and black pepper, not too much pepper as *funghi* pick up strong flavours very easily. She lets the pan simmer away on a medium flame until the mushrooms start to give up their liquid. Then she allows them to cook gently for about fifteen minutes until they are thoroughly tender. Again this makes an exquisite dish in its own right. Silvana would serve it alone or perhaps with a plain *frittata*. I have eaten this same dish cooked until the liquid is reduced, used as a sauce in the most perfect of *lasagne*, the *funghi* taking the place of the meat and tomato sauce and a creamy béchamel flavoured with *parmigiano* making up the rest of the dish between the layers of pasta. This is also a Tuscan recipe, but from a more elaborate establishment.

 To prepare the **Porcini in Umido** you will need, to serve four people, 500 g or 1 lb 2 oz of *funghi porcini*, two cloves of garlic, a branch of *nepitella* or a handful of chopped parsley, three tablespoons of olive oil, salt and black pepper.

Clean the *porcini* and cut them into pieces about the size of a large almond in its shell. In a shallow pan heat the olive oil and in it soften the garlic; if you are using the *nepitella* put it in the pan at this point to perfume the oil. Do not allow the garlic to brown. Next add the *porcini* and the parsley if that is the herb that you are using. Turn the *porcini* in the oil then lower the flame and let the mushrooms simmer; they will eventually release their liquid. Season them with a little salt and a very little black pepper. Cook until the *porcini* are tender. Before serving remove the sprig of *nepitella*. This makes a very luxurious *contorno* to eat with a plain grilled steak or on its own as a supper dish.

 What to do if there are no *porcini*? You may still make a very delicious *contorno* using *champignons*, **Funghi Trifolati**. For four people you will again need 500g or 1 lb 2 oz of firm button mushrooms, three cloves of garlic, three tablespoons of olive oil, a handful of chopped parsley and one heaped dessertspoon of tomato concentrate, salt and black pepper.

Clean and trim the button mushrooms and slice them finely. Clean the cloves of garlic and slice them too. Heat the olive oil in a shallow pan and put in the garlic to soften, then add the mushrooms and turn them well in the oil; lower the flame and let the mushrooms give up their liquid. At this point add the tomato paste and mix it in well with the *funghi* juices. Sprinkle on half of the parsley and season with the salt and pepper. Be careful with the pepper, as *funghi* take on flavours very easily. When the mushrooms have cooked for about ten minutes and the liquid is evaporating, they are ready to serve. Sprinkle on the rest of the parsley and take them to the table.

Finally, to complete the triad of basic ways to cook the glorious *porcino*, there is the deep frying method. This again has its own particular delights. Silvana follows the basic cleaning rules and cuts the *funghi* into small fat segments. These she rolls in a light covering of hard flour then plunges a few at a time into fiercely boiling olive oil: this is not an occasion to economise by using cheaper vegetable oils. The result is a delicious crisp exterior and the soft flavoursome flesh inside. *Porcini* cooked in this way are good on their own or as an especially rich *contorno* to accompany a plain grilled meat dish. Sometimes when there is a plentiful supply of *porcini*, for a special supper when guests are expected Silvana will serve the *funghi* cooked in all three different ways to make a *funghi* feast. Good white wine, fresh bread and a piquant green salad are all that is necessary to complete the meal. Although in England the *porcino* is seldom seen, all these methods can be used successfully with cultivated and field mushrooms, although the dishes will have a very different flavour.

 To make deep-fried button mushrooms, **Funghi Fritti**, for four people you will need 400g or 14oz of small compact button mushrooms, a plate of seasoned flour or *polenta* flour, a pan of boiling arachide oil and wedges of lemon to serve with the *funghi*.

Clean the *funghi* and roll them in the flour. A few at a time plunge them into the hot fat and cook them until they are golden brown. Drain them well then serve them with the pieces of lemon, which must be freshly cut and juicy.

The other most favoured *funghi* are the *guatelli*, or *Cantherellus Cibarius* (*chanterelle*), which are a delightful golden yellow and have a firm flesh which is never prone to attack by grubs. They are shaped like small fat trumpets, the stalk thickening out into the flat top with its frilled edge. These *funghi* have a delicate sweet flavour and a scent of apricots. Invariably Silvana cooks them *in umido* with parsley, garlic and oil, in exactly the same manner as the *porcini*. Very occasionally she might add some diced *prosciutto* to the dish. I have some across recipes for them which include *dragoncello*, tarragon, a herb which is not used in Italy except in the Tuscan town of Siena. It is a tempting combination.

Silvana is always quite pleased when she finds a cluster of *famigliola* growing on a log. They are golden brown turning to cinnamon-coloured mushrooms with small almost conical button caps decorated with darker brown granules and have long fibrous stalks. They have rather a rich flavour and Silvana likes to chop them into quite small pieces and cook them in olive oil until she has a fairly dry mixture. The stalks are not used as they are very fibrous and tough. For an especially festive Sunday lunch, Silvana will use this *funghi* mixture to spread on top of the customary *crostini* in place of her usual chicken liver pâté.

She is also quite pleased to find examples of the *biete*, which have such spectacular colours that can run from a gentle yellow orange to maybe a fierce persimmon red and on to a dull pinky purple. Their skin glistens with a shallow viscous slick. Their gills are a rare creamy yellow colour, like old ivory, and have a texture which is pleasant and crisp like that of flaked almonds. Only their stalks are white and pithy. Care has to be taken in gathering these particular mushrooms as they can be confused with the *Russula Emetica*, which is toxic but not deadly. Silvana cooks them *in umido* in the usual way with garlic, oil and parsley. They make a very unusual dish with their vivid colours sparked off by flecks of bright green parsley. The flavour too is very unusual and likely to be an acquired taste as they are inclined to be bitter as some forms of salad greens are in Italy and also in the Middle East. I am not totally convinced that the *biete* are *Russula Vesca* because their flavour is so bitter. They are not toxic, so cannot be *Russula Emetica*. Personally I do not cook them unless Silvana has inspected them and approved.

The parasol mushrooms, or *scaroce* as Silvana calls them, are probably next on their list of favourites. These large pretty mushrooms that are also native to England grow invariably in the same place each year and once or twice a season Silvana will make a special trip to see if any have appeared. They can grow to an amazingly large size and when young and still furled, when it is best to gather them, they have the appearance and colouring of a speckled thrush. They are best cooked over the open fire and Silvana treats them in the same way as the *porcini*, with a copious drenching of olive oil, a little garlic, *mentuccia* or parsley. They have their own mild flavour but in no way compare to the full-bodied taste of the *porcino*. It is like the difference between the flavour of a Verdicchio, a fresh white wine, and a seasoned Barolo, a heavy rich red. They are both excellent in their own way, but if a choice had to be made the Barolo must win.

Among the commonest *funghi* to be found in Orlando's fields are the *Lycoperdon Giganteum*, puff balls, which are called locally *puzzarella*, or 'stinkers'. Although they can grow to enormous sizes, large enough to weigh ten kilos, the small ones are much more common. They have a crisp outer skin to their globular shape and inside have the texture of a marshmallow. When they are ageing the inside takes on a greenish-yellow hue which rapidly becomes an olive-green thick liquid, finally drying into a dark olive powder which explodes in the air if they are knocked. From this description it is easy to see why they have the common names of puff balls and *puzzerella*. Their flavour is very mild and pleasant and Silvana will willingly use them mixed into a dish of scrambled eggs, which Orlando may occasionally eat for his breakfast on a Sunday. He is however more likely to want an egg fried in bubbling green olive oil to which has been added a clove of garlic. The small pink-gilled field mushrooms Silvana will prepare in the same manner as the *puzzarella* mixed in with a mild egg dish.

This catalogue of mushrooms provides of course only a small example of all the *funghi* that are available wild in Italy, but they are the ones that grow on Orlando's land and the ones which both he and Silvana recognize and happily cook and eat. This is another reason why their cuisine is so particular to them and Tuscany.

September is the last month in the year when the sun is really hot, hot enough to dry any *porcini* which are left over and can be used to store for the winter. When the season has been particularly good every household has a box or sheets of cardboard outside the door in the sunniest place. The boxes will be spread with fine slices of *porcini*, which will turn a rich cream colour in the sun. Sometimes they are strung on cotton threads and allowed to hang in the fresh air and sunlight. These dried *funghi* have a strong rich scent and when all traces of moisture have disappeared the housewives including Silvana will pack them into paper bags or cardboard cartons and hang them from the beams in the pantry. As they are needed through the winter Silvana will fetch down the bags and soak a handful of the slices to flavour her sauces. Some years, when the *porcini* crop has been overwhelmingly abundant, she has dried kilo upon kilo of the mushrooms and has sold them to local stores. The money she earns in this way, as well as the money she earns from the sale of her cheeses, is hers to keep. She rarely goes to market or to the shops but she looks forward to the visits of the Moroccan carpet seller who comes around to outlying farms about twice a year. In the back of his battered old car he has a stock of carpets, counterpanes and all manner of linens from elaborate lace tablecloths to white linen hand towels edged with embroidery. It is Silvana's great joy to offer the salesman a cup of coffee or lunch as the time might indicate and then to pore over his selection of pretty things. Usually she buys something, maybe a warm blanket or some dainty towels which she stores away in her linen chest and brings out gleefully for special occasions.

The last hot sun of the year is good to dry figs as well as the *funghi*. During August the fig trees, both white and black varieties, that grow at the back of the chapel have been laden with ripening figs. The air around the trees has been full of the hot sticky sweet scent of the fruit. The family and the farm workers have eaten great quantities of them but there are still many left over so Silvana sets to and picks the remaining fruit. She splits the figs in half to make the drying quicker and lays them in rows on cardboard in the sun. She also has some long oval shallow twig baskets which are made especially for the purpose and can be used every year. It takes an extremely hot sun to dry figs; the best dried figs come from southern Italy and Greece where the heat is greater than here in Tuscany, so to aid the drying process Silvana prepares the brick bread oven. She uses it to cook a large joint of meat and when the oven has lost its first heat she puts in the figs to desiccate in the gentle dry warmth. The temperature must be just right or the figs will cook instead of drying. Sometimes as an extra treat she puts an almond into the middle of each fig and when the figs are sufficiently dry she takes them out, puts them in a large bag of veiling sugar and shakes them vigorously until they are covered in a fine sweet dust. She can then pack the fruit in wooden boxes or thread them on twine to eat through the winter.

She remembers her childhood when in a country family of eleven children there was no money to buy sweets and chocolate even if they had been available in wartime Italy. Their Christmas stockings were filled with a few of the figs, some nuts and a small home-made toy. She also remembers a neighbouring family who were fortunate to have several splendid fig trees. The mother would spend hours drying the fruit, some of which she sold, and the rest she fed to her children sandwiched between two slices of the coarse wartime bread. This was regarded as the food of the really poor.

❧OCTOBER

Orlando sniffs the air anxiously now, on the clear starlit nights. He is secretly willing away the first light frosts so that he can gather in all of his tobacco crop before the glittering crystals destroy the remaining tall plants. Already the leaves of the cherry and pear trees have turned colour and been whisked off the branches by brisk winds. The hillsides are stippled with gold and the skies are cold blue. For the past week or so all around the valley the farmers and ordinary householders who have a few vines around their houses have been cleaning their barrels and fetching out their *follatore*, the grape crushing machines. The grapes are ripe, as plump and sweet as they can be expected to be, and on the first day when the tobacco kilns are full and no more can be gathered, Orlando judges that the *vendemmia* can begin. The moon is in the right phase, on the wane, so they can begin to pick the grapes with easy minds.

Silvana enjoys the *vendemmia* and always arranges her work so that she too may join in the picking. At six-thirty in the morning Orlando drives the large tractor down the hill to the fields below. On the trailer behind are stacked large square containers and a heap of baskets. Silvana and her friend Nena are perched among the baskets and following along behind come Menchino, round like a *putto*, and blond with bright blue eyes, and Guido's twin brothers Tonio and Alfredo, whose dark bobbed hair makes them look like a couple of Renaissance pages. They are all armed with iron clippers in the shape of secateurs, some with curved handles that cradle the fist. Most of their baskets are of brightly coloured plastic, large and oval with one deep handle. However Silvana has a real twig basket made for her by an elderly relative who still makes the *canestre* in the long winter evenings. This craft dates back to Roman times, when it was advocated by Cato as a seemly activity to keep the farm workers busy on cold winter nights. Silvana's basket is a curious shape. Its handle is cut from a branch with four prongs, two of which make the curved handle. The two smaller branches are left and trimmed off to make small projections that can be conveniently used to hang the basket from the vine, so leaving the two hands free for picking; the body is made from woven twigs. As soon as the basket is full it can be emptied into the large wooden cases and plastic containers and the whole process started again.

In this part of the valley, the fields are flat and narrow, lying in horizontal bands widthways across the valley floor. The vines grow along the edges of the fields, supported by wooden posts, props and wires. Some are fifty years old and they are mostly Trebbiano and Sangiovese grapes. Some of the fields are still full of tobacco and alternate with those left for pasture. Andrea the shepherd is helping with the picking too and his flock graze a few yards away. He has to keep a sharp eye on them as they love to eat the grapes. He is a large man, with shambling gait and green goat eyes, his shiny bald head always covered by a greasy large-brimmed hat, pulled well down around his ears. Always ready to smile and show one stained brown tooth, he is easygoing; all year round he is to be found outside, spreadeagled in a flower-strewn summer meadow or crouched under a dripping tree, his greatcoat pulled over his head, in the wet months. He sometimes carries an illustrated paper or his cracked transistor radio which he keeps tuned to a station that plays old-fashioned *vecchia Romagna* tunes. His sheep always surround him, a woolly army whose rhythmic chewing and pattering hooves can be heard fields away. His three dogs, one a very aged black mongrel bitch with a friendly disposition, and two ill-trained young Alsatians, will win no trials.

Silvana works next to Nena, both of them neatly and quickly stripping the vines, laughing and talking all the while as they cut the bunches easily with the sharp clippers. They work carefully, not tearing away at the boughs which will be left to die back until it is time for Guido to prune them again next March or April. As the day wears on they move to the higher fields which are smaller and are planted in the antique

manner with pergolas holding good quality grapes. They group themselves in fours and fives working together around one large arbour,
bending and stretching amongst the livid gold leaves and blue-black
grapes as on some animated Attic frieze. The cases of grapes become
fuller and fuller, mountains of fruit, green and black, covered with
bloom and oozing juice from their own weight. The pickers' hands are
sticky and there is a heavy scent of fruit in the warming air. The men
discard their darned woollen jumpers and their muscles strain under their
faded shirts. Nena and Silvana, both by now bare-armed, take care not
to get stung by the nettles or torn by the odd bramble that winds itself
around the roots of the vines. The vines are too many and the labourers
too few to spend time cleaning around each plant, and so in the further
fields the grapes flourish among hedgerows choked with field flowers,
stray corn and tall grasses. They stumble on a hide made by some passing
hunter. The once green leaves of the broken branches are withered and
brown, the trodden ground littered with spent cartridges. Orlando mut-
ters under his breath about thieving hunters. Silvana wants to keep some
of the grapes apart for eating. Tonio reaches for the most luxuriant
bunches and cuts them off with a T-shaped piece of the hard vine still
attached so that she can hang the clusters from the nails in the storeroom
beams. These will keep well until December.

They halt for a break and sprawl themselves in the shade of a large
arbour, the sun playing through the leaves onto their red flushed faces.
Silvana passes around the flasks of last year's wine and Orlando drinks
from the bottle, the wine trickling down his broad chin and staining his
shirt a dull pink. Andrea is perched on the edge of the group, his shirt
tied in the fashion of fifteen years ago in a knot under his belly, exposing
a vast expanse of grubby woollen vest. His three dogs have followed the
progress of the pickers and, as soon as they move on, the animals root
and sniff at the base of the stripped vines, searching for and eating the
grapes that drop to the ground and escape the baskets. Silvana says that
they eat the fallen figs too and every day they come around to the fig
tree. So do the foxes, says Nena, and they steal the grapes from the vine,
she has seen them. But she says this is better luck for the chickens: the
foxes are less likely to rob the hen coops when there is fruit on the vine.
Orlando, interested in the conversation, says that he has heard from a
professor in Cortona that in the very old days, the Roman *contadini*
would fatten young foxes on grapes and eat them. There is a general
groan of disgust at this piece of information. Even in the worst years of
the war they had not sunk to such unappetizing depths.

After they have gathered the last grape and the cases are loaded onto the trailer, the black and green grapes always kept separate, they all make their way back to the *fattoria*. The day's grape gathering has nothing to do with the greater world of wine, vintages, labels and commerce. This is simply a group of country people, timeless in their attitudes and expressions, and as their forefathers did, they have gathered in the fruits of their labours. After all the ancient Greeks' name for the Italian peninsula was Oenotria, the land of wine.

Now they set to to make the wine that is as necessary to their lives as bread and water. Behind the chapel and down a slope under some walnut trees is the *cantina*, the cellar, which is long and cool with a shallowly vaulted ceiling. Here the grapes are pressed and the wine kept in the huge oak barrels that line the walls. The tractor is driven round to the *cantina* and the cases unloaded, and the pressing of the grapes begins immediately. It is already dusk and the men work on into the night. The long room is lit by two dim lightbulbs dangling on dusty wires from the crumbling bricks, the walls are encrusted with aged dust and the cobwebbed barrels are immense in the shadows. The three men, Guido, Menchino and Tonio, watched by Sauro, move in the gloom operating the machinery like warlocks in some vast devil's kitchen. The shadows on their faces deepen in the faint light and if it were not for their clothes it would be difficult to put a date to the scene.

First they tip the cases of green grapes into a funnel-shaped apparatus outside the *cantina* wall, then they turn a handle like that of a mangle at the base of the funnel which half presses the fruit and sends the liquid and skins cascading through a window into a deep-walled stone trough inside the *cantina*. Here Tonio stirs the must with a long pole and rakes over the skins. This funnel-shaped machine, the *follatore*, is a simple form of the *égrappoir*, the machine used for the same purpose in more elaborate vineyards. The Cerottis' version has however no refinement to remove the stalks from the grapes, it is just a simple crushing device. The juice or must is filtered from the stone trough into the wooden vats through a large plastic pipe, the liquid sent on its way by a hand pump. The skins are then put into presses shaped like barrels with open slatted sides. A screw is turned at the top and this forces a plate down on to the skins, squeezing the remaining juice out between the side slats. A turgid yellow-green froth bubbles sluggishly from the base of the presses. This press wine, which is strong and full of tannin from the skins, is later added to the must in the fermenting barrels. The wrung-out skins, which some farmers use to make a rough *grappa*, in much the same way as

French farmers make *marc*, are finally thrown out onto a field well away from the house as they would harm any poultry that ventured to eat them.

The black grapes are crushed in a separate machine and their must is put into an oak barrel together with the skins. The longer the skins are left in, the darker the wine will be. The wine will clarify, the sugar turning into alcohol, in about ten days' time, but the vats will remain unsealed for about a month in order to complete the fermentation. When this happens the barrels will be sealed properly with an air-tight clay seal to prevent the alcohol content of the wine dissipating and the wine turning to vinegar.

Back at the house the kitchen is rosy red from the huge log fire. Orlando hangs a long square blackened tin from the hook on the chimney chain ready to boil up some fresh chestnuts. This month is the time when the ripe heavy brown nuts fall from the tall trees and Sauro has been industriously collecting them by the sackful to store in one of the upper attics so that they may enjoy roasting them during the coming winter. Everyone gathers around the fire, drinking wine and eating the nuts which, being so fresh, have milk-white soft flesh. The skins they save for the animals, as Silvana sees to it that nothing is wasted in the household. The men have washed away the juice of the grapes and combed their hair ready for the supper which everyone will eat together in celebration of a successful day. Nena, clean and neat in a new pinafore, her hair covered with a spotted scarf, is helping Silvana. She lays a white cloth on the long wooden table, then places the glasses, plates, bowls and cutlery, three huge crusty loaves of bread, massive bowls of fruit and walnuts and the last of the old wine.

Meanwhile Silvana is cooking the supper. She makes two dishes of *funghi* cooked *in umido*, one of *porcini* flavoured with garlic and *mentuccia* and the other of *guatelli*, chanterelle, flavoured with parsley. There is also a large *Frittata di Cipollo*, an onion-flavoured omelette, country sausages grilled with sage leaves over the fire, and after, walnuts and one of the last soft fruits of the year that ripen during this month, the *cachi*, the beautiful vermilion-coloured Japanese persimmons. Sauro picks the fruit from the tall, elegantly shaped tree at the end of the kitchen garden. When the leaves have fallen the tree looks spectacular with its large round glowing fruit hanging on the bare silver-grey branches. Eventually the food is ready and everyone takes their place at the table. By this time they are all hungry and enjoy the spicy butcher's sausages crisp from the fire and the succulent mushrooms with their rich sauce that everyone mops up with the fresh bread.

To make the **Guatelli in Umido**, stewed *chanterelles*, for two people you would need about 250 g or 9 oz of *chanterelle* mushrooms, three tablespoons of olive oil or butter, one clove of garlic, a small bunch of parsley, salt and black pepper.

Clean the mushrooms with a damp cloth and split them into pieces following the grain of the mushroom from the base of the stem to the top. Slice the garlic finely and heat it in the olive oil or butter until it smells sweet; do not let it take on colour. Add the mushrooms to the oil and let them sweat gently. When they start to give up their juices add a little salt and a very little black pepper and a sprinkling of chopped parsley. Let the *funghi* simmer gently until they are tender. When you bring them to the table sprinkle on a little more of the parsley. They make an excellent *contorno* with simply cooked breast of chicken.

 Silvana makes her **Frittata di Cipollo** in the following manner. For two people she would use two tablespoons of olive oil, one onion, four fresh eggs, salt and black pepper. Slice the onion into thin slices and set it to soften in the olive oil in a thick-bottomed omelette pan. Beat the eggs up with a fork in a small bowl and season them with the salt and pepper. When the onion has become transparent but before it has started to brown, raise the heat under the pan and spread the onion out evenly over its surface. Next pour in the eggs and allow them to set on the bottom of the pan; lower your heat and let the eggs cook through slowly. They should be firm but soft in the centre. When the *frittata* has arrived at this point slide it out of the pan onto a hot plate. Raise the heat again, adding a little more oil if necessary, then tip in the *frittata* raw side down and allow it to cook for a few minutes to set the bottom into a crust. To serve the *frittata* put it onto a round plate and cut it into wedges. You may also cover it with some sharp tomato sauce flavoured with basil and then it will be called a **Frittata Affogata**, a smothered omelette.

After the meal is finished Orlando decides to make some hot spiced wine. He reaches for a small cauldron and fills it with three or four litres of red wine. Meanwhile Silvana has been sent to the *dispensa* to fetch some cinnamon sticks, cloves, an orange, a lemon and a bag of sugar. She also brings a bottle of brandy from the *tinello* in the dining room. Orlando tips a generous measure of sugar into the wine, then breaks a few cinnamon sticks and scatters in the fragments. He adds a few of the *chiodi di garofani*, the cloves, and some lemon and orange peel which he pares off with his pocket knife. Then the cauldron is slung over the fire to heat while Orlando watches to see that it does not boil and lose its alcohol. The last ingredient to go in is a big glass or two of brandy.

Orlando is in an expansive mood, well pleased with his year's harvests and ready to talk and relax a little. When the wine is hot enough he ladles it out into the toughened glass wine glasses which are the traditional trumpet shaped type, to be seen in any country bar and in most country kitchens. He and his men laugh and talk on, their faces becoming more animated and their voices louder with the conversation and the hot wine. They are feeling their masculinity, asserting their opinions, sure of their worth and their own importance, displaying the confidence that has been instilled into them with their mother's milk, products of a religion that worships the Boy Child. The fire dies down and Silvana sits at the end of the table, her head propped in her hand, trying to keep her eyes from closing. At last, aware that the next day begins at six, the men cease their talk, heave on their coats and start out into the cold night air to their homes. Orlando pokes his nose outside the door and is happy that he cannot smell any frost in the air.

Wine to an Italian is a completely normal commodity, easily and cheaply available even to those who are city dwellers and unable to make their own. Wine and water are the daily drink with meals, coffee and tea, which latter is only now becoming quite popular, are taken at other prescribed times during the day: a *caffè latte* in the morning and a tiny cup of strong *espresso* coffee at other times of the day when a small stimulant is needed. Wine is seen as something to be drunk, not fussed over. Country people like the Cerottis invariably drink their own. It certainly is not the best of wines, but it is genuine, made of nothing but grapes. Of course there is the other world of Italian wine, the famous wines from the best growing areas in Italy, the wines that can be tasted in places like the celebrated *enoteca* at Siena where there are examples of all the best wines of Italy and in all the superior restaurants of Italy's main cities. There is a vast army of dedicated wine lovers who take endless pains to see that their wines match the luxurious dishes served at the myriad sophisticated tables in the land; good food and wine are an Italian passion. Tuscany itself is the home of many of the most renowned and valued of Italian wines, for example the superb *Brunello di Montalcino*, which comes from a small area within the Chianti district and is a great red wine with a fine full flavour and perfumed bouquet. It can be kept indefinitely and the small quantity of it that is exported fetches an outrageously high price. It should be drunk with rich roasts and game or on its own after dinner. There is also the *Vino Nobile di Montepulciano*, which again is an excellent dignified wine with long ageing properties. The Chiantis themselves, from the normal cheerful sort to the most serious *riservas* of the exclusive houses in the *classico* area, are certainly to be respected and enjoyed. Tuscany is also fortunate in having the white vine of Orvieto and the gentle whites of the Val di Chiana, and Tuscany is only one area of Italy and these are just a few of the wines of Southern Tuscany so it is evident the subject can be continued in many volumes.

However the Cerottis are not concerned with this elaborate and sophisticated world of wine. They drink what they produce themselves and although they may treat themselves to a special wine for an important occasion and enthusiastically consume bottles of *spumante* from Piedmonte with their cakes and sweet dishes, in the end they prefer their own brew. Its alcohol content is not so high that a glass or two will make them drunk and they are used to their thin red wine and the sharp clear taste of the white.

As we have seen, throughout the year, wine is an indispensible ingredient in Silvana's cooking. She uses it to moisten a great many of her sauces and the meat dishes that she cooks *in umido* or *in padella*. White wine is dashed over the roasting chestnuts to make them tender, splashed on to grilled meat and Orlando always drinks hot white wine flavoured with sugar if he has an incipient cold or sore throat. Brandy, a whole range of *digestivos*, digestive mixtures of herbs and alcohol and *mistra*, an anice-based liqueur, are always to be found in the *tinello*. Silvana serves them after a meal and some of them in coffee to make a *caffè corretto*. Brandy and *mistra* are suitable for this purpose and the *mistra* she also uses to flavour her sweet fried cakes, the *castagnole*, and sometimes to douse the sponge fingers in her *Zuppa Inglese*. Orlando is also very fond of *grappa* and when he discovers that he has one barrel of white wine too many for their needs he calls in a distiller to convert the wine into *grappa di vino*, which is a potent clear white liquor, prized as an after-dinner drink. The distiller will arrive and set up his still in the courtyard. They call the still the '*serpente*', probably because of its serpentine pipes, if not for the sting in the liquid it produces. In Italy good *grappa* is a drink for the *cognoscenti*. Famous vineyards distill their own from the best wines. There are endless varieties and flavourings such as strawberry and cherry and those produced from different sorts of grape, and the prices vary from a few pounds to twelve or fifteen pounds a bottle.

There is a marked difference in the qualities and the flavours and home-made *grappa* like that of the Cerottis is in a different and far superior class to the ordinary commercial brands. This drink is again offered to guests at the end of a meal. It is very strong.

Another drink that the Cerottis always have on hand to offer visitors is a good *vin santo* or 'holy wine'. The Cerottis do not make their own *vin santo* but rely on Silvana's brother Paulo for their supply. This wine is made from grapes that are stored for many months after the *vendemmia* before they are pressed. It is kept in small barrels for four or five years or more and it is always rather a gamble as to whether the wine will mature successfully. Paulo says it is the most difficult wine to make and the one most liable to spoil. His *vin santo* is usually a red-gold colour and has a sweet lemony taste. Contrary to popular belief, *vin santo* is not always a sweet wine. There is some very excellent dry *vin santo*, for example the *Vin Santo di Caratello* of Francesca Colombini from Montalcino. This is reminiscent of a very good dry sherry. There are various stories as to why this wine came by the name of *vin santo*. Some people say it was the wine that priests used to have specially made for the celebration of the mass. Others say that the grapes that were harvested in October were dried sufficiently to make the wine by the following Easter and that this is the reason why the wine is called holy wine. *Vin santo* is also made in the Trentino and Alto Adige areas of Italy but I think it is much more characteristic of Tuscany. Silvana will often serve this pleasant dessert wine at the end of a meal with *biscotti secchi*, very dry biscuits. These delicious biscuits, which are specially made to serve with the wine, are called *cantuccini* or *biscotti del prato* and they are small, full of whole almonds and extremely hard, intended to be dunked into a glass of the *vin santo*. A glass of the luscious golden wine and a few of the crisp nutty biscuits make a splendid and simple end to a dinner. *Vin santo* and *cantuccini* are also good things to take home from a visit to Tuscany, but be sure to buy *vin santo* that comes from a good vineyard. The famous Chianti houses usually offer good examples; the sort sold in two-litre bottles can be very sweet and rather nasty.

One of the last harvests of the year also occurs in October, that of the Indian corn or *gran turco*. All summer the tall green plants with their rich brown top-knots have been rustling in the fields. Now the corn cobs are ripe, the beads of corn golden yellow, purple and cream, the leaves just crackling parchment husks. Every year, as for the grain harvest, a man brings around a large machine to each farmyard to strip the corn from the cobs. Only in the very smallest establishments are the cobs left whole and strung in yellow bunches under the eaves and in the barns to be stripped by hand when needed. The *gran turco* is grown chiefly to feed the domestic farm animals and fowl, so Silvana and Nena take a particular interest in the harvest and enjoy counting their sacks of corn. The husks will be collected together and used for bedding in the sheep-pens. The poultry will benefit from this excellent diet and the eggs will have deep-yellow flavourful yolks.

Ground *gran turco* provides the excellent yellow flour for making *polenta*, a dish which was a speciality of the Veneto, and used there in the same way that Tuscans use their bread as a staple in their cooking, but has now spread in fame and is enjoyed very much in Tuscany. Silvana looks forward to the season when she can buy fresh maize flour. Her favourite way of using the *polenta* flour is in a dish which is arranged in the same way as *lasagne*. To make the basic *polenta* she first boils up a large saucepan of salted water. When the water is at a rolling boil she starts to pour in the yellow maize flour; it must be poured very slowly in a steady stream and mixed as it is poured with a wooden spoon to prevent lumps forming. She stoops over the fire, her face pink with the heat as she concentrates on the all-important mixing with the long-handled wooden spoon. The mixture becomes thicker as she pours in the flour and at last it resembles a soft potato purée, coming away from the sides of the pan easily as she stirs. The dish must be cooked gently for about thirty-five to forty-five minutes. She has ready and hot beside her a pan of her normal meat and tomato sauce and a large heap of grated *pecorino* cheese. When the *polenta* is cooked Silvana ladles a layer of it into an oiled oven dish; on top she sprinkles a handful of grated *pecorino*. Next comes a layer of *ragù*, more cheese, then *polenta* and so on layer after layer until the dish is full. This *Polenta al Sugo* she serves in place of the *pasta* course and its texture is soft and rich. If there is any left over she puts it into the oven to heat up for supper. By then the *polenta* will have taken on a more solid character but will lose none of its flavour. Of course this dish could also be made with a sauce of fresh or dried wild mushrooms. Silvana also uses *polenta* to make a flat solid cake. For this she makes a similar but thicker mixture of the flour and salted water and pours the cooked mush onto a large board. She leaves it to dry, then cuts the flat cake into slices as she needs them. This form of *polenta* she sometimes uses in the bottom of the soup dish instead of a slice of bread, or more usually she toasts pieces over the fire to go maybe with a *salmi* of pheasant. She sometimes serves spit-roasted small birds with a slice of grilled *polenta*. Around Venice a slice of *polenta* often forms a base for a dish of *seppie*, or squid, cooked in their own inky black sauce.

 To make a dish of this **Polenta al Sugo** for six people you will need for the *polenta* itself, about 1½ litres or 2¾ pints of water, 500 g or 18 oz of coarse ground maize flour (the coarse ground flour will make the softer *polenta* which is needed for this dish, the fine ground maize flour gives a harder *polenta* which is more suitable for the cakes of *polenta* that are served grilled with various meat and game dishes), and salt.

To make the *polenta*, boil the salted water in a large thick pan. When the water begins to boil, slowly pour in the flour with one hand, stirring the pot with a long-handled wooden spoon with the other. Do this slowly, a little flour at a time, or you will find lumps forming in the mush which are difficult to get rid of. The *polenta* must be smooth and thick. When all the flour is in, leave the *polenta* to cook for about thirty-five minutes, stirring it frequently to prevent it sticking. When it comes away from the side of the pan easily when the pan is tipped, it is ready for the next step. You must have ready a good pint of *ragù*, either the recipe given in January's chapter for Silvana's normal *ragù*, or possibly her sauce made with dried *funghi*. As well as the *ragù* you must have a plate of grated parmesan or *pecorino* cheese, about four heaped tablespoons. In an earthenware oven dish which you have greased with olive oil, pour a layer of *polenta*; on top of the *polenta* spread a layer of the sauce, then sprinkle on some of the grated cheese, continue in this fashion until you have finished up the ingredients, topping the dish with a final sprinkling of cheese. Then put the dish into a hot oven for about ten minutes. This will make a substantial dish to be served as a first course instead of pasta. You may also serve the *Polenta al Sugo* by simply putting two or three spoonfuls of *polenta* into individual bowls, then a few spoons of *sugo*, the cheese, a little more *polenta*, more sauce and a final dusting of cheese, and taking it immediately to the table, omitting the step of finishing the dish in the oven. The result will be softer and lusher.

On Sunday, Orlando and Silvana like to go visiting. After their large Sunday lunch they both dress in their best clothes, Orlando in his formal suit and wide-brimmed hat and Silvana in her best dress of soft brown wool jersey. She also wears the heavy gold bracelet that Orlando bought her for their twenty-fifth wedding anniversary, her prettiest hoop earrings and a spray of the scent that her sister sent her from Paris. They lock up the house carefully and while Orlando gets out the car, she picks some Michaelmas daisies from the little flower patch; she also takes a bottle of clean water, because on their way they will visit the small local cemetery. They drive up the hill slowly, the tyres crunching on the loose gravel of the dirt road. Eventually, after twisting ever higher into the mountain, they arrive at the quiet walled cemetery where Orlando's ancestors are buried. The cemetery is built on a small saddle of ground and the view down into the next valley is breathtaking. The old walls enclose a small grass courtyard which is filled with wrought-iron crosses dating from the middle of the last century. At the end of the enclosure are arranged the tiers of tombs, almost like drawers in a filing cabinet. Each place has an engraved stone in coloured marble giving the dates of the birth and death of the occupant, their names and a small framed photograph of the dead person. There are little red lights by each tomb and small vases of flowers. Silvana has brought her flowers to put beside the tomb of her son Piero. She and Orlando come here every Sunday to bring fresh flowers. They either know or are related to everyone buried in the cemetery and are acquainted with the stories of their lives. Most are the tombs of the elderly, buried after long lives of eighty and ninety years, but there are one or two tragic exceptions, such as the occupant of a large turn-of-the-century tomb set apart from the others. In it, so Silvana was told by her grandmother, lies the body of a beautiful girl of sixteen. She had been courted by a young man, but her father had disapproved of the match and refused to let the couple marry. In desperation the young man took his gun and shot her then himself. He is buried outside the churchyard but within sight of her grave. Silvana was very impressed by this sad and romantic story when she herself was a young girl.

After they have finished arranging the flowers they close the heavy iron gates of the *campo santo* and drive on to the next village. Here there is a small grocery store combined with a bar, and it is here that on Sunday afternoons several of the Cerottis' friends and neighbours stop for a glass of wine and a chat. Silvana sits with some of her friends and cousins and they exchange family news while Orlando stands at the bar with his cronies. Whilst there Silvana buys some chocolates and small bags of sweets before they move on to their next stop, Orlando's family home. This rather grand and large stone house is even further up in the mountains and is occupied by Orlando's mother, who is very old, and Orlando's brother and his wife and their two pretty daughters. The sweets are for them. Orlando is his mother's favourite and he causes chaos in the large kitchen, with its noble tall fireplace, by demanding all sorts of cakes and pastries and *digestivi*, which his mother hurries to fetch him.

As the afternoon is wearing on they say their goodbyes and, loaded with *cenci* and two loaves of the bread that Orlando's mother still bakes each Saturday, they drive on through the hills to the *paesino*, the hamlet where Silvana was born. This tiny place is situated on a small hill above a river. The houses are almost totally surrounded by the *macchia*, the deep forest, but the meadows that circle the houses are pretty in spring and are dotted with olive trees. The hamlet consists of four houses and a chapel, which was built in the early years of the last century and contains the tombs of Silvana's grandmother and great-grandmother. The main house, in which her grandparents lived, but which is now empty, is very fine and is built on three floors over the stables. The old kitchen is cavernous and has an enormous fireplace. The floors are made of vast planks of wood hewn from large tree trunks and finished by hand with adzes. At the back of the house, with a view down the valley, there is a tiny parlour with a pretty carved stone fireplace. This *signorile* feature shows that the inhabitants of the house did not always have to work, they had time to sit in comfort like ladies and gentlemen. The upper rooms of the house are again floored with wood whose patina is now covered by dust as the house is no longer lived in. In one of the rooms there is an old loom on which Silvana's grandmother wove the cloth that made their clothes and the heavy linen sheets that covered their beds. When Silvana was a girl she and her sisters used to carry the linen a mile or so down the hill to the river where they would do the washing. They sang as they worked; each task had its own special song in those days. Sometimes in the summer they would strip to their petticoats and bathe while the washing dried in the sun. If the weather was damp it was very hard work to carry the water-heavy washing back up the long steep hill to their home.

In a smaller adjacent house Silvana's sister lives with her numerous family who all come out to greet them as Orlando's car inches its way down the narrow drive. This is the house in which both Silvana and Sauro were born. On the walls of the outside stone stairway that leads up to the main door there are pots of basil and night-scented stock. Through the wide wooden door one steps straight into the large long kitchen which is still equipped with an old carved stone sink. On a shelf above the sink are arranged the brass water jars with which the girls fetch water from the spring. The house is lit with oil lamps and candles

and the light of the leaping wood fires. It is a warm and friendly place.
Orlando remains outside and amuses the younger children by jumping
onto a very ancient bicycle and riding it full pelt down into the meadow,
his portly form precariously balanced on the saddle. Silvana goes into
the kitchen to help her sister with the supper. They are going to eat
Zuppa di Ceci, a thick soup of chick peas flavoured with anchovies, garlic
and rosemary, then chicken marinated in olive oil and lemon juice,
flavoured with bay and rosemary leaves then grilled over the open fire:
Pollo alla Brace.

To make *Zuppa di Ceci* as Silvana's sister does it, for six people you
will need 350 g or 12 oz of softened *ceci* or chick peas, 350 g or 12 oz
of *bietole*, spinach beet, three tablespoons of olive oil, one clove of
garlic, one onion, two anchovies, a dessert spoon of tomato concentrate, a sprig of rosemary, salt and pepper.

The evening before, you must set the dried chick peas to soak in
abundant cold water. Wash the *bietole*, discarding any yellow leaves,
and cook it in just the water that clings to the leaves until they have
wilted. Drain it well, squeezing away all the moisture with your hands,
and chop it up into small pieces. In a large pan heat the olive oil and
in this set the clove of garlic and the chopped onion to just turn colour,
then add the anchovies. Crush them into the onion until they disintegrate but do not allow them to burn. When they are well mixed in
add the drained *ceci*, let them take on the flavour of the *soffritto* (the
chopped onions and anchovy) by stirring the mixture with a wooden
spoon and leaving it to simmer for a few minutes. Then add the *bietole*,
the spoonful of tomato concentrate which you may dilute in a little
hot water and the sprig of rosemary which must be kept whole so that
it is easily removed well before the end of the cooking. You must not
use dried rosemary for this recipe. Season with pepper and taste for
salt as there will be some from the anchovies. Finally cover the ingredients with water, mix it all together, cover the pan and allow it to
cook gently for about three hours until the *ceci* are tender. To serve
the soup, toast pieces of bread, one for each person, lay one in every
soup bowl and pour on a ladleful of the hot soup. A dribble of the
best olive oil makes a good addition.

To prepare the *Pollo alla Brace* for four people you will need a
maize-fed chicken of about 1 kilo or a little more in weight, about 2½ lbs,
one glass of olive oil, the juice of a large lemon, two cloves of garlic,

a small bunch of parsley, a bay leaf, a sprig of rosemary, salt and black pepper.

Split the chicken down the back, open it out and press it flat. In a large flat dish mix up a marinade of the oil and lemon juice, adding the garlic which you must chop up finely with the bunch of parsley. You chop up the garlic together with the parsley so that the garlic juice will be caught on the parsley leaves and not be left on the chopping board. Then give the marinade extra flavour with the bay leaves, the rosemary and the salt and pepper.

Let the chicken marinate in this mixture for about two hours, turning the fowl occasionally so that each side is flavoured. Then cook the chicken on a hot grill over an open fire, or alternatively, use a barbecue in the garden.

When the food is almost ready Silvana helps to lay the long kitchen table. The two women, Sauro and his seven cousins all crowd onto the wooden benches; Orlando sits at one head of the table and his brother-in-law at the other. By now it has grown dark and the oil lamps have been lit, giving a soft light brightened by the flickering flames of the log fire. They eat the soup with its base of home-made toasted bread, then the chicken, which is accompanied by a simple salad. After supper is over and the children have enjoyed Silvana's chocolates, Orlando starts up the car as it is time for them to return to the *fattoria*, where Monday morning's work will begin before six o'clock.

❦ NOVEMBER

The wooded slopes of the valley and the highest hills behind the *fattoria* are planted with immense chestnut trees; old pathways, now overgrown, run along the hillside between the lines of trees, brambles choke the way and autumns of fallen leaves lie feet-deep in places, providing fertile mould for the *funghi*. The chestnuts and the paths to reach them were planted and laid out many, many years ago when times were much harder. People then would harvest the nuts, dry them in the heat of fires of oak leaves and grind them into flour. This together with other grains was made into an unappetizing bread which the Cerottis call *castagnaccia*, a poor food that still brings back memories of deprivation. This chestnut flour is still available. It is finely ground, a pale beige in colour and has a faint sweet flavour.

During this month, when there is a little more time for repose, Orlando's mother comes to stay with the family for a short while. She is an exceptional woman with great vitality and force of personality, a very animated ninety-one-year-old. She is totally deaf but incredibly talkative and easy to communicate with as she skilfully asks questions that require one-word replies. In the evenings they all sit together around the fire. She knits the traditional black and white flecked wool socks, her old hands flicking continually as she sits in the warmest seat in the hearth, a privilege of the elderly in Italian country households.

More logs are brought in and the fire roars up the chimney. Sauro suggests roasting some chestnuts and fetches some from one of the upper storerooms. Guido goes into the pantry to get the huge iron pan, the *briscia*. It is shaped like a large frying pan with a yard-long handle ending in a curlicue and the bowl is pierced with a pattern of round holes. It is made of iron. They put some chestnuts in this then hold it over the flames that are roaring fiercely; this is the reason for the handle being so long. Guido tosses the chestnuts until they are hot and bursting, and now and then Silvana splashes on some white wine to make them tender.

Orlando's mother starts to reminisce about the days when she was newly married and living in a large household with her mother-in-law. She says that in the days before commercial mouse poison was available the mice were a great enemy, always trying to insinuate themselves into the storerooms, where their sensitive noses smelt rich pickings from miles away. To combat the greedy creatures she would fetch a wooden tub; it had to be made of wood so that the mice would be able to climb up it. Then she would fill the tub to the top with water and on the surface would sprinkle a thick layer of chestnut flour. The mice, attracted by the heady scent of the flour, would be drawn into the tub to eat where, tricked by the seemingly solid surface, they would promptly fall into the water and drown.

As well as for baiting this bucolic mouse-trap, she also used the flour for making sweet cakes, one of which is called *Baldino di Castagna*. Silvana makes the *baldino* too as she remembers it from her childhood. The cake is made by mixing the soft sweet flour into a loose paste with water and some warm olive oil. When the paste is well mixed Silvana pours it into a round flat tin which has been oiled, again with olive oil. Sometimes Silvana flavours the cake by scattering rosemary over the top and sometimes a little lemon peel cut into tiny splinters. To cook it she puts the flat tin on top of some embers beside the fire then covers it with an old saucepan lid, on top of which she piles more hot embers. In this way she has constructed a very primitive oven. This is how the cake was cooked when she was a girl, though now she very often puts it into her new oven on a medium heat. The cake is done when the top has become a dark chestnut brown and has a cracked surface. There is also a delicious smell of nuts and chocolate. In fact the cake has a mild faintly chocolaty flavour. The olive oil and the rosemary, so often the garnish for meats, impart a curious very old-fashioned taste. Another version of the cake, which is rather richer and a recipe that is probably more in general use in Tuscany, adds currants and sultanas, pine kernels and nuts. These are mixed in with the paste and then scattered in decorative patterns on the top of the cake before it is put into the oven.

 To make a **Baldino di Castagna** you will need about 500 g or 1 lb 2 oz of chestnut flour, a pinch of salt, enough water to convert the flour into a rather liquid dough, two dessertspoons of olive oil, a few fresh rosemary leaves or a dessertspoon of lemon peel cut into tiny splinters.

Put the flour into a mixing bowl and slowly add water, stirring all the time with a wooden spoon. When the mixture is even and of a consistency to pour easily add the spoons of olive oil and mix them in well. Have ready a round shallow cake tin which you must oil with olive oil, both the sides and the bottom. Bring your oven to a medium heat then pour the chestnut mixture into the cake tin to the depth of about half an inch. Sprinkle the rosemary or the lemon peel over the top and put the cake into the oven until you can smell a delicious scent and the top of the cake is a deep crusty brown.

Silvana, although she always makes a *crostata* for their Sunday lunch, has far more time to bake cakes in the winter when she has less work than the daily feeding of her army of work people. She is very fond of a nice *ciambellone*, which is a sort of plain sponge cake. In a large mixing bowl she beats up three of her fresh eggs together with some sugar, then she slowly adds flour in which she has mixed some baking powder. There is no such thing as self-raising flour in Italy; *lievito* for cakes is bought in paper packets and is often flavoured with vanilla. With the flour she adds half a cup of milk into which she has poured about 70 g of melted butter. Then she adds a small glass of brandy or *vin santo*, maybe *mistra*, whatever her mood indicates. Sometimes she also adds some currants. She has ready a deep round tin which she has thoroughly greased with butter and then sprinkled with very fine breadcrumbs. Sometimes she puts an old cup without a handle into the tin to produce a cake with a hole in its middle. She pours the cake mixture into the tin and then cooks it in a fairly hot oven.

 To make a **Ciambellone** you will need 500 g or 18 oz of flour, three eggs, 250 g or 9 oz of sugar, six level teaspoons of baking powder, half a teacup of milk, 70 g or 3 oz of melted butter and a small glass of liqueur, *mistra* or brandy or possibly rum.

In a large mixing bowl beat up the eggs with the sugar then add a little at a time the flour, the milk which has been mixed with the melted butter and the liqueur. Have ready a cake tin or mould which you have greased with butter or olive oil. Pour the mixture into the mould and place it in a fairly hot oven for about half an hour. Check to see if it is cooked through by piercing the cake with a skewer; if the skewer emerges dry it is time to take the *ciambellone* out of the oven.

Silvana's *crostata* is really a sort of a tart but it is made from a more cake-like mixture than an ordinary pastry. She makes the cake dough with melted butter, flour, a little sugar, eggs, salt and a sachet of baking powder. She works all the ingredients into a soft dough and leaves it to rest for half an hour or so. Then on her wooden table in the pantry she rolls out the dough fairly thickly, about 1 cm, and lays it in a floured flat tin, pressing it down well and making a small wall around the sides of the tin. Sometimes Silvana flavours the tart with a layer of *marmellata*, jam, then she uses scraps of dough to make a latticework over the surface of the jam. At other times she will lay on a layer of thinly-sliced apple which she then sprinkles with sugar. In the autumn when there are heaps of fresh walnuts in the attic she will crush up the nuts and mix them with honey and use this to fill the *crostata*. Whatever its form, it is then put into the oven to bake. This homely, rather solid tart is very popular in Tuscany in country households. Most country women will either make or buy one from the local baker to eat after the heavy Sunday lunches and to offer to friends and family who come visiting on Sunday evenings.

 To make a **Crostata di Marmellata** you will need 300 g or about 12 oz of flour, 150 g or 5½ oz of sugar, 150 g or 5½ oz of butter, two large eggs, two scant teaspoons of baking powder, a pinch of salt and three or four tablespoons of apricot jam.

In a bowl mix the flour, sugar, melted butter, the beaten egg, salt and baking powder into a soft dough. Roll this *pasta frolla* into a ball and leave it to rest for about half an hour in a cool place. Meanwhile choose a shallow baking tin and grease it well with butter. After the dough has rested cut a little more than a third of it off and leave it aside. Take the larger portion and press it into the shape of the base of your baking tin; push the dough into the tin and press it well with your fingers so it completely covers the bottom of the tin. Roll out most of the rest of the dough on a floured board into one long strip which you must use to build a shallow, half-inch wall around the edge of the baking tin. Into the well that you have made spread the apricot jam with a knife. Roll the remainder of the dough out and cut it into strips; make a lattice with these strips to decorate the jam. Have your oven heated to a medium heat and cook the *crostata* in it for about half an hour.

Silvana also likes to bake apples in the oven which she takes from wooden trays where they have been laid to keep during the winter. She prepares the apples simply by removing the cores and filling the hole with sugar and lemon peel, then she puts the apples with some melted butter and a little water into a dish which she places in the hot oven. She bastes the apples occasionally with their juice and they are done when soft and bursting. Another simple sweet dish that she makes is more in the nature of a restorative than a pudding, her *zabajone*. To concoct this she beats up the yolk of an egg with a spoonful of sugar until it is smooth and creamy, then very slowly she beats in a glass of Paulo's lemony-sweet *vin santo*.

 To prepare **Mele in Forno** for four people you will need four large apples, four dessertspoons of sugar, the peel of half a lemon cut into tiny splinters, a tablespoon of butter and half a glass of water.

Core the apples and fill their centres with the sugar and lemon peel mixed together. Put the apples upright in a baking tin or terracotta dish, arranging them so that they fit fairly tightly and support each other. Melt the butter and pour it around the base of the apples, then add the water. Cook them in a medium oven until they are soft and bursting. If you leave a little room in the dish then you will be able to baste the apples every now and again with their own juice.

 To make Silvana's **Zabajone** for two people you will need two yolks of egg that are absolutely fresh, two heaped teaspoons of fine sugar and two glasses of marsala or excellent dry *vin santo*. Beat the egg yolks and sugar together until they are frothy and creamy, then slowly add the *vin santo* or marsala, beating the mixture as you pour in the liquid. Pour the *zabajone* into two of your prettiest glasses and serve it on a small tray.

As well as the rather conventional baked cakes, there are many Tuscan recipes for fried sweet cakes. In February, as we have seen, Silvana makes copious amounts of the *castagnole*, which have nothing to do with chestnuts or chestnut flour but are rather like small dense doughnuts. Silvana also makes *cenci*, for which she needs flour, butter, sugar, eggs, rum or *vin santo* or brandy. She forms these ingredients into a dough which she works for a long while, this step being necessary for the correct elastic texture of the raw *cenci*. When the dough has rested for half an hour she rolls it out to the thickness of a coin. With a little pastry wheel she cuts the dough into ribbons which she twists into knots; other pieces she cuts into odd shapes as the fancy takes her. When the pastry is all cut she plunges the knots a few at a time into boiling oil and fries them until they are a golden brown. When they are done, well drained and cool she sprinkles them with vanilla-flavoured icing sugar.

 For a nice big bowl of **Cenci** you will need 250 g or 9 oz of flour, 25 g or 1 oz of melted butter, 30 g or 1½ oz of fine sugar, two eggs, a little brandy, rum or *mistra*, a little grated orange peel and a pinch of salt.
  In a large mixing bowl add to the flour and sugar all the wet ingredients, the salt and the small spoonful of grated orange peel. Work all these things into a firm dough. You must work the dough for a long while with your hands on a floured board to give it the necessary elasticity. When you are satisfied that it has the correct texture, which will allow it to be easily tied into knots, then leave it aside in a cool place for about half an hour, covering it with a clean cloth. After this period roll out the dough to the thickness of a coin, then with a sharp knife or a bevelled pastry wheel cut the dough into strips about half an inch wide and about five inches long. Twist these strips into simple knots. Now you must have ready on the stove a pan full of bubbling arachide oil. Do not use corn oil as this will leave a nasty greasy coat upon the *cenci*. Plunge the knots a few at a time into the boiling oil and cook them until they are a golden brown; scoop them out of the oil with a perforated spoon and let them drain on kitchen paper. When all the knots are cooked put them into a large bowl and sprinkle them with sifted sugar.

The recipe and the method of cooking the *castagnole* and the *cenci* are very similar, however, the *castagnole* are made with a raising agent so that they form plump little cushions, whereas the *cenci* must remain flat.

Cenci in Italian means rags, small pieces of cloth, and your bowl full of the cakes should look like a bowl of twisted golden rags.

Although Silvana does not any longer make her own bread as her mother-in-law still does once a week in the old stone bread oven, she still has time for and enjoys making *schiacciata*, which is a flat pizza-type bread that can be flavoured in different ways. When she has a mind to bake the bread, she makes sure that the fire is burning brightly then goes to the pantry to find the *pannaio*. This is a round slab of heavy earthenware about fifteen inches in diameter and three inches thick. Growing out of the top is a ridge that serves as a handle: the *pannaio* is exceedingly heavy. These old-fashioned clay slabs are hard to find. Silvana bought hers from a very old man on the Umbrian side of the valley who is famous for his handiwork. Modern ones tend to be made of circular pieces of concrete with a thin metal handle embedded on one of the surfaces. She sets the *pannaio* right on the brightly burning fire to heat up.

In the pantry Silvana scoops out flour from the sack. Her scoop, hand-carved from wood, holds about a kilo of flour. She also has several smaller scoops that hold different measures, one of which she uses for sugar. She never bothers to calculate her amounts exactly: time has taught her what quantities are needed, how many handfuls of this and that, how big a pinch is and what the size a glass should be. The only time she uses her balance is when she weighs a cheese for selling and then she calculates accurately enough. Her balance is of the old-fashioned sort which the stall holders in the markets use and which can still be bought from country ironmongers. It works on the same principle as the yard balance. From one end of a square thin rod marked out in 100-gram divisions there hangs, by three chains, a flat circular brass dish; at the other end of the rod there are a couple of hooks from which weights can be hung. The cheese is put in the pan then an appropriate weight is chosen, probably a kilo, and hung upon the hook. Any difference in the two weights is made up by sliding a piece of metal along the rod with its divisions of grams to the opposite place. The balance is held in the hand by a central decorative handle.

Silvana makes a dent in the mound of flour she has heaped on the scrubbed old wooden table. Into the dent she pours some yeast that has been fizzing gently in a glass of warm water. Orlando buys the fresh yeast from the village shop. She adds a small amount of olive oil and some salt. The *schiacciata*, unlike the ordinary Tuscan bread which is made of three ingredients, flour, yeast and water, is flavoured with salt and enriched with oil. *Schiacciata* must be eaten fresh. Bread is kept, so the absence of salt which would attract water makes the bread become dry rather than mouldy. When the liquid has been poured in she starts to fold the flour in; quenching the water, she works the dough, kneading it strongly and rhythmically, pushing with the heel of one hand and pulling back with the other in a rocking motion. When she is satisfied with the texture of the dough she wraps it in a clean cloth and returns to the kitchen to set it in a pan to rest in the warm stone cavity under the hearthstone. It will rest there for about half an hour and should increase to about twice its size.

The *pannaio* becomes white hot as it has to be to cook the bread. To test the heat Silvana sprinkles flour onto the stone: the flour browns immediately. She punches the risen dough into a rough circular shape and then slaps it onto the scalding stone; this needs practice. The next step is to prick the bread all over with a large fork. After a few minutes she puts a huge saucepan lid right over the *pannaio* and on top of this heaps glowing embers, which will serve to cook the top of the bread. It can, of course, be cooked in the conventional oven but Silvana enjoys using the old-fashioned method. She makes the bread with several different flavours too. Sometimes she will anoint the surface with olive oil and sprinkle on coarse salt and rosemary leaves. Then sometimes she spreads the dough with a little *concentrato di pomodoro* and maybe a little finely-sliced onion. Occasionally she will add some small pieces of anchovy. These flavoured breads are very popular in Tuscany. In Cortona during the *Carnevale* before Lent they sell a special bread strongly seasoned with ground black pepper and small pieces of crunchy roasted *prosciutto*. In Arezzo there is one baker who makes small round loaves of brown bread stuffed with green olives which are delicious and very pretty to look at and arrange on the table. The basic reason for these seasoned breads is that in years long gone by, when bread was the basic daily food, on festive occasions it could be made more interesting quite cheaply with small additions to the ordinary dough. Whatever their history, these savoury breads are still deservedly popular.

There is one sort of bread that Silvana remembers from her childhood which is really an old *piatto povero*, poor man's food, a term used in Italy to describe dishes that certainly were eaten by poor people but are no less delicious for that. These particular bread-cakes are called *ficattole* and are made from pieces of bread dough left over from the weekly baking. The dough must be rolled out and cut into strips about 10 cm long with a slash down the centre. Then they are fried in copious amounts of olive oil until they are a golden brown and have swollen slightly, and then drained well on kitchen paper; Silvana's mother would have used brown paper. When they are cooked they can be used in two ways, sweetened or salted. They can be sprinkled with a little sugar and used to dip into milky coffee or sprinkled with salt and dipped into white wine to accompany a supper dish. Either way Silvana becomes quite nostalgic when she remembers the treat they used to be on baking day when she was little.

 To make the *Schiacciata* you will need, for 350g or 12½ oz of hard flour, 15g or a little more than ½ oz of fresh yeast, water and olive oil sufficient to mix and a pinch of salt.

Crumble the yeast into a glass and add to it a little warm water. Mix it into a paste, then add more water and keep mixing until the glass is nearly full. Let the yeast fizz away to itself for a few minutes. Meanwhile heap your flour onto the pastry board and make a dip in the middle; into this dip scatter the salt, pour the glass of yeast and the oil, about a spoonful, and gradually mix the liquid into the flour by pushing the flour inwards into the pool of yeast. Knead the dough until it is smooth and elastic, work it on the floured board and when you are satisfied with the texture put it into a flour-sprinkled earthenware crock, cover it with a clean cloth and leave it in a warm place to rise. Silvana puts hers under the fireplace. She leaves her dough to rise for about half an hour or so, but to make it rise completely it will need more like two hours. While the dough is rising, heat your oven to Gas mark 6 or 400F or 200C. Have a baking sheet ready, which you must cover with a film of olive oil. You may also have ready some salt, a saucer of olive oil and a pastry brush, maybe a little tomato concentrate, a few very thinly sliced onion rings or even some sage leaves. When the dough has risen put the ball on a board and work it with your hands into roughly the shape of the baking sheet. Transfer it to the sheet and prick holes here and there with a large fork. Alternatively you can make small round dents here and there with your finger. Dip the pastry brush in olive oil and paint the surface of the dough, then as you please sprinkle on a little salt and few rosemary leaves, or tomato concentrate and onions, whatever takes your fancy. Put the baking sheet into the hot oven and let it cook for about ten minutes or more depending on the thickness of your dough. It should be a golden brown colour when it is done, and you must eat it hot from the oven. Split it if you like and make sandwiches filled with thin slices of *prosciutto*. Silvana often makes it plain with just oil and salt and serves it hot with *prosciutto* or *salame* for the morning *merenda*. You may also use this dough for making *pizze*, but leave out the salt and oil.

The narrow paths that criss-cross among the chestnut trees in the forests are now used mostly by the *cinghiale*, the wild boar who have their dens in the thickest parts of the wood. Normally these animals stay hidden away in the woods but occasionally at night they venture into the cultivated part of the valley. Orlando, who is a fine shot and a member of a Cortonese hunters' society, sometimes organizes a boar hunt on his land. The boar are never hunted by one man alone; they are too dangerous and prone to turn and attack with their sharp tusks when angered and frightened. So from time to time Orlando's companions will come from Cortona for some sport. The hills resound with the harsh cries of the twenty or so men who join in the hunt. They beat the forest and yell as loud as they can to drive out a boar that has been recently spotted. They are successful; shots crack through the air and a great cheer rings out. From a thicket at the edge of the meadow the men stumble dishevelled into the open, two of them proudly carrying their prize, a medium-sized specimen with grizzled bristles and ugly yellowed tusks. They all march in a line back to the *fattoria* to celebrate.

Silvana is always delighted when she has a piece of *cinghiale* to cook if the animal is a young one. An old male has a disagreeable scent which is very hard to get rid of and besides the flesh is tough and requires days of marinating to make it tender enough to eat. Most recipes for wild boar in Italy are fairly involved and contain instructions for elaborate marinades that are highly spiced and flavoured. Then after the marinating the meat is usually cooked *in umido* to avoid the tendency to toughness.

 When Orlando bags a boar, Silvana cooks it in quite a different way. She will take some pieces from the loin of a young animal; the meat is pale and coarse-grained, looking more like *vitello* than domestic pork. She washes it carefully, not bothering to dry it very thoroughly, then she cuts it up into chunks and puts it into a pan in which some chopped garlic and some sage leaves have been stewing in olive oil. After she has turned the meat over to seal it on all sides she adds a large glass of white wine and leaves the meat to simmer slowly, adding more wine if there is a danger of the meat drying out. When it is done the flesh is tender and has a more subtle flavour than ordinary pork. Maybe Silvana can successfully cook the *cinghiale* in this simple manner without the long complicated preparations and highly seasoned ingredients that are suggested in cookery books because she knows the state of the animal when it is brought home. She is not buying a piece of meat on a butcher's slab whose age she has no accurate way of telling. Perhaps it has always been felt that a strong selvatic animal like a boar deserves a rich, time-consuming treatment. However Silvana prepares this meat with excellent results and the minimum of fuss. And there again is an example of her particular style of Tuscan cooking.

The wind-driven clouds sweep over Orlando's fields, now as bare as the large-leafed trees. His worries are over; the tobacco is safely in, now he can look forward to the old-fashioned olive harvest and the festive month of December. But this month there is still the ploughing to be considered and the sowing of a few fields of winter wheat. Soon his tractors are ripping into the dark soil, ploughing under the tall thick tobacco stalks and disturbing the light green of the fields that have been left fallow. The men sow the seed by hand, walking through the furrows with an old satchel under one arm, scattering the seed with the flinging gesture that men have used since it occurred to them to till the land, a gesture repeated in the valley every year from times before the Romans.

The sweet-smelling bales of tobacco, each weighing a *quintale* or 100 kilos, have been stored in every conceivable part of the house since the last picking was dried. The attics, the room off the pantry where the telephone is kept, even the chapel is stacked high. Today they expect the government official who will inspect the tobacco and offer a price for it. Orlando will be pleased when he has struck a bargain, the bales have been taken off in lorries and the cash is safely in the bank. Silvana is preparing an excellent lunch for the official, knowing quite well that these city men often have a sentimental nostalgia for country life and a good lunch would be likely to put him into a mellow mood, all the better to bargain with.

One of her enormous Tuscan chickens would seem to be the answer, well cooked over the open fire. Having cleaned the bird, Silvana splits it down the middle with her iron cleaver but not quite through so as to separate the halves, then she flattens the carcass slightly with her hands. She makes quite deep cuts into the joints and slits small pockets in the chicken breasts. Then on her enormous four-inch thick chopping block, dark with use, hollowed in the middle from the *mezzaluna*, its handle swallow-tailed like the crenellations on a ghibelline tower, she chops eight huge cloves of garlic, a handful of fresh sage leaves and two walnuts of sweet butter. This she mixes together with a good teaspoonful of coarse salt and half a teaspoonful of ground black pepper. The fragrant hot pepper she buys in paper bags of about a pound in weight. When the seasoning is well mixed she stuffs it energetically into the cuts in the chicken. The spices and sage will season the bird and the butter will keep it moist and tender. Then she rubs the chicken well with some olive oil and sprinkles on more coarse salt and places it on a large trivet over some hot wood cinders. As the chicken browns she turns it, taking care that it does not burn, adding more hot cinders when the fire cools, and she sprinkles it occasionally with more olive oil and sometimes a little wine vinegar. This has the effect of slowing down the cooking if the fire is a little too hot and also makes the flesh tender.

To go with the chicken, Silvana decides upon some *Patate in Umido*. To make them Silvana slices the pared potatoes as thinly as they can be without dissolving into a mush; it is preferable to use the sort of potato that is waxy, not floury. She rinses the slices, pats them quite dry and puts them into a deep china bowl. Then she makes a mixture of some of her basil-flavoured tomato *conserva* and a glass of white wine. She pours this sauce into the potatoes and mixes them well until they are evenly coated. At this point she adds a couple of bay leaves to the mixture. In a large deepish *tegame* she browns some cloves of garlic in olive oil until they are a pale gold, no darker in case they catch. Then, having seasoned the potatoes with salt and freshly-ground black pepper, she tips them into the hot oil and lets them cook gently until the potatoes are soft. She turns them carefully to prevent them from breaking up too much, and if they are in any danger of sticking she adds a little more of the tomato conserve. Potatoes have never been completely accepted by the Italians, who already have their traditional staples from the rice of the north, to the *polenta*, the Tuscan bread and the southern pasta. However they certainly have a place in Italian cuisine. Potatoes roasted in a pan underneath a spit-roast of lamb or veal, flavoured with rosemary and the rich drippings from the meat, are a truly Tuscan delight, in this area so famous for its grilled meats.

 To cook a ***Pollo al Salvia e Aglio***, the chicken flavoured with sage and garlic, you will need to feed four people one plump free-range maize-fed chicken, a bunch of fresh sage leaves, six cloves of garlic which should be white fleshed and fresh, 50 g or 2 oz of saltless butter, coarse salt and freshly ground black pepper.

On your chopping block, chop the sage and garlic together, and add about two level teaspoons of salt and one of pepper to the sage and garlic mixture. Add to this little heap of stuffing the cold butter which you must cut into small dice. Mix these all together. If you are going to roast the chicken in the oven in your normal way, prepare it in this manner. Slit the skin over the breast and loosen it from the flesh. Into these two pockets put half your stuffing, push it well into the slits so that it covers the two breasts. Make deep cuts where the legs of the chicken join the body and stuff these with the rest of the sage mixture. Truss the chicken, rub it with a little olive oil, sprinkle it with coarse salt and roast it in the oven in the ordinary way. You can also treat half or quarter chickens in the same way and cook them on the charcoal grill in the garden, sprinkling them from time to time with olive oil and a few drops of wine vinegar. If you do not like the flavour of sage use fresh parsley instead, which tastes even better.

To make a dish of **Patate al Pomodoro**, potatoes flavoured with tomatoes, you will need 500 g or 18 oz of thinly-sliced potatoes of the waxy sort and half a pint of tomato *conserva*. You can use *passato di pomodoro*; Parmalat make a good version called *Pomi* which is available in some Italian food stores in London, or tinned tomatoes which have been thoroughly drained and chopped, or the same quantity of the pulp of fresh skinned tomatoes. Also a glass of white wine, two bay leaves, salt and black pepper, two cloves of garlic and half a glass of olive oil.

In a china bowl mix the potatoes (which you have rinsed and dried) with the tomato *conserva* and the wine, and then add the bay leaves and season with salt and black pepper. In a large deep frying pan cook the chopped garlic in the olive oil until it is a pale gold colour; do not let it burn. Next tip the potatoes into the hot olive oil. Let them cook on a very low flame, and turn them frequently so that they all cook through. If they show any signs of sticking add a little more tomato or wine.

Whether it is the good quality of Orlando's tobacco or the excellence of Silvana's cooking that influences the inspector is debatable, however he and Orlando strike a satisfactory bargain and the family fortune is secured for another year. The inspector drives off, happily clutching one of Silvana's best *pecorino* cheeses. He also had a chance to taste the new wine; in fact there were a group of them gathered in the kitchen when Guido, who is the chief vintner, brought in a jug of the new vintage for them all to taste and pronounce judgement upon. Silvana, Orlando, his mother, the inspector, the postman Ugo, Menchino and Guido all had a glass to taste the new brew which is now ready to be sealed into the barrels. Orlando is pleased. The red wine is very dark, almost black: in fact, red wine is often called *nero* not *rosso* in this part of Italy for that reason. He is also delighted that the wine is a degree stronger than last year's. The white is up to its usual standard but this year appears especially limpid.

The nights are becoming cold. At about nine-thirty each evening Silvana brings out some small tin pots with wire handles rather like small paint pots and she fills them with red embers from the fire. She takes the pots upstairs, shivering in the cold air of the stone stairway. She turns back the covers of their huge high bed and exposes the priest laying between the linen sheets. This *prêté* is made of curved slats of wood fashioned into a boat-shaped cage inside which can be hung the pots of embers. Carefully hanging the pot so as not to scorch the sheets, she covers the *prêté* over again with the bedclothes, leaving a large hump in the centre of the bed looking exactly as if someone were lying there. This antique device, still on sale in country stores, will warm their bed beautifully before they retire to sleep.

❧ DECEMBER

Now is the time to collect fuel for the home fires. Orlando's labourers turn from the ploughs and set to work in the forests felling trees and cutting up trunks that have been left in their fallen state over years to season. Now that the sap is finally dry, the wood is suitable to be cut into logs and sold in the cities. Huge lorries arrive at the Cerottis' to collect the wood and all day the shrill sounds of chain-saws break the silence of the hills. The tractors grind down the pathways with their loads of logs and it is only when the heaviest rains turn the earth to sticky clinging mud that the machines are put away and in some farms the few remaining white oxen are harnessed to their wooden sleds and used to haul the timber.

This is also a good time of year for planting new trees before the ground hardens with the real winter cold and the snow appears. This year Orlando plans to plant several cypresses to fill some gaps in his drive. A lorry laden with trees arrives from a *vivaista*, a plant and tree seller in Cortona. Orlando has also ordered five new cypresses to replace five dead trees that form part of a semi-circle around the little stone monument at the crossroads. This monument was erected after the war to the memory of the ten men and one woman from the village who were executed by the Nazis on that spot. These villagers were in the Resistance and were caught, some in the cornfields, some in the woods, after they had attacked a German army patrol. They were herded into a house that stood beside the cross-road and the house was then dynam- ited. Miraculously one man escaped alive, sheltered under a massive beam that fell diagonally from the roof to the floor. He still attends the yearly memorial service for the dead. Strangely enough this remote valley was on the path of the allied advance in Italy and there was much hand-to-hand fighting and gunfire around the quiet fields.

December is the month when Orlando usually chooses to gather his olives, although many gather their's in November and even in late October. It all depends on the area and on the extent of ripeness that the farmer wants from his crop. Some olives are picked when they are immature and green and are preserved in brine, others are left until they are a strange, almost porphyry-purple colour. This is the state in which, although the olive is not completely ripe, it is more nutritious and will make more deliciously flavoured oil. The berries become a shiny black when they are totally ripe.

There are two basic methods of collecting the olives. Some farmers prefer to spread nets under the trees and allow the ripe olives to drop into them. This method is obviously not labour-intensive but the olives gathered in this manner do not make the best oil. Orlando and Silvana prefer the old-fashioned, finger-numbing method of gathering the olives by hand. Silvana excavates the old olive baskets from a corner of the attic. These baskets are of a very particular apron-like shape; constructed of small branches and osiers, they are flat on one side and curved in a semi-circular bowl on the other. The flat side is held against the stomach with the aid of the gatherer's belt and a wooden catch. The semi-circular basket sticks out in front ready to receive the olives; in this way both the hands are left free for picking. The men, each with a basket slung at his waist, climb up to the grove on the terraced slope above the *fattoria*, taking a couple of rough wooden ladders to reach to the tops of the gnarled old trees. After all the olives are picked, Orlando will take them to Cortona to the *frantoia* where they will be pressed, then he will bring back the oil to be stored in large pottery jars in the ground-floor store-room next to the pantry. One hundred kilos of oil will be sufficient to last the household for about a year.

The best quality olive oil comes from olives that are hand-picked before they are completely ripe and black, and the oil must be the product of the first pressing in a cold press, that is, ground between stones in the old-fashioned way and not in a machine. This is called *Olio di Prima Spremitura*; it is pure olive oil, unaffected by heat and is the most flavourful and easily digestible of all cooking oils. It is also extremely expensive and not easily found in normal shops even in Italy. However some of the most superior food stores in the large towns and cities do sell this oil; very often it comes from the olive groves of famous vineyards and wine producers. Its good flavour some-what depends on the type of soil and the area in which the olive is grown and the test of its purity is that it contains 1% or less of oleic acid.

There are several grades of olive oil and they are again distinguished by the percentage of acid they contain. *Olio Extravergine d'Oliva*, the best olive oil that is available normally, contains not more than 1% oleic acid. *Olio Sopraffino Vergine d'Oliva* has not more than 1.5%, then there is *Olio Fino Vergine d'Oliva* with 3% and, finally, *Olio Vergine d'Oliva* with not more than 4% acid content. Obviously the *Extravergine* will have the best flavour; it will be the most expensive, but is the most excellent and flavoursome oil to pour over a salad or onto a hot vegetable. The cheaper olive oils are splendidly adequate for frying and other types of cooking.

The yield of oil from a *quintale* of olives, that is 100 kilos, is a source of much discussion. Some farmers claim as much as 16 kilos for every 100 kilos of berries, others insist that nine is more usual. About ten to twelve is probably the average, though much depends on the quality of the olives themselves and the soil on which they are grown. In one exceptional year Orlando obtained 19 kilos per 100 and was delighted. Italians are fiercely partisan about the quality and flavour of their oils. Lucca in the north of Tuscany claims to have the best oil in Italy, a claim hotly disputed by southerners who say their oil is the richest and best. Personally I find that the green oil from the hills around Florence has the truest, sweetest, most fruity flavour of all, though the Aretini would not agree. In short the Italians prefer their own. Silvana certainly does; in her opinion olive oil bought from shops and coming from other parts of Italy is a suspect substance. She knows her own oil contains nothing but good olives. Choosing oil therefore remains a question of personal taste. When buying olive oil it is worth remembering the different grades of oil and to go for an *Olio Extravergine d'Oliva* if possible. The greener and darker the oil, the fruitier and more flavourful it is likely to be. Avoid pale yellowish Italian olive oil as it can be too refined, with a resulting loss of flavour. Price, too, is a good guide: the best is usually the most expensive.

Olive oil belongs to the warm Mediterranean. It complements the fiery flavours of garlic and peppers and the oily aromatic wild oregano that are used in Provence, Spain and Greece. Although there is a belt of butter based cooking in its northern regions, Italy firmly belongs to the list of countries cooking in the Mediterranean way. Tuscan food depends upon oil. Bread and olive oil together are a foundation of Tuscan cooking and this is well demonstrated by the numerous olive groves that cover the landscape. Olive oil is another of the basic ingredients that is always in copious supply in Silvana's kitchen and which gives her cooking its character. She of course uses it in nearly all her cookery from salads, roasts and grills, and dishes cooked *in umido* right through to soups. The only things for which she will select a lighter oil are deep-fried *polpette* or vegetables coated in flour and egg and sweet fried cakes. For these she uses an arachide oil or one made from mixed vegetable oils. However when she wants the dish to be extra delicious she will use olive oil, as in years gone by when everything was cooked in olive oil including the *castagnole* and *cenci*.

It is of course very easy in France and Italy to obtain excellent olive oil from even the simplest of food stores. In countries which do not produce their own olives matters are a little more difficult. However good oil can be obtained and it is worth the extra expense involved. The oil used in a dish is basic to that dish's taste and texture. It is a false economy to cook an expensive piece of meat in cheap cooking oil. However it is not always necessary to use the finest grade of olive oil in a dish where the oil plays a small part and a strongly flavoured oil would impinge on other delicate flavours. But this is no excuse at all to use another 'vegetable oil', as is often suggested in even the most prestigious of cookery books. As well as the flavour of the oil you must consider its texture; vegetable oils such as corn oil leave a disagreeable clinging film of grease on food, which can spoil an otherwise well prepared dish. In short, it is best to use the very finest *Olio Extravergine d'Oliva* in salads, to garnish soups and in dishes where a simple vegetable provides a medium to enjoy an exquisite oil. The less expensive grades of olive oil are perfectly adequate for dishes cooked *in umido* and some fried dishes. Arachide oil can reasonably be used for deep frying as it has no taste and a light texture. Unsalted butter of course can be used instead of olive oil in certain dishes but it is not a traditional cooking medium in Tuscany. So, good olive oil can be added to the list of things to be taken home from a trip to Tuscany, but treat it like expensive scent; use it when it is fresh and new. Nothing will be gained by hoarding it in the larder until its flavour has started to deteriorate.

One of Silvana's favourite snacks when she is on her own is a simple slice of the good fresh bread onto which she has dribbled a green-gold rivulet of olive oil. The bread and oil have a satisfying flavour which is hard to improve upon even by the most talented cook. When it is very cold, olive oil solidifies and Silvana says that this solid oil tastes even better when spread on bread like butter.

 One of the traditional dishes that is always eaten at the time of the olive harvest when the oil is at its sweetest and freshest is **Bruschetta** or **Fett'unta** as it is called by the Florentines, which literally means oiled slice. Silvana often serves it for lunch at this time of year. To make it she toasts thick slices of the saltless bread over a bright fire; she browns them quickly so they are golden and crisp outside and soft within. On the chopping block there are fat cloves of garlic which she halves and rubs vigorously over both sides of the toast. Laying the slices on a large plate she drenches them with warm olive oil and sprinkles on good pinches of coarse salt. This simplest dish is the epitome of Tuscan cookery, using just the most basic ingredients of the absolute best quality and allowing them to mix together and still be themselves. The *bruschetta* can of course lend itself to additions, such as the paper-fine slices of black or white truffles so beloved of the Umbrians.

 Another surprisingly tasty luncheon dish combines the *bruschetta* with the dark long-leafed *cavolo nero*, which is a type of winter cabbage very popular in Tuscany. Silvana cooks the cabbage in boiling water for about twenty minutes. When it is done she has ready the slices of hot toast rubbed with the garlic; she dips each slice into the cabbage water to moisten it then on top of each slice she puts a small heap of drained cabbage. Over the vegetable goes the olive oil, salt and a sprinkle of black pepper. **Bruschetta al Cavolo Nero** is a very old-fashioned favourite but one really only to be found in people's homes. I have never seen it appear in a restaurant although *bruschetta* is often served as an *antipasto*.

 One of the nicest ways to eat good olive oil is in a **Pinzimonio**. This is simply a small bowl of olive oil flavoured with a very little black pepper and a small pinch of salt into which you dip a selection of fresh raw vegetables such as celery, fennel cut into small pieces, radishes and carrot sticks. It makes a lovely start to a light summer meal.

Orlando and Silvana keep their olive oil in large pottery jars and straw-covered glass demi-johns that have wide necks. The jars must be very carefully sealed with heavy lids or tight-fitting corks. This precaution is taken because mice love olive oil. If they can dislodge a lid they will climb into the jars and naturally they cannot get out again; this means that the whole jar containing twenty-eight litres will be spoilt. Silvana says that this disaster befell her family during the war and that the polluted oil could not even be used to light the little pottery lamps that they burned with old oil as fuel and a scrap of cotton as a wick.

December is of course the great month for entertaining. Festivities seem to start on the Sunday before Christmas and extend to Epiphany. On this Sunday, Silvana's brother Paulo, her sister-in-law Anna and their young son Roberto are expected from Castiglion Fiorentino for a family lunch. Silvana loves to have company as an excuse to cook a special meal and she enjoys hearing all the family news. She gets up early to make some fresh *tagliatelle*. Silvana uses the traditional recipe for making the pasta, using six eggs to one kilo or two and a half pounds of flour. Normal *pastasciutta* like spaghetti is not made with eggs but the home-made pastas and the ribbon pastas bought from the stores are often enriched with egg and this gives them a different flavour and texture. She heaps the flour onto the scrubbed pantry table and into a well in the middle she breaks the eggs; she mixes these ingredients if necessary with a little water into a firm dough. Strictly speaking the dough should then be rolled out on an enormous board or table with a very long rolling pin, one metre in length and made of wood. The dough is rolled very thinly, then rolled again until it is almost transparent; by then it hangs down the edges of the table like a tablecloth. This takes an exact texture of dough and years of experience to achieve. Next, the sheet must be rolled into a loose swiss roll shape and then, using a very sharp long knife, the roll is cut into thin slices the size of wide baby ribbon; this is the *tagliatelle*. *Tagliarini* is cut into finer strips and *pappardelle*, a favourite in Arezzo, into ribbons half an inch wide. The coils of pasta are then left to rest a while before being plunged into turbulently boiling water for the brief cooking that fresh pasta requires. It needs space, time and practise to make *tagliatelle* in this manner, so many housewives have a pasta machine like a small mangle into which they can feed already rolled out sheets of dough to achieve the required exquisite fineness.

The fine sheets are then put through a second set of rollers which cut the pasta into ribbons. Silvana uses one of these little old-fashioned machines which she has had since her marriage. She normally only makes fresh pasta for guests and family Sunday lunches. For every day, when there may be twenty or more people to feed, she uses ordinary pasta bought in vast quantities from the village shop.

As the cauldron of boiling water bubbles over the fire ready to receive the *tagliatelle*, Silvana bastes the chicken grilling on a trivet and stews some pieces of pork fillet in a pan with white wine, sage and garlic. With the chicken liver she intends to make one of her *crostini* recipes. She mashes the previously poached livers into about four ounces of softened butter to make a smooth pomade seasoned with salt and black pepper, then spreads the mixture onto thin small rounds of bread. To add variety she mixes some more butter with anchovy paste and again spreads it on more rounds of the white Tuscan bread, topping each piece with a fat caper that she has pickled herself in their own wine vinegar.

To make the **Fegatini al Burro**, you will need three large chicken livers, 3 oz of saltless butter and several capers. Poach the chicken livers in a little white wine. When they are cooked, mash them and mix them into the softened butter to form a smooth pomade. Spread on rounds of bread and top each *crostino* with a caper. The *crostini* flavoured with anchovy are made by mixing unsalted butter with either pounded anchovies or more simply anchovy paste. They are very delicate and delicious.

Silvana has several other variations on the theme of *crostini* and particularly those made with *fegatini*, chicken livers. One of her basic recipes is as follows. She chops some *odori*, onion, carrot and celery and parsley, very finely and allows them to soften in a spoon or two of olive oil. Then she adds the whole cleaned livers, a sprig of rosemary and a little white wine. She lets this simmer for a few minutes and then adds a small amount of tomato *conserva*, salt and pepper. After about ten minutes of gentle cooking she removes the livers and chops them up fairly finely and returns them to the saucepan adding too some capers. She stirs the mixture well; then it is ready to be spread on the rounds of bread one of whose surfaces she has dipped into a bowl of stock to moisten; this helps the chicken liver pâté to adhere well. Some Tuscan cooks add finely chopped *milza* or spleen to their *crostini neri* but Silvana does not have this habit, although it does add a very particular flavour.

 This more traditional recipe that Silvana often uses for the **Crostini Neri** requires the following quantities. One small onion, one small carrot, half a rib of celery, a small sprig of parsley. Three tablespoons of olive oil, five chicken livers, a sprig of rosemary, a heaped teaspoon of tomato concentrate, salt and pepper, and a glass of white wine.

Chop the *odori* and the parsley very finely and let them soften in the olive oil; add the chicken livers and the sprig of rosemary. Let the livers cook gently through then remove them from the pan; chop them finely and replace them. Next add the tomato concentrate, season with salt and pepper and add a little wine to moisten. Let the pan cook softly for ten minutes or so. Add more wine if the mixture is too dry. Remove the sprig of rosemary and spread the mixture on to your pieces of bread as already indicated.

Sometimes Silvana will simply poach the livers in white wine flavoured with rosemary and sometimes she prepares them with finely chopped onion, splinters of lemon peel, a little lemon juice and capers. These make an excitingly sharp and good contrast to the rich liver flavour. She also makes excellent *crostini* using butter, mayonnaise, chopped *sott'aceto* (crisp vegetables bottled in wine vinegar), and a little parsley, all amalgamated into a soft paste. In whatever form they come, these small piquant appetizers always start their Sunday meal. Then comes the pasta, the meat course and a salad still picked from under a cloche in the kitchen garden. As it is Christmas time, for dessert there will be the *panettone* or *pan d'oro*, which is a richer version. This is a large buttery light sponge which is the Italian equivalent of our Christmas cake, not in its appearance or taste but in the importance that it has during the festivities. The *panettone* comes in large bell-shaped boxes and is sprinkled with vanilla flavoured veiling sugar; invariably it is eaten with an *amabile*, pleasantly sweet, sparkling white wine from Piedmonte. The Italians do not treat this sparkling wine as a second-rate champagne but as what it is, a delicious fruity drink in its own right and an excellent choice to go with the dessert for a jolly celebration lunch party. After the *panettone* they will all eat various biscuits and cakes, the *ricciarelli*, rich, soft and almond flavoured, sugar covered *cenci* and they will drink Paulo's excellent dark honey-coloured *vin santo*.

While the adults gossip over the remains of their meal, Sauro and his young cousin struggle into the warm kitchen carrying a young fir tree that they have taken from the woods. They set it in a pot under the dining-room window and pester Silvana to find the Christmas decorations for them. Eventually, after rummaging around in a cupboard she finds the boxes of spun glass baubles and painted wooden figures. The boys crinkle up some brown paper to make rocks and place it beneath the tree as a foundation for the *presepio*, the crib. Among the decorations there is a small stable made of painted wood, fashioned like an old Italian house with sloping roof and overhanging eaves and beside it a dark green woolly pine tree. Then emerging from the tissue paper come beautifully modelled sheep, shepherds, angels with delicate pink, blue and gold edged gowns, the magi with splendid robes and crowns, Joseph, Mary and the child in a tiny manger. The style of the figures is copied from Botticelli's nativities. Sauro and Roberto arrange the figures in their rocky setting but leave the Christ child aside until the night of Christmas Eve. The Christmas tree is a newcomer to Tuscan country celebrations. It has become popular only during the last ten or so years and to some extent this is also true of the *presepio*. In the old days Epiphany, on January 6th, was the occasion when children were given small presents. Christmas was never a great commercialized festival and in the Tuscan countryside Christmas day is still celebrated in a quiet way.

When Sauro was a little boy and his elder brother Pietro was still alive, the family would sit around the fire late on Christmas Eve and Orlando would find small Christmas gifts for the children up in the chimney with the aid of the *ceppo*, the Christmas log. This he would do by poking the long log up into the depths of the huge chimney then bringing it down with great expressions of surprise to reveal the small toy that he had concealed up his sleeve or in his pocket. This was a source of enormous delight to the children, who could not conceive how such wonders came to be hidden in the dirty old chimney. Before they went to bed they would hang their small woolly socks from nails on the chimney piece to be miraculously filled with nuts and clementines and sweets. Always Silvana and Orlando would walk out into the cold crisp night air and down their cyprus-lined drive to the small church at the cross-roads. Here they would join their neighbours in welcoming the newly-born Christ child at the midnight mass.

In Tuscany and Umbria most families eat *tortellini* at Christmas, especially on Christmas Eve. They also eat it all the year round but Christmas time is the traditional time to eat the filled pasta. Perhaps this also dates back to the period when people spiced the bread to make it special and maybe, in the same way, enlivened their basic pasta with a filling to make it rich and festive. The small cushions of pasta have different names in diverse parts of Italy, different shapes and different fillings. *Tortellini* can also be called *tortelloni*, if they are very large, sometimes they are known as *cappelletti* or *agnolotti* and sometimes as *ravioli*; this is not such a common name as might be supposed, although it is well known in Britain in the form of the tinned variety, which bears absolutely no relationship to the real thing. Ravioli is usually filled with a mixture of ricotta cheese, a mild soft sheep's cheese, and very finely chopped spinach or *bietole*, spinach beet. It is normally served with butter, a sage leaf or two and some parmesan sprinkled over the surface. The other filled pastas, the *tortellini* and the *capelletti*, are usually filled with some sort of meat mixture: either a mixture of lean veal and pork ground very very fine, spiced with parmesan, garlic and parsley or possibly ground beef mixed maybe with *mortadella*, flavoured with rosemary, bound with red wine, enriched with parmesan and nutmeg. There are many varieties in these fillings and the pasta is usually served in a bowl of well-flavoured bouillon. They can of course come with a *pomaruola* or *sugo*, but personally I find that a heavily flavoured sauce masks the taste of these delicious filled pastas and they appear to greater advantage in *brodo*. Silvana's favourite filling is of chicken breast shredded and pounded very fine, garlic minutely minced, parsley, parmesan cheese, salt, pepper and nutmeg, the ingredients bound together into a smooth tight paste with an egg. To make her *tortellini* she uses the same dough as for her *tagliatelle* but in this case cuts out rounds of fine dough with a small circular scalloped pastry cutter. On half of the circle she places a small spoon of filling then she folds the pasta over to make a semi-circle, moistening the edges and firmly pressing them down. The *ravioli* are generally square in shape and the *tortellini* and *cappelletti* can be made by folding a square over diagonally with the stuffing inside the triangle produced, then by taking the corners of the triangle and drawing them together to form a small ring. Legend has it that one night Venus stayed at an inn in central Italy. The cook, beguiled by her beauty, stared in at her while she slept; he was so overcome with the shape of her navel that he invented *tortellini* in honour of it. Actually these small round folded bonne-bouches are rather reminiscent in shape of belly buttons. Of course they are exceptionally good when served simply with butter and some slices of truffle, especially the cheese-filled *ravioli*. In Torino it is possible to eat the subtlest and most delicious kinds of *ravioli*, sometimes filled with delicate mixtures of salt water fish, finished in sauces of butter and pine kernels, which add an interesting texture to the soft *ravioli*, or filled with *fonduta*, the rich mixture of melted cheeses that is a triumph of Italian culinary art.

 To make Silvana's **Tortellini** for six or seven people you will need 300 g or 10½ oz of poached chicken breast, 80 g or 2½ oz of grated parmesan cheese, a few sprigs of parsley, two cloves of garlic, salt, pepper and nutmeg, one egg, 300 g or 10½ oz of plain flour, and three more eggs.

Chop the chicken, the parsley and garlic very finely and mix them with the grated parmesan, the salt and pepper and a little grated nutmeg. Reduce this stuffing into a very fine paste in a pestle and mortar and bind it together with one egg. Next make a hard dough with the flour and three eggs. Roll the dough out thinly on a floured board then with a circular pastry cutter or a glass cut out rounds of dough. On to one side of each round put a spoonful of the chicken stuffing. Fold the rounds in half so that you are left with small semicircles of filled dough. Press the open semi-circular edge of each *tortellino* well together with a fork so that the stuffing will not fall out into the cooking water.

Have ready on the fire a large pan of boiling salted water; cook the *tortellini* in this until the pasta is cooked through. If the *tortellini* are fresh this will not take more than a few minutes; they will float to the top when they are done. Drain the *tortellini* thoroughly as water will dilute any sauce that you may serve them with. Now divide them between individual plates and onto each plate pour a little melted butter in which fresh sage leaves have been allowed to float; leave one leaf on each plate, then sprinkle on a spoonful of freshly grated parmesan cheese and take to the table immediately.

After her Christmas dish of home-made *tortellini* Silvana likes to serve *faraona*, a guinea fowl. This game-like domesticated fowl with its tiny head and beautiful dappled grey black plumage is rather noisy and likes to perch in trees, so Silvana, who has work enough already without the care of wayward animals, does not have them in her farmyard. Instead Orlando will buy a pair from a neighbour who specialises in them. Orlando enjoys the guinea fowl *in salmi*, so first Silvana makes a *soffritto* of *odori* to which she adds a bay leaf or two. She browns the fowl which is cut up into pieces and then adds them to the *soffritto* and lets them cook for a few minutes; then she adds the chopped liver of the fowl and a chicken liver and on top of this she pours some red wine. The bird is then left to cook until it is tender and the sauce is reduced. She puts the pieces on a hot dish and covers them with spoonfuls of the rich thick sauce. This is the same recipe that she uses for the *Fagiano in Salmi* and is given in detail in September's chapter.

 As well as serving the *Faraona in Salmi*, Silvana might prepare a dish of turkey breast cooked with *prosciutto* and *groviera*, a **Filetto di Tacchino al Prosciutto**. To make this dish for Orlando, Sauro and herself she will buy three fillets of turkey breast which are neatly trimmed and flattened. She will cook the fillets in a large flat pan with a little unsalted butter; after she has turned the fillets once so that they have changed colour on both sides, she lays on each fillet a slice of parma ham and on top a thin slice of *groviera* or *fontina* cheese and leaves the pan to cook on a very gentle flame. The dish is ready when the cheese starts to melt down into the buttery pan. Their own *prosciutto* and *pecorino* cheese are not suitable for this more elegant dish, which needs the paper-thin, sweet slices of the best *prosciutto* from Parma and a cheese which will melt into softness.

Another speciality of this winter season are the *cardi*, cardoons, or what are known locally as *gobbi*. These are the long greenish-white thistle-like vegetables which are eaten in the south of France as the special Christmas Eve food and are called *cardon*. They are to be seen growing in rows in the country gardens, their grey-green artichoke-like leaves sprouting out of earth or rags that have been wrapped and banked around the long stalks to bleach them. The cardoons need careful preparation before cooking. First the long inner stalks, (it is better to discard any very tough damaged outer ones), must be stripped of the silvery incipient leaves and membranes as these are extremely bitter and will spoil the delicate flavour of the dish. When this has been done and the stalks are cut into lengths of about two inches they must be immediately put into acidulated water to prevent them turning colour and spoiling the appearance of the dish. The water can be made acid with lemon juice or wine vinegar. After this preliminary treatment the *cardi* must be cooked in boiling salted water until tender. This takes about half an hour, longer, if the stalks are tough. After this the vegetable can be treated in different ways. Silvana likes to put layers of the *cardi* in between layers of grated parmesan and bake them in the oven. Occasionally she will dip the pieces in beaten egg and flour and deep fry them in olive oil until they are crisp. Both methods are very delicious. The cardoon has a subtle taste of the heart of artichoke, the tender part that one never seems to be able to get enough of when eating the summer vegetable.

 Cardi alla Besciamella, cardoons in a béchamel sauce, are also an excellent way to serve this delicious vegetable. To serve four to six people you will need one large cardoon, 50 g or 2 oz of butter, 50 g or 2 oz of flour, half a litre or a scant pint of milk and 50 g or 2 oz of grated parmesan, salt and pepper.

Prepare the cardoon as already indicated and cook it for at least thirty minutes in boiling salted water. It will be sufficiently cooked when it is easily penetrated with a fork. With the butter, flour and milk make a béchamel sauce, season it with salt and pepper and if you care to, add some of the grated cheese. When the cardoon is tender drain it well in a colander and add it to the béchamel; mix the vegetable well into the sauce. Tip the sauce coated cardoons into a buttered oven dish, then on top sprinkle a thick layer of the grated cheese. Put the dish into a medium oven until the top has melted and starts to brown.

On Christmas day Orlando, Silvana and Sauro will usually have a quiet lunch together, enjoying the special dishes such as the *Faraona in Salmi* and the *Filetto di Tacchino*. They will exchange gifts; this is the time when Sauro will be given a new bicycle, or some such important present. But on the whole Christmas for the Cerottis is not the extravagant gift-giving celebration that it is elsewhere - Silvana and Orlando appreciate a quiet day in their otherwise crowded year. Later in the day they may go visiting or receive relatives.

Over the long holiday period the *fattoria* will be full of guests for lunch and dinner. Silvana will certainly serve the *cardi* in one of its forms. Just as certainly the *tinello* in the long dining room will be laden with piles of sweet home-made biscuits, bowls of walnuts, clementines and dried figs. There will be several large *pannettone*, some filled with candied fruit and some with small pieces of bitter chocolate embedded in the light sponge. Silvana will also serve the delicious *zabajone* when the spirits flag and delicate glasses of *vin santo* to moisten the almond biscuits. Orlando will open an impressive number of bottles of *spumante d'Asti* to toast their guests and all the friends who will drop in to wish them well for the new year that is dawning.

NOTES

Measurements

Like many Italian cooks, Silvana does not use a strict system for measuring ingredients. I have given the recipes in pounds and ounces and kilograms. The other measures I have used are as follows. By a tablespoon, I mean a classical English tablespoon which is large and has a pointed bowl; it contains two American tablespoons. By dessertspoon, I mean the classical English dessert or soup spoon, two of which make a tablespoon. A tea cup is an ordinary sized cup, not an American cup. When the word glass is mentioned it means an ordinary wine glass.

Ingredients

Tuscan cooking is based on olive oil and there is no substitute for this; if the dish is to taste as it should then it must contain the best olive oil in the case of salads, soups and vegetable dishes. Try to obtain oil with the words *Olio Extravergine d'Oliva* on the label.

Prosciutto when served alone for an *antipasto* is always cut in thin slices; however for cooking it needs to be cut into dice. Italians who do not have their own *prosciutto* often buy the ends of *prosciutti* in the stores for this purpose. You can substitute bacon or *pancetta* that is not too fat.

Herbs

Use fresh herbs, especially in the case of rosemary. In many recipes rosemary should be put into the dish in the form of a small whole sprig, and should be taken out well before the end of the cooking time if this is lengthy. This is because individual rosemary leaves can be bitter and strong in the mouth. If they are loose in the pot then they will be impossible to discard, so do not use separate dried rosemary leaves and remember to take out the sprig before the leaves drop off.

Tomato Preserves

Use the sort of tomato preserve that is indicated in each recipe. For a description of the different types of tomato conserves and their different uses in Tuscan cooking, see the chapter on August. Fresh tomatoes should be the marmande variety or fresh garden tomatoes if you grow them.

Bread

Where possible make your own out of strong white flour or buy good baker's bread. Wholemeal brown bread is not suitable for the Tuscan bread based dishes; nor, of course, is commercial sliced bread.

Equipment

Tuscan cooking does not demand very complicated equipment. To cook pasta well you will need a very large saucepan that can take at least four litres or seven pints of water and leave room for the pasta. You will also need long-handled wooden spoons and forks to stir the pasta and a large colander with a base and handles to drain it. Other items are a cheese grater, several heavy bottomed frying pans and small pans for sauces, small wooden spoons and forks and at least two good sized chopping boards. To make your own pasta you will need a large pastry board or a wooden table, a long rolling pin and possibly a simple pasta machine to roll out the dough thinly. Two or three sharp knives, small ones for vegetables, larger ones for meat, and a straight long bladed knife for *prosciutto* and *salame* are essential, so is a knife sharpener. A *mezzaluna* or double-handled curved chopping tool will make short work of chopping garlic and herbs, a pastry wheel is nice to cut pasta and a mouli is useful for pureéing vegetables and beans for your soups. A great many grilled meat dishes can be cooked very well on a garden barbecue. A little espresso coffee machine such as the one that Bialetti make is good for making the little cups of black coffee for after dinner and lunch. In fact nothing more exotic is needed than what a reasonably well-equipped kitchen already possesses.

INDEX
FOR SILVANA'S RECIPES

Only those recipes given in small type are listed below. The general topics discussed in the text are listed under the chapter titles on the Contents page.

For discussions of the dishes that are indexed, see the pages adjoining the recipes.

CPSIA information can be obtained
at www.ICGtesting.com
Printed in the USA
LVHW090207010819
626129LV00001B/49/P

9 780865 473874